D1391892

CAPTAINS OF WAR

by the same author

Non Fiction
A Damned Un-English Weapon.
The Killing Time.
The Devil's Device.
Few Survived.

Fiction
No Survivors.
Action Atlantic.
Tokyo Torpedo.
Last Command.
Fighting Submarine.
Devil Flotilla.
Diving Stations.
Crash Dive 500.

CAPTAINS OF WAR

EDWYN GRAY

Leo Cooper
London

First published 1988 by Leo Cooper Ltd

Leo Cooper is an independent imprint
of the Heinemann Group of Publishers,
10 Upper Grosvenor Street, London WIX 9PA.

LONDON MELBOURNE AUCKLAND

ISBN: 0–85052–246–3

Photoset by Deltatype Ltd, Ellesmere Port
Printed by Mackays of Chatham Ltd, Chatham, Kent

To Vivienne with Love

Contents

Illustrations

Author's Note and Acknowledgements

'We had competent administrators, brilliant experts of all descriptions, unequalled navigators, good disciplinarians, (and) fine sea officers . . . but at the outset of the conflict we had more captains of ships than captains of war.'
(Winston S. Churchill)

Unlike other warships a submarine has no peacetime role. She cannot 'show the flag' or be used to entertain foreign dignitaries. She is unsuitable for the pomp and ceremony for which war vessels of all nations are in such great demand and she is hardly the ideal vehicle for carrying a Head of State on official visits. She has no facilities or surplus space available to enable her to provide aid when natural disasters such as earthquakes, floods and volcanic eruptions occur in remote areas; and she can only offer limited assistance in a rescue situation. The submarine, unlike her surface sisters, is solely a vessel of war. Thus, by definition, her Commanding Officer is, in Winston Churchill's stirring phrase, a Captain of War.

In my previous books on underwater warfare I have been at pains to stress that submariners of all nations, both friend and foe, share the same dangers and discomforts whether they are at sea in times of peace or on combat patrol during times of war. And, indeed, their techniques, reactions, and attitudes are virtually identical, no matter under which flag they serve. This book, which spans both World Wars, is an attempt to delve more deeply into the characters and personal achievements of seventeen individual submarine captains drawn from the navies of Britain, the United States, Germany, Italy, Poland and Japan. And, although these officers represent only a tiny sample, their actions will, I hope, demonstrate the common bond of courage, determination and dedication that unites all those who fight beneath the sea.

Material has been drawn from a large area of published and unpublished sources and I must thank, as always, Cdr Richard Compton-Hall, MBE, RN (Retd) and Mrs Marjorie Bidmead of the

Royal Navy's Submarine Museum for their assistance in tracing facts and photographs. My thanks also to my shipmates in the Wymondham branch of the Royal Naval Association and to Ray Rimell, the Editor of *Sea Classic International*, for permission to adapt my articles on Norman Holbrook and Otto Kretschmer which first saw light of day in his magazine. Finally may I express my appreciation to Leo Cooper and Nat Sobel for their continued support, and, of course, to Vivienne for putting up with me while this book was being researched and written.

Mention must be made of certain works which have provided valuable background information to supplement my research and I wish to acknowledge my debt of gratitude to their authors: *Will Not We Fear* by C. E. T. Warren and James Benson for details of *Seal's* last mission; the biography of Otto Kretschmer *The Golden Horseshoe* by Terence Robertson; *Orzel's Patrol* by Eryk Sopocko; and *Sunk* by Mochitsura Hashimoto.

My grateful thanks are also due to the following publishers for the use of copyright material listed in the *Quotation Sources* at the end of the book: Doubleday & Co Inc; The Amalgamated Press; Thornton & Butterworth Ltd; Hodder & Stoughton Ltd; Conway Maritime Press Ltd; Leo Cooper; Peter Davies; Mews Books Inc; Seeley Service & Co Ltd; Constable & Co Ltd; The Hogarth Press; Oxford University Press; Herbert Jenkins & Co; Sidgwick & Jackson Ltd; William Kimber Ltd; Methuen & Co; John Murray Ltd; George G. Harrap & Co Ltd; Evans Brothers Ltd; Ian Allen Ltd/Podzun Verlag; Andrew Melrose; Pyramid Books Inc; Hutchinsons Ltd; Longmans Green & Co Ltd; William Heinemann Ltd; Manor Books Inc; and Arthur Barker Ltd. My apologies to copyright holders included in the above list whom I have been unable to trace due to mergers, amalgamations and cessations of trading in the years since original publication.

Photographic material has generally been supplied by the National Archives in Washington and the Royal Navy Submarine Museum, Gosport. It has, however, proved impossible to trace the copyright holders of four of the illustrations used.

It continues to be my humble belief that the men who fight beneath the sea are the bravest of the brave. It is therefore to the submariners of the world – past, present and future – that this book is dedicated.

EDWYN GRAY
Attleborough, Norfolk.

April, 1987

—ONE—

Captains of war

'It was an effort of genius'

In the autumn of 1620 the Pilgrim Fathers made landfall in a deserted bay to the north of Cape Cod. And, together with other like-minded pioneers, they planted the seeds from which was to grow the most powerful nation the world has ever seen. In that same year a Dutch physician working as a tutor to the children of King James 1 of England, Cornelis van Drebbel, demonstrated his 'submarine' on the River Thames and thus set in motion a chain of technological development that would ultimately lead to the nuclear-engined ballistic missile submarine – the most powerful warship and weapon-system on earth. These two events, linked by the same birthdate yet separated by nearly three thousand miles of ocean, are proof indeed of the ancient adage that from the smallest of acorns can grow the mightiest of oaks. And, together, they mark a convenient starting point for this account of submarine warfare and the men who fight beneath the sea.

Van Drebbel was not, of course, a Captain of War in the Churchillian definition of that phrase. He was an inventor and scientist who foresaw the advantages of underwater navigation. Neither was his vessel, built from wood and covered with greased leather, a true submarine, for, at best, it was little more than an oar-propelled diving bell similar in shape to an upturned boat. According to a contemporary German chronicler 'the part of the ship where the rowers sit has no bottom so that the water is at all times visible to the rowers who . . . sitting on the seat a little above

1

the water never touch it with their feet'. This description, however, may be a little fanciful, for, bearing in mind the laws of hydrostatics, it seems far more likely that the oarsmen sat with their heads inside an air-pocket while their lower extremities were immersed in freezing cold river water. Van Drebbel's submarine certainly did not dive nor even submerge and, in the opinion of modern experts, it probably only ran awash during its famous trip from the Whitehall Palace to Greenwich.

The Frenchman De Son was the first person to visualize the submarine as a potential weapon of war but his vessel failed dismally when its clockwork-powered paddle-wheel proved inadequate for the task demanded of it. And in 1648 – exactly three hundred years before Admiral Hyman Rickover set up the Nuclear Power Division of the Bureau of Ships as the initial step in the construction of the world's first nuclear-engined submarine *Nautilus* – John Wilkins, a brother-in-law of Oliver Cromwell and a subsequent Bishop of Chester, wrote in his *Mathematical Magick* that the submarine 'may be of very great advantage against a Navy of Enemies who, by this means, may be undermined in the Water and blown up'.

The history of submarine warfare is full of oddities and it comes as no surprise to find that the first underwater Captain of War was neither a sailor nor a captain but a soldier and a sergeant – by name Ezra Lee. A member of General Samuel Parsons' Colonial Army, Lee volunteered to pilot David Bushnell's *Turtle* in an attack against the British flagship *Eagle* as she lay at anchor 'off the town of New York' when the inventor's brother fell ill. His feat was destined to win him an honoured place in the annals of sea warfare, but, as is so often the case, the reality of Lee's attack on the *Eagle*, which took place on 6 September, 1776, is far removed from the history book version of the event.

Bushnell, the son of a Connecticut farmer and a graduate of Yale University, was an inventor of considerable talent. His youthful interest in new forms of agricultural machinery and improvements in construction techniques soon waned and, while studying at Yale, he turned his attention to underwater explosives. Bushnell, in fact, is credited with the invention of the modern sea mine and reliable evidence exists to show that he supplied the rebel colonists with small watertight wooden casks filled with gunpowder and detonated by a simple clockwork mechanism which they floated down rivers and estuaries against their English enemies. And it was from this promising beginning that he moved on to the natural corollary – the design and construction of a submarine.

2

In a letter to Thomas Jefferson some years later Bushnell described the *Turtle* in the following words: 'The external shape of the Submarine Vessel bore some resemblance to two upper Tortoise shells of equal size, joined together . . . the inside was capable of containing the operator and air sufficient to supply him (for) thirty minutes . . .' And as no drawings have survived this is all we know about the external appearance of this revolutionary underwater machine.

The submarine, built secretly on the family's Saybrook Farm, took four years to complete and swallowed up most of Bushnell's money. When finished it resembled a seven-foot-tall egg made from oak planks shaped like the staves of a barrel. It was driven through the water by means of a flat-bladed propeller, similar to the vanes of a windmill, which was worked by a manual crank. Experts have failed to agree whether this crank was operated by hand or by foot but the latter method seems more likely. The speed is estimated to have been between two and four knots.

Although designed to run awash, so that the operator could navigate visually through glass ports in the upper part of the shell, it was possible to submerge the vessel several feet beneath the surface by means of a system of valves, ballast tanks and pumps. Air was supplied to the interior via tubes similar in principle to the modern snorkel. A compass and a depth-gauge were added to assist the operator while submerged, and for armament the *Turtle* relied on a primitive form of limpet mine which it was intended to attach to the enemy's wooden bottom with the aid of an auger. A simple clockwork fuse provided sufficient delay for the submarine to get clear before detonation. It is impossible to describe all the various ingenious devices which David Bushnell incorporated into the *Turtle* but, without mechanical power of any sort, everything devolved upon the operator who had to use both hands and feet to propel, steer and dive the Water Machine, and who must have possessed the dexterity of a one-man band plus the muscle-power of a weight-lifter.

Trials were conducted on the Connecticut River with Bushnell's brother at the controls and these were sufficiently successful for George Washington and General Putnam to approve of its use against the British. But in August, 1776, Bushnell's brother was taken ill and Sergeant Ezra Lee volunteered to take his place. Over the course of the next few weeks Lee was taught how to operate the submersible and, finally, on the night of 6 September, he and his device were launched from the Whitehall Stairs near the Battery on Manhattan Island.

According to legend Lee propelled the submarine through the

harbour in an awash condition and, on approaching *Eagle*, he submerged in order to get beneath the frigate's keel. It had taken him two hours to reach the target and his disappointment can be imagined when the auger failed to penetrate the copper-sheathed bottom of the British warship. To make matters worse the Sergeant was convinced that the enemy had seen him and, pedalling madly, he headed back towards Manhattan. On coming abreast of Government Island a twelve-oared barge packed full with armed Redcoats gave chase and, in a desperate attempt to lighten the submarine, he released the explosive charge which proceeded to drift into the East River where it ultimately detonated without harming either friend or foe. Lee himself managed to reach the Whitehall Stairs and when the upper hatch had been unbolted from the outside he was lifted out more dead than alive after his ordeal.

Modern research suggests that, despite his brave efforts, Ezra Lee never reached his target. Contemporary records indicate that the *Eagle* did not have a copper-sheathed bottom in 1776 and her log contains no reference to any suspicious happenings near or under the ship that night. And it must be added that the Marine sentries who acted as lookouts when the flagship was anchored in harbour were of the highest order – their alertness being renowned throughout the fleet. It is also a scientific fact that within thirty minutes of leaving the Whitehall Stairs the unfortunate sergeant, sealed inside his egg-shaped Water Machine, would have been so befuddled with carbon dioxide poisoning that accurate navigation, or even manipulation of the controls, would have been impossible. And the exertion of pedalling the contraption for such a distance would have probably been beyond the limits of his physical strength.

But although Lee's attack on the *Eagle* did not meet with success the fact that he set out on his hazardous mission with the firm intention of attacking an enemy warship with the submarine is beyond dispute. And even after the layers of embroidery and inaccuracy are stripped away from the legend of the *Turtle* enough substance remains to confirm Sergeant Ezra Lee as a true Captain of War. For as George Washington observed in a letter he wrote to Thomas Jefferson after the event: 'It was an effort of genius'.

Bushnell's *Turtle* served to inspire many other inventors in the decades that followed the abortive attack on the *Eagle* although only two, Robert Fulton and Wilhelm Bauer – a Bavarian-born corporal serving in the Prussian army – proved able to design and build seaworthy underwater vessels capable of destroying enemy ships. For various reasons, however, neither Fulton's *Nautilus* nor

Bauer's *Der Brandtaucher* and *Le Diable Marin* were ever tested in action. And it was not until the advent of the American Civil War some ninety years after the *Turtle*'s adventure that a submarine took part in combat operations.

The *Hunley* was the brainchild of three ardent Confederate patriots – Horace L. Hunley, after whom it was named, James McLintock, and a civilian engineer, Baxter Watson. It was constructed from a 25-foot long and 4-foot diameter boiler cylinder which was cut into two horizontal lengths and heightened by the insertion of two 12-inch iron strips to give a headroom of five feet. Propulsion was manual with eight brawny seamen turning a cranked shaft which rotated a propeller in the stern – and the full nine-man complement was made up by the captain who steered and controlled the vessel from a small conning-tower in the bows. It was originally intended to employ a form of towed explosive device similar to the Royal Navy's Harvey torpedo but problems with tangled lines led to the adoption of an even more suicidal weapon – the spar torpedo.*

Hunley's first captain, Lieutenant John Payne, survived three accidental sinkings which cost the lives of nineteen men and he was ultimately replaced by Horace Hunley who took over command from Payne only to die himself when the ill-omened vessel sank for a fourth time on 15 October 1863, taking Hunley and another eight men to the bottom. A further crew of seven men was lost when the submarine sank during a practice attack on the Confederate ship *Indian Chief*. But with reckless bravery more volunteers came forward and, on the night of 17 February 1864, having been raised and dried out, the Hunley sailed against the Union corvette *Housatonic* as it lay at anchor in Charleston Roads.

Now under the command of her fourth skipper, Lieutenant George E. Dixon, she reached the target without mishap and, having submerged, thrust her spar against the enemy's hull below the waterline. The impact triggered the detonator and the resulting explosion ignited the corvette's magazine with disastrous consequences. On this occasion, however, fortune did not favour the brave. At the very moment of the submarine's triumph the brooding jinx struck once again and the gallant *Hunley*, entangled in the wreckage of the *Housatonic*, went to the bottom with her victim. But not even this final tragedy could alter the fact that a

---

* A thirty-foot wooden spar which projected from the bows of a vessel – usually a steam launch – like a medieval jousting lance. A canister of explosives was fastened to the outboard end of the spar and this could be triggered by a simple impact detonator. Intended for use by surface vessels it was the most frightening and unsuitable weapon ever fitted to a submarine.

submarine had engaged and sunk an enemy ship for the first time in the history of sea warfare.

By the turn of the century the submarine had progressed sufficiently to be accepted, albeit grudgingly, into the navies of the world, thanks to the pioneering work of John Philip Holland and Simon Lake in the United States, Maxime Laubeuf in France, and Dzhevetsky in Russia. France took an early lead but was soon followed by the United States and, reluctantly, by Britain who was forced to build her first underwater vessels under licence from the owners of the Holland patents – a situation quickly rectified when the giant Vickers Company got into its stride and began constructing boats to its own design. By 1906 there were 114 submarines in service world-wide and although they were beset with frequent accidents – at least 277 submariners lost their lives between 1900 and the outbreak of the war in 1914 – it was clear that they would exercise a considerable and baleful influence on the future conduct of the war at sea.

The first modern submarine to launch a torpedo attack in anger was the 295-ton Greek *Delphin* which fired an 18–inch Whitehead weapon at the Turkish cruiser *Mejidieh* off the Dardanelles on 9 December 1912, during the First Balkan War. Although virtually unknown outside his native Greece her captain, Lt-Cdr E. Paparrigopoulos, certainly rates his own particular niche in the archives of those who fought beneath the sea. On this occasion the torpedo missed its target, a not unusual occurrence, and the *Mejidieh* survived to enjoy a somewhat chequered career thereafter. Sunk by mines in the Black Sea in April 1915, she was salvaged by the Russians who repaired and refitted her. She was seized by an Austro-Russian army at Sebastopol in 1918 who returned her to the Turkish Navy and she was still in service as late as 1945 as the *Mecidiye*. Like old soldiers, some old ships never seem to die.

The submarine came of age in the world-wide conflict that followed less than two years after the *Delphin*'s historic attack, and the underwater threat soon dominated every aspect of the war at sea. Britain's flotillas were hampered by a lack of targets for there were virtually no German merchant ships on the High Seas after August, 1914, and the Kaiser's war vessels proved equally shy of salt water. Most of the Royal Navy's successes came either in the Baltic – where captains such as Max Horton and Noel Laurence ran riot and forced the enemy on to the defensive – or in the Dardanelles and the Sea of Marmora, the favourite hunting grounds of Holbrook, Nasmith, Boyle and other commanders. And, with the exception of Dick Sandford's heroic mission with the veteran *C.3* at Zeebrugge in 1918, all of Britain's five underwater Victoria Crosses were won in Turkish waters.

But it was the U-boat arm of the German Navy that really demonstrated the awesome power of the submarine. Otto Weddigen's destruction of three cruisers in the course of a single September morning in 1914 frightened the Admiralty to its core and the reverberating echoes of the incident had a profound effect on Britain's maritime strategy for the rest of the war – especially on Jellicoe's handling of the Grand Fleet. The war on Britain's trade routes was, if anything, even more shattering. Aces such as Lothar von Arnauld de la Perière and Baron von Spiegel almost brought the British Empire to its knees. Jellicoe, who was by that time First Sea Lord, warned the Cabinet in June 1917, that, if losses continued at the current rate of some half a million tons per month, it would be impossible to continue the war into 1918! And there is little doubt that the U-boats were only defeated by the narrowest of margins.

A few bare statistics must suffice to illustrate what skilled and determined submarine commanders could achieve: U-boats sank a world total of 5,708 ships grossing 11,018, 865 tons between 1914 and 1918 and 13,333 non-combatant merchant seamen and passengers paid with their lives. But the U-boats did not restrict themselves solely to defenceless merchantmen, for, as Appendix One reveals, German submarines also sent nine British and French battleships to the bottom plus fourteen cruisers and a host of smaller warships.

Other than Germany and Britain few countries achieved any major successes with their submarines and only the relatively small Austro-Hungarian Navy produced comparative results. France and Italy, despite their large submarine fleets, had little to show for their efforts while the Russians, beset by political turmoil, proved to be disappointingly indisciplined and hopelessly inept. Finally, and unfortunately, the United States Navy entered the conflict too late for her submarines to have an adequate opportunity to show their worth.

The interwar years produced an alarming succession of under-water disasters – in 1925, for example, five submarines were lost as the result of accidents in which 156 men lost their lives. There was some combat activity during the Spanish Civil War when German and Italian submarines carried out operations in support of Franco's forces which involved attacks on non-combatant cargo ships. And with typical British eccentricity the Royal Navy employed submarines from the Hong Kong Flotilla to fight Chinese pirates – an unusual example of the poacher turning

7

gamekeeper which has its own special place in this volume.

So far as the submarine was concerned the Second World War virtually began where the First had ended. Apart from technical refinements, British and German underwater vessels were basically similar to their First World War counterparts. So, too, during the initial months of the conflict were their tactics. Royal Navy submarines were under strict orders to operate in accordance with International Law and were required to stop suspect ships, examine their papers, and to ensure the safety of their crews before sinking them – a wholly impractical procedure with the ever-present danger of aircraft patrols. Germany's U-boats, while instructed not to attack passenger vessels, were given a freer hand, although, under the stress of war, this soon degenerated into a policy of sinking on sight and without warning – the dreaded *spurlos versenkt*** of the 1914–1918 conflict. In addition submarines on both sides continued to be employed as minelayers, a role that was later taken over by aircraft, and it was on one such mission deep inside enemy waters that the British *Seal* met her doom.

Doenitz's introduction of the wolf-pack was the first break with the traditional role of the submarine as a lone hunter. This was quickly followed by night attacks on the surface – a tactic pioneered by Otto Kretschmer which decimated Allied convoys in the North Atlantic. Both methods produced such impressive results that they were later copied by American submarine captains in the Pacific. Some leading U-boat commanders achieved quite dramatic successes: Kretschmer himself sinking 43 ships totalling 263,682 tons while Luth was credited with 46 ships grossing 212,036 tons. But improved weapons such as the depth-charge and the anti-submarine ahead-throwing mortar, the introduction of asdic and sonar detection systems, the development of radar and the employment of aircraft, together with the tried-and-tested convoy system, prevented the second generation of U-boat commanders from challenging the dazzling success of the First World War aces: von Arnauld, for example, sinking an incredible 194 ships totalling 453,716 tons and Forstmann 146 ships of 384,304 tons.

German U-boats were equally successful against warships and sank two battleships, eight aircraft carriers and no fewer than fifty destroyers. Faced by a much smaller enemy fleet, British submarines could not compete with this scale of wholesale destruction. But when targets were relatively plentiful they could give a

* Sunk without trace.

8

good account of themselves – the Royal Navy's top commander, Malcolm Wanklyn, sending two destroyers, two submarines and 129,529 tons of enemy shipping to the bottom.

Italy's submarine force, one of the largest and most modern in the world, achieved little, although her human torpedo units, led by officers such as Luigi de la Penne, did much to maintain the Nation's naval honour. The French Navy's boats, as in the previous conflict, sank no enemy warships whatsoever and showed a distinct lack of enthusiasm for underwater warfare, surprising for a nation that had originally led the world in the development of the submarine. Russia, too, met with little success, despite overwhelming numbers, due, in part, to the operational restrictions placed upon her captains by the High Command which at one stage of the war forbade submarines to submerge in waters deeper than the safe diving limit of the boat. Had such a ridiculous order been issued to the German Navy no U-boats would have operated in the Atlantic!

The minor navies had little to show for their efforts although brave deeds abounded as they struggled to resist the brutal onslaught of Hitler's war machine. And Poland's Jan Grudzinski provides a good example of what can be achieved by a determined captain and a courageous crew fighting single-handed in a hostile sea with their bases destroyed and their homeland occupied by the enemy. The escape of the *Orzel* must certainly rank as one of the world's great submarine epics.

Japan's contribution to the underwater war was disappointingly ineffective – a failure caused by the tactical misuse of her submarines together with an appalling lack of scientific aids such as radar, sonar and torpedo data computers. Of her many highly trained combat commanders only Mochitsura Hashimoto and a few other fortunate captains had an opportunity to prove their skills in the face of the enemy.

By contrast the Submarine Service of the United States Navy surprised everyone – except, perhaps, itself and the American people. Making use of night surface attacks and wolf-pack tactics, and adopting a 'sink on sight' policy from the very first day they entered the conflict, America's superbly built fleet submarines dominated the waters around Japan and made an incalculable contribution to Allied victory in the Pacific. Men like 'Mush' Morton and Dick O'Kane wiped enemy convoys off the face of the ocean – often making their attacks within sight of the Japanese mainland. Others, such as Sam Dealey, preferred warship targets. As a yardstick of their achievement American submarines actually sank more enemy fighting ships than Hitler's vaunted U-boats. In the midst of battle new heroes were created and new legends born. But none was more glorious than Commander Howard Gilmore who deliberately sacrificed his own life in order to ensure the survival of the *Growler* and her crew. It was an act of herosim that will be remembered for as long as submarines exist. And probably even beyond that!

The submarine, today, is the prime weapon of the nuclear age. It is a miracle of modern technology capable of circumnavigating the world without coming to the surface or refuelling and can remain submerged for three months or more. Able to travel beneath the polar icecaps, it can dive to prodigious depths – the Russian *November*-class boats are said to have a maximum diving limit of 1,650 feet – and the destructive power of its doomsday weapon-system almost defies belief. A single vessel can turn major cities to ashes, inflict millions of human casualties, and lay waste to vast areas of the earth's surface at the literal touch of a button.

In terms of sheer size it dwarfs the battleships which ruled the seas when the first pioneer submarines joined the American, British, and French navies at the turn of the century. The new *Ohio*-class submarines, for example, built as launch vehicles for the Trident missile, displace 18,700 tons submerged and have an overall length of 560 feet. By contrast the British *Canopus*-class battleships, completed in 1900, were only 418 feet long and displaced 12,950 tons. Even the revolutionary *Dreadnought* of 1906 was smaller at 17,900 tons, as well as being 33 feet shorter. And while the *Dreadnought*'s 12-inch guns had a range of just over 20 miles the *Ohio*'s Trident missiles can hit targets 4,000 miles away from their firing point. Such is the measure of the submarine's progress since van Drebbel's jaunt down the Thames in 1620.

* * *

On Sunday 2 May, 1982, Commander Christopher Wreford-Brown took the nuclear-powered *Conqueror* to within 4,000 yards of the Argentine cruiser *General Belgrano*. And at 4.01 pm precisely, in obedience to political orders from London, he fired three Mark VIII torpedoes at his victim. Two struck home and 368 men died.

It was just seventy years since Lt-Cdr Paparrigopoulos had attacked the Turkish cruiser *Mejidieh* in 1912. Despite the carnage of two World Wars nothing had changed. . . .

—TWO—

Commander Max Kennedy Horton, RN

'Please stand clear while I sink this ship.'

In common with many other superstitious men Max Horton regarded thirteen as his lucky number. And when he brought *E.9* to periscope depth on 13 September, 1914, he was quietly confident that Dame Fortune was about to smile upon him. For, like all dedicated gamblers, he had a touching faith in that legendary lady.

It was a dreary day. Despite a relatively calm sea the weather was unpleasantly thick and it was raining hard. Having spent the night resting peacefully on the seabed 120 feet down – and uncomfortably near to the enemy's coast – the submarine was now only some six miles to the south-south-west of Heligoland. Not that the close proximity of the island worried Horton. A few days earlier *E.9* had penetrated inside Heligoland's harbour and, finding no suitable targets, he had taken the submarine to the bottom and remained *inside* the embracing shelter of the moles, under the very guns of the fortress, for several hours. 'We played auction bridge while we were waiting,' Horton confided in a letter to a friend. And, he added jubilantly, 'I won 4/11½d.'

Suspecting that an enemy submarine had managed to creep into the harbour, Heligoland's naval commandant alerted the defences and set about organizing an underwater search using sweep-wires and grapnels. One probe actually came into contact with *E.9*'s hull during the hunt but was safely diverted away by the boat's jumping-wire. Horton, on hearing the ominous scraping noise of

11

the sweep, merely shrugged off the danger and calmly continued his game of cards.

His subsequent comment that 'I knew nothing would happen to us' suggests a conceit born out of hindsight. But Max was no blustering braggart. His unshakeable confidence in the good offices of Fate was inspired, like his addiction to the number thirteen, by superstition. For example he always wore a 'lucky' signet ring on his finger – a ring that carried the Horton family crest of a dolphin rising from the sea impaled on a spear and the motto *In Deo Confido*. And Max had told his brother D'Arcy, who had given him the talisman when he first joined the submarine service: 'If it ever comes off I know my luck will run out!' As uncanny proof of its protective powers two boats which Horton subsequently commanded later in his career, *J.6* and *M.1*, were both lost in tragic circumstances after he had left them.

Having enjoyed a brief respite on the bottom, Horton returned to periscope depth at 7.15 am and almost immediately sighted a cruiser some two miles to starboard. Thirteen minutes later he had closed to a position 600 yards abeam of his target. 'Submarine very lively (while) diving,' he noted in his log. 'Fired both bow torpedoes at her starboard side at intervals of about 15 seconds. 7.29 am. Heard single loud explosion. Submarine at 70 feet, course parallel to cruiser.'

Horton had observed several other vessels in the vicinity while he was preparing to launch his attack and he wisely remained hidden beneath the waves for a few minutes before bringing *E.9* back to periscope depth at 7.32 am. Almost immediately he found himself under fire from unseen enemy ships and, seeking safety in the deep, he hurriedly submerged to 70 feet where he picked up his trim and lay doggo. Having almost certainly obtained a hit with one of his torpedoes, Horton could have quite justifiably retired quietly from the scene on his electric motors. But he was determined to confirm that the attack had been successful with his own eyes and he held *E.9* at seventy feet while he waited an opportune moment to inspect the situation on the surface.

Over an hour passed before he dared to raise the periscope and, when he turned the upper lens onto the relevant bearing, there was no sign of the cruiser, although he saw 'trawlers where cruiser had been – four or five in number in a cluster'. Satisfied that he had sunk the enemy ship, Max took *E.9* back to 70 feet and for the next thirteen hours played tag with the destroyers and trawlers hunting him on the surface. Fortunately, depth-charges had not been developed at that stage of the war. Had the Germans possessed such a weapon in September, 1914, the submarine could never have survived. But, as ever, Max was lucky and when he finally came to the surface at 9.26 pm he found the horizon clear of the enemy. Coupling up the diesel engines, he recharged his exhausted batteries and, after a quick meal, set course for home.

Hela was the first ship to be sunk by a British submarine and for that reason alone Horton had earned his place in history. But there were greater things to come. Only seventeen days later Max brought *E.9* to periscope depth in the middle of a German destroyer patrol off the mouth of the West Ems. From this hazardous position he coolly observed their tactics which he subsequently reported back to his flotilla commander – an early instance of underwater surveillance and intelligence-gathering as practised by Nato and Warsaw Pact submarines in the Cold War conditions of today.

On 6 October, having aborted his search for German heavy units, Horton altered the depth-setting of the *E.9*'s torpedoes so that they would run shallow and set off to look for smaller prey. Navigating cautiously in and out of the shoals and sandbanks of Germany's North Sea coast, he found a likely target, the destroyer *S116*, but had to belay his first two attacks in their final seconds when the enemy vessel altered course unexpectedly. With the submarine's batteries seriously depleted by the exertions of the underwater hunt Horton had nearly given up hope of success when his elusive prey suddenly turned towards him. There was only just time to pull *E.9* clear of the oncoming vessel and Max took a snap shot more in desperation than hope. But the Horton luck held. 'She went up beautifully,' he told a friend later, 'and when I had the chance of a good look around about five minutes afterwards all that could be seen was about fifteen feet of bow sticking vertically out of the water'. And, duly acknowledging his debt to Dame Fortune, he added: 'To hit a destroyer always requires maximum luck.'

His Commodore, Roger Keyes, was more inclined to credit the success to Horton's skill as a submarine commander. 'To get one of these wriggling destroyers is like shooting snipe with a rifle,' he explained in his *Naval Memoirs*. And, by a debatable coincidence, Horton celebrated his victory by returning to Harwich with the emblem of the Skull and Crossbones flying from *E.9*'s periscope standard, a gesture which many read as a punning reference to his Commanding Officer's name. Whether intentional or not, Horton's Jolly Roger began a Royal Navy tradition. British submarines returning from a successful patrol now always fly the notorious pirate flag on entering harbour, the most recent occasion being Commander Wreford-Brown's arrival at Faslane with the *Conqueror* after his attack on the *General Belgrano*.

Despite the relatively recent introduction of submarines, Horton

13

was, even in 1914, something of an underwater veteran. Except for a two-year interval of compulsory 'big ship' duty on the cruiser *Duke of Edinburgh*, during which he had taken part in the rescue of the Princess Royal after the P&O liner *Delhi* ran aground off Cape Spartel, he had served in submarines continuously since joining the Branch in October, 1904. He had commanded four pioneer boats: *Holland No. 3: A.1*, following her salvage after being sunk with all hands off Spithead; *C.8;* and *D.6* before moving to *E.9* on 16 March, 1914, less than six months before war was declared.

His early career, despite being somewhat uneventful, showed considerable promise, although some of his more madcap escapades did not always go down well with senior officers. A report from his Flotilla Commander in October, 1907, described him as 'Good at his boat but bad socially' – an enigmatic comment that could have meant almost anything. And there is little doubt that Horton's half-Jewish parentage counted against him in English Society which, despite the efforts of King Edward VII, was in those days strongly antisemitic. A contemporary who served with him on *C.8* wrote: 'His reputation as a poker player was second only to his credit for coolness and sobriety as a submarine commander, in which capacity he was . . . the superior of most.' The same officer also observed: 'The qualities essential for first-class poker playing have their undoubted value in the conduct of war where successful bluff may, on occasions, be the only way to victory in the face of odds.' It is interesting to note that Admiral Isoroku Yamamoto, the architect of the Japanese Navy's attack on Pearl Harbor in 1941, was another dedicated poker player.

In the 1912 fleet manoeuvres, while in command of *D.6*, Horton successfully penetrated the Firth of Forth, navigating most of the route at periscope depth, and torpedoed two 'enemy' ships anchored above the bridge. Later, during the same exercises, he encountered the battlecruiser *Indefatigable*, carried out a dummy attack, and then surfaced to inform the infuriated captain: 'I have sunk you!' In the course of the ensuing argument between the young Lieutenant and the senior post-Captain, Horton, who thoroughly enjoyed such confrontations, carefully omitted to explain that, according to the rules, *D.6* had already expended her complete outfit of torpedoes during the foray into the Firth of Forth. Instead he told Captain Leveson that his flotilla-mate *D.4* was in the vicinity and that if the battlecruiser remained stopped much longer she would find herself being torpedoed again!

His adventures during the 1913 manoeuvres, when Commodore Keyes gave him a roving commission to do as he pleased, led to a complete reappraisal of Britain's previous strategy of close block-ade and resulted in many old ideas being discarded. Thanks to Horton it was decided that, in any future war, only submarines would operate close to the German coast, while surface ships would excercise a 'distant' blockade supported, many hundreds of miles in the rear, by the Grand Fleet.

And so Britain's pioneer submarines, once castigated by a senior admiral as 'underhand and damned un-English', were now given pride of place in the Royal Navy's war plans. In the face of intense opposition from the Establishment a major revolution in strategic thinking had been accomplished by a determined band of young officers* who, like Horton, recognized the real significance of the submarine and who were prepared to exploit this new and terrible weapon to its fullest potential.

* * *

The suggestion that British submarines should be sent into the Baltic to bolster the Russian war effort first came up for discussion at a special conference held on board Jellicoe's flagship *Iron Duke* on 17 September, 1914. And it had the merit of being a far more practical proposition than many other schemes already lying on the table for consideration. The First Sea Lord, Prince Louis of Battenberg, for example, favoured a plan which involved the assault and capture of the island of Sylt, a proposal he first mooted in 1913, while the political head of the Navy, Winston Churchill, wanted to land on Borkum and seize the port of Emden. Sir Arthur Wilson was more inclined to storm the fortress of Heligoland, Germany's Gibraltar, while Admiral Fisher, still on the retired list and not yet recalled to office, recommended despatching the entire Grand Fleet to the Baltic in support of a landing on the Pomeranian coast.

The final plan adopted by Jellicoe proved to be considerably less ambitious but far more practical than the wild schemes put forward by the Navy's other senior admirals. A flotilla of submarines would be sent into the Baltic where, operating from Russian bases, they could attack German shipping engaged in the vital iron-ore trade with Sweden on which the Kaiser's war economy depended. Submarines were chosen for the task because they had a longer endurance and were more self-supporting than surface ships. In addition they were the only war vessels that could, given the right conditions, make the passage from the North Sea into the Baltic without detection.

* Other notable pre-1914 submarine captains included Martin Nasmith, Geoffrey Layton, Cecil Talbot and Noel Laurence.

Leaving aside the awkward fact that the Kaiser's navy exercised undisputed control over both the Kattegat and the Skagerrak, the major obstacle facing the Admiralty's planners was The Sound, the stretch of shoaling water that connected the narrows of the Kattegat to the Baltic. For the charts showed that, even at high tide, the depth of the water in The Sound was insufficient for a submarine to fully submerge. And this meant that it was virtually impossible to pass through undetected. Lastly, and certainly not least, the enemy was known to be guarding the eastern exit of The Sound with strong destroyer patrols.

Nor were German forces the only problem. Jealous of their neutrality, the Danish and Swedish navies also maintained constant surveillance over The Sound. Shore batteries and search-lights, both enemy and neutral, could range over every yard of water once the alarm was raised. It was a far from encouraging prospect. Yet, despite their inability to remain submerged while making passage through The Sound, submarines still seemed the most suitable vessels for the operation. The planners con-cluded that the best way to break through into the Baltic was to make an optimistic dash through The Sound on the surface during the darkest part of the night with the submarine trimmed low in the water to avoid detection by the thousands of watching eyes along the coast. It was a calculated gamble, but it was one which the submarine crews of the Royal Navy were eager to take.

On 13 October, less than a month after the conference on board the *Iron Duke*, Commodore Keyes, in command of the Harwich submarines, was ordered to put the plan into action. Once again the 13th proved to be Horton's lucky day for he was one of the three submarine commanders selected for the operation, his companions being Noel Laurence with *E.1*, who was to act as Senior Officer when they arrived, and Martin Nasmith with *E.11*. Engine trouble quickly eliminated the latter, however, and, at dusk on 15 October, Horton and Laurence left their temporary base at Gorleston and headed out into the cold bleakness of the North Sea at a steady ten knots.

But the early submarines were sadly unreliable and, as the two boats approached the Skagerrak, *E.9*, like *E.11*, developed mechanical problems and Laurence was left to continue alone while Horton and his crew stopped to carry out makeshift repairs to a broken shaft – a hazardous task for a submarine deep inside enemy-controlled waters.

Laurence successfully rounded the Skaw and crept into the Skagerrak, diving each time his lookouts sighted the smoke of an approaching ship. And as it was still daylight when he reached the approaches to Ore Sound he took *E.1* to the bottom to await nightfall. Unlike those who were to follow in his wake Laurence had the good fortune to enjoy an easy run through The Sound and, with *E.1* trimmed low in the water so that her conning-tower was awash, he succeeded in passing through the main danger area without being detected. He entered the Baltic soon after midnight and, once safely into deep water, he took the submarine to the bottom so that his crew could have a welcome, if belated, supper.

Horton's passage was, by contrast, a hair-raising experience. Delayed by the broken shaft, he did not reach the entrance to The Sound until the evening of the 17th, too late to pass through during the hours of darkness. With enemy patrols criss-crossing the area, he was forced to postpone his attempt until the next night. Taking *E.9* to the bottom, he lay doggo throughout the following day and only returned to the surface as dusk began to shroud the northern sky.

The submarine was successfully conned as far as Malmö without being spotted and, on approaching the shallow waters of the Flint Channel, Horton shut down the noisy diesel engines and switched over to the electric motors for the next stage of their hazardous journey. Moving almost silently on one motor, *E.9* edged her way down the narrow channel while Horton and the lookouts scanned the darkness for enemy patrols. Danger loomed at every hand. Searchlights swept the surface of the sea and German patrol-boats could be seen scouring the area. It was uncomfortably apparent that the enemy knew British submarines were trying to break through into the Baltic. But how? Had German Intelligence discovered their plans – or had Laurence and *E.1* been discovered and sunk?

Max guided *E.9* carefully through the shoals and shallows of The Sound with the calm confidence of a local pilot and the submarine weaved first to port and then to starboard as he struggled to keep her in the deep-water channel. Suddenly the horizon darkened and the anxious lookouts picked out the lean shape of a German torpedo-boat some 150 yards away on the starboard bow. Horton snapped an order to submerge, but, as the flood valves opened, *E.9* scraped her keel plate on the bottom. In reacting to the stress of the situation Max had overlooked the shallow depth of the channel in which he was operating and he had tried to dive in just *fourteen feet of water*!

Scarcely daring to breathe, the British sailors waited for the torpedo-boat to ram them. But, incredibly, nothing happened. By some miracle, or, perhaps, thanks to Horton's lucky ring, the German lookouts had failed to detect the low silhouette of the submarine in the darkness and the enemy warship steamed past unaware of its presence.

After an interval of thirty minutes Horton cautiously trimmed *E.9* off the seabed. But, to his consternation, the enemy ship was still lurking in the vicinity. Although the distance between the two vessels was now less than 75 yards the enemy lookouts were still apparently ignorant of the British submarine under their very noses – a very rare example of German incompetence. Taking advantage of this unexpected piece of luck, Max submerged *E.9* to ten feet and, with her conning tower awash and a bare four feet of water under her keel, she crept past the sleeping sentinel on her electric motors.

Once clear of danger and into deeper water, Horton tried to make up for lost time by starting the submarine's diesel engines and making a dash on the surface, but the appearance of another destroyer quickly persuaded him that more haste meant less speed and he completed his epic passage at periscope depth, finally reaching the relative safety of the Baltic in the early hours of the following morning.

In their rush to send submarines to Russia, and with typical bureaucratic blindness, the Admiralty planners neglected to pay sufficient attention to both the calendar and the local weather situation, so that, almost as soon as *E.1* and *E.9* arrived in Reval, Horton and Laurence found themselves engulfed by the fierceness of the Baltic winter. With drifting blizzards reducing visibility to zero and ice thickening over the sea all submarine activity ground to a halt and the seasoned experts of the Tsar's Navy politely explained that no underwater operations would be possible for at least the next four months.

But Horton soon became bored by the enforced inactivity and, persuading an icebreaker to clear a passage out of Reval harbour, he set course for the open sea, watched by his sceptical Russian allies. It was desperately cold and within minutes *E.9* was encased in glare ice. Frozen slush clogged the vents while valves seized solid. But the Arctic conditions merely warmed Horton to the challenge.

Running on the surface was unadulterated hell. Spray froze on the stanchions and huge icicles hung down from the rigging wires; great wedges of ice formed on the bridge and both the periscopes and torpedo-tube caps froze immoveably. Horton had to station men on the fore casing and the conning-tower to chip the ice away with hammers and one man was given the specific task of keeping the upper hatch clear. The acid test would come when the submarine submerged and everyone on board, including Horton, kept their fingers crossed as *E.9* dipped beneath the surface. If the ice caused a failure in the intricate series of vents and valves upon which their lives depended the outcome of the exercise would be disaster.

The additional top-weight led to the boat submerging more rapidly than normal, but the relatively warmer temperature of the water beneath the surface quickly melted the ice and within minutes *E.9* was her usual efficient self again. It had seemed like a madcap gamble to the watching Russians, but Max had weighed the odds carefully and was confident that he would succeed. *In Deo Confido* – although he, perhaps, may not have expressed it in quite the same way.

Satisfied that the Russian winter held no terrors for a well-disciplined crew, Horton took *E.9* on a hunting expedition and, in the approaches to Kiel Bay, well inside Germany's home waters, he found the destroyer *S-120* going about her business. Fighting to control the submarine in a heavy swell that continually threatened to lift the boat to the surface, Lieutenant Chapman, *E.9*'s Number One, balanced the trim with praiseworthy delicacy while Horton conned the vessel closer to its target. After eleven minutes, when the range was down to 600 yards, a single torpedo streaked from the starboard bow tube. But at that precise moment *E.9* lost trim. Her nose plunged down and Horton lost sight of the enemy ship. However, exactly to the second, the muted sound of an under-water explosion was heard inside the submarine and, when Horton rose to periscope depth to check the success of his attack, there was no sign of the German vessel.

Max justifiably claimed to have sunk the *S-120* and the victory was duly confirmed by both the British Admiralty and the Russian Navy. But, in fact, the enemy destroyer had escaped destruction and she owed her survival to a piece of luck that even Horton must have envied. A submerged sandbank had lain invisibly between the submarine and its prey and, acting as a defensive barrier, it had caused the torpedo to detonate prematurely just a few yards short of its target. It was the sound of this explosion that misled *E.9*'s crew into thinking that they had hit the enemy. Thus warned of the submarine's presence, the German vessel had promptly, and wisely, decamped from the scene as fast as it could steam and was already out of sight by the time Horton's periscope broke surface.

The particular attack, having taken place so close to their main fleet base, thoroughly alarmed the German High Command. Their heavy ships operating in support of the army's seaward flank were hurriedly recalled and destroyers and other small craft were given the task of searching the Prussian coastline for a mythical base from which British submarines were thought to be working. For although only *E.1* and *E.9* had actually reached the Baltic the German C-in-C, Prince Henry, was convinced that he was under threat from an entire flotilla!

'I consider the destruction of a Russian submarine to be a great success,' he told his U-boat captains operating in the Gulf of Finland. 'But I regard the destruction of a British submarine as being at least as valuable as that of a Russian armoured cruiser.'

That the British Admiralty shared the enemy's high regard for *E.9*'s captain was soon apparent when the New Year's promotion list included the following small but significant entry: *Lt-Cdr M.K. Horton DSO to be Commander.*

The Russians, however, remained sourly unimpressed. Their attitude, like the weather, was decidedly frigid and the two British submarine commanders soon found themselves being blocked in every direction and at every level. Horton's own experience was typical. Both *E.1* and *E.9* had exhausted their official rum ration and in the bitter cold of the Russian winter the crews needed something to warm their inner cockles while on patrol and on their return to harbour. The local Russian commander refused to supply them with vodka, a commodity strictly reserved for the wardroom, and Horton pursued his request to the highest possible levels. His persistence finally reached the ears of the Tsar himself. But the 'Little Father', enjoying the comfortable warmth of the Winter Palace in St Petersburg, was unconcerned by such trivialities. Surely, he asked cynically, the British had been sent to the Baltic to fight, not drink? 'If they are so cold,' he observed unsympathetically, 'why can't they wear two shirts?' The story is probably apocryphal, but it serves to demonstrate the attitude of the Court to the humble sailor and helps to explain the resentments that caused the Revolution. But, politics aside, and via channels which no one cared to investigate too closely, Horton obtained a plentiful supply of vodka for his 'troops' and the traditional spirit ration continued. Poker playing with the Russians could be a useful occupation!

The Spring of 1915 found Britain's two lone submarines scouring the Baltic for targets. Horton was initially ordered to attack the seaward flank of the German advance on Libau, but the port had fallen by 10 May and he was told, instead, to patrol the enemy's lines of communication out of Danzig. Within hours of receiving his new instructions Horton sighted three transports escorted by three cruisers and a number of destroyers. With typical bravado, he dived under the destroyer screen and, coming to periscope depth, loosed his two bow torpedoes at the cruiser *Roon*. But the range was 1,000 yards, a considerable distance for weapons of that period, and both torpedoes missed.

Undismayed by the failure, Max took *E.9* across the bows of the approaching transports in order to gain the advantage of the sun and, as the troopships came into his sights, he fired his port midships torpedo at the leading vessel. But luck had deserted him that day and, although his aim was true, the weapon ran too deep and passed harmlessly under the target's keel. Then, while *E.9*'s torpedo-men were struggling to reload the bow tubes, Horton swung the submarine through eight points and scored a hit on the second of the troopships with his stern tube. Alerted by the bubbling tracks of the torpedoes, the enemy destroyers quickly found *E.9*'s periscope and every time Max rose to take aim he came under heavy fire from the escort ships. Refusing to give up, he fired his bow tubes at the third transport, once again convinced that he had found another victim.

Sadly, his efforts had all been in vain. One of the torpedoes which he thought had struck home had, in fact, nosedived to the seabed and exploded on hitting the bottom. The others had all missed their targets and German naval records, when examined after the war, showed that no ships had been lost in the attack.

Subsequent events seemed to confirm that Horton's luck had finally run out and he suffered a series of disappointing failures over the course of the next few days. Due to a shortage of British-made torpedoes, *E.9* was now carrying a number of Russian-built weapons and when he fired one at the transports *Indianola* and *Ikula*, two of the ships that had escaped unscathed in the earlier convoy attack, it shot to the surface and careered towards the target like a miniature speedboat giving the enemy ample time to take evasive action. On his next patrol he sighted the German submarine *U-26* on the surface, but the enemy lookouts were equally alert and both vessels dived simultaneously. Without such modern aids as sonar gear and hydrophones, Horton had no chance of finding the U-boat under the water and, as another British submarine commander had observed in a similar situation: 'Neither of us knew what to do'. In the circumstances it was hardly surprising that *U-26* made her escape.

But fortune smiled on Horton again when, only a few hours later, he encountered the cruiser *Thetis* with four destroyers and the collier *Dora Hugo Stinnes*. To his amazement, the latter stopped to refuel two of the destroyers, leaving the three remaining warships to circle defensively while the sacks of coal were transferred. This particular attack demonstrated Horton's undoubted skill as a tactician. Having studied the movements of the enemy ships for several minutes, he suddenly realized that he could make a double killing, for the relative positions of the vessels were such that there was one point in the geometry of the circle where he would be able to fire his port beam tube at the cruiser while, simultaneously, launching the bow torpedoes at the collier.

Unfortunately the torpedo aimed at the *Thetis* performed erratically and missed its target, but the two British-built weapons despatched from the bow tubes met with more success. The first hit the *Dora Hugo Stinnes* squarely in the stern, throwing up a choking cloud of black coal dust and inflicting a wound that was to send the collier to the bottom a few hours later. The second torpedo struck the destroyer *S-148* in the bows, causing serious damage, although, thanks to the strenuous efforts of the crew and the fine seamanship of her skipper, the vessel was kept afloat and eventually reached harbour. It is not surprising that, by this time, the Germans were calling the Baltic 'Horton's Sea'!

Thick fog affected submarine operations for the next few weeks, but on 2 July, while patrolling off Danzig, *E.9* sighted two large warships escorted by destroyers. The sea was smooth as glass and this made it difficult to conceal the telltale feather of spray spuming from the periscope as Horton stalked his prey. However, thanks to his consummate skill, the submarine remained undetected and, having closed to a bare 400 yards, an incredible achievement in the circumstances, he fired his two bow torpedoes at the leading ship. But, in turning to bring the port beam tube to bear, *E.9* lost trim and wallowed to the surface. In Horton's own words: 'We hit her . . . with two torpedoes. She was going pretty fast, about eighteen (knots). . . . Saw the first explosion by the foremast, fine show, débris and smoke up to the tops of the masts. I was keeping a somewhat anxious eye on a destroyer, pretty close, doing its best to ram us. Dirty dog!'

It was a letter typical of Horton. No mention of the skill needed to put two torpedoes into an escorted armoured cruiser or the terrible danger they faced when *E.9* broke surface under the guns of the avenging German destroyers. In fact Horton only escaped destruction by a hair's breadth and *E.9* dived so rapidly that she plunged her bows into the muddy bottom of the seabed 45 feet below before she could be trimmed level. Yet, despite the brilliance of his attack, Max only succeeded in damaging the *Prinz Adalbert*, for, although he secured two hits on the armoured cruiser, her hide was too tough to succumb to the puny 200-pound warheads of the 18-inch RNTF Mk VIII torpedoes with which *E.9* was armed. Nevertheless, the enemy boat was badly damaged and remained in dockyard hands for several months. When she finally emerged on 23 October she promptly fell victim to Lt-Cdr Goodhart and *E.8*, who, luckier than Horton, put a torpedo into her forward magazine. An horrendous explosion literally tore the unfortunate vessel apart and within eight minutes she had vanished.

The Russians were delighted by Horton's run of successes and any disappointment that he may have felt over his failure to sink the *Prinz Adalbert* was amply assuaged when, by order of the Tsar, the Russian C-in-C, Admiral Kanin, presented him with the country's highest military honour, the Order of St George.

Recognition of the important work being carried out by Laurence and Horton took a more concrete form in Whitehall where it was decided to send *E.8* (Lt-Cdr Goodhart), *E.13* (Lt-Cdr Layton), *E.18* (Lt-Cdr Halahan) and *E.19* (Lt-Cdr Cromie) into the Baltic via the Kattegat, Skagerrak, and The Sound – a passage which the unlucky *E.13* failed to complete – while four older and smaller submarines, *C.26, C.27, C.32* and *C.35* were towed to Archangel and then shipped overland to St Petersburg on canal barges!

The reinforcement of the Frozen Flotilla also coincided with a change of strategy when it was decided to launch an all-out offensive against the German-Swedish iron-ore trade and other Baltic shipping routes. Both Goodhart and Laurence scored a number of early successes and, finally, on 17 October, 1915, it was Horton's turn to join the hunt. The first ship he stopped after leaving Reval turned out to be a Danish merchantman bound for Stockholm with English coal and, having examined the cargo manifest, Horton allowed the neutral trader to proceed unharmed. His second victim was the German *Soderhamm* carrying a shipment of wood for Holland. She was a legitimate prize under International Law and, having given the crew time to abandon ship, a boarding party was sent over to open the seacocks and rig demolition charges. In fact, the stoutly built *Soderhamm* failed to sink and, drifting onto rocks in Norrkoping Bay, she was subsequently salvaged.

When Horton caught up with the iron-ore carrier *Pernambuco* her German crew hastily left the ship before he had even issued the mandatory challenge. But again the demolition charges proved inadequate and he had to despatch her to the bottom with one of his precious torpedoes. *Johannes Russ* fell victim to *E.9* at dawn the next day and this time Horton's experts succeeded in scuttling the vessel with explosives.

But, despite the destruction which Horton was wreaking along the Swedish coast, he took care to keep within the rules of

International Law. And after this particular foray he reported to the Admiralty that: 'Due and proper warning was given in every case. . . . Ample time was allowed for placing personal gear, food, and water, into the boats and in no case was the weather unsuitable for small boats or the distance to the nearest shore more than 15 miles . . . no casualties occurred or were reported.'

Nevertheless, an incident that same day showed that Horton did not intend to be browbeaten by an unfair application of the rules relating to neutral rights. He had gone after the German vessel *Dal Alfoen* and, having stopped her, was waiting for the crew to pull away from the ship in their boats when the Swedish destroyer *Wale* suddenly appeared on the scene full of bustling importance. Thinking that the intruder was a German warship, Horton promptly submerged and, determined not to be robbed of his prize, he tried to sink the *Dal Alfoen* with two torpedoes. But both weapons missed in the confusion and when recognized the Swedish ensign flying from the destroyer's masthead he brought *E.9* to the surface. The exchange of signals that followed revealed an unexpectedly ruthless side to Horton's normally happy-go-lucky character:

Wale: You are in Swedish waters.

E.9:   I make myself six miles from land.

Wale: I make you five.

E.9:   Neutral limit is three miles. Please stand clear while I sink this ship.

True to his word, and in full view of his captive audience, Horton turned *E.9* around, aimed his stern tube at the German vessel and sent her to the bottom with a single torpedo. Although he had acted strictly within the law, his action certainly showed a lack of tact and it did little to endear him to the Swedish authorities.

When the Russian winter shut down submarine operations until the following spring both Laurence and Horton received recall telegrams from the Admiralty in London informing them that they were 'urgently required for service in new submarines in home waters'. For Horton this meant command of *J.6* and, later, the monster submarine monitor *M.1*. It was the first step in a long ladder of promotion that ultimately led him to flag rank and command of the Royal Navy's submarine service from 9 January, 1940, to 9 November, 1942, followed by an equally important appointment as C-in-C Western Approaches during the most crucial period of Britain's battle with the U-boats for control of the Atlantic.

All this, however, lay in the future. Recognizing his worth, the Russian Navy urgently requested that Max should remain at Reval as the Senior Naval Officer, Baltic. But the British Admiralty thought otherwise, and, with memories of the Jolly Roger which the *E.9* had flamboyantly flown after sinking the *Hela*, the Second Sea Lord acidly, and certainly unjustifiably, noted the minute relating to the request: 'I understand that Commander Horton is something of a pirate and not at all suited for the position of SNO in the Baltic.'

But Max clearly had friends in high places and even Sir George Buchanan, Britain's ambassador to St Petersburg, interceded on his behalf in a telegram to London: 'I learn that Commander Laurence and Commander Horton are under orders for England. The latter gets on particularly well with the Russians which requires special qualifications, and his experience in the Baltic is also valuable. Would it not be possible for him to remain?'

But even this plea failed to move Their Lordships and on 31 December, 1915, Horton packed his bags and prepared to depart for England. Leaving *E.9* in the capable hands of her new skipper, Lt-Cdr Hubert Vaughan-Jones, and travelling overland through neutral Sweden and Norway on a false passport, Max finally arrived in Newcastle wrapped in an enormous sable coat and smoking some evil-smelling Russian cigarettes that kept both friends and Customs' officials at a respectful distance. In addition to his normal luggage he was carrying a small leather jewel case. It contained: the Order of Vladimir with Swords, the Order of St Ann with Swords and Diamonds, the Order of St George, the Distinguished Service Order, and the accoutrements of a *Chevalier* of the *Legion d'Honneur*.

It was, indeed, a veritable treasure-trove of loot. But the man whom the Admiralty had once described as a 'pirate' richly deserved every single honour that had been bestowed upon him. For throughout 1915, as the German Navy itself admitted, the Baltic had been – Horton's Sea.

—THREE—

Kapitanleutnant Otto Weddigen

'We wish no lives to be lost'

Secured to the line of rust-streaked buoys that stretched south-eastwards from the island fortress of Heligoland, and forming a barrier across the main seaward approach to the German Bight, the ten U-boats that made up the First Flotilla rolled gently with the ebbing tide as the evening of 2 August, 1914, drew to an uneasy close. It had been a pleasant summer's day with just the hint of a breeze blowing off the sea. And sheltered behind the canvas screens of the submarines' open bridges officers and lookouts alike anxiously searched the western horizon for the first warning of a British attack.

Germany was already at war with Russia and, as the Kaiser's armies massed on the borders of Belgium, it was quite certain that France would enter the fray the following day. Only Britain and her Empire stood alone and undecided. Would she, as the German Government hoped, remain aloof from the conflict that was spreading hourly across Europe in the wake of Archduke Ferdinand's assassination in Sarajevo? Or would the British Cabinet, meeting in secret session at that very moment to consider Sir Edward Grey's latest diplomatic efforts to pull the Central Powers back from the brink of the abyss, agree to act against Germany, should von Molkte's divisions violate Belgium's borders?

Otto Weddigen, the captain of *U-9*, one of the boats standing guard over the sea approaches to Wilhelmshaven, was uncomfort-

ably aware of the international situation. But, like many professional officers whose only duty was to obey orders without
question, he took little interest in politics. So far as he was
concerned the month of August, 1914, marked only one event of
any significance – his forthcoming wedding. Despite his un-
questioned patriotism he fervently hoped that the war could at
least be delayed for a few weeks until he had made Irma his bride.
After that he was content to let the gods do their worst!

Weaned on a diet of Anglophobic hysteria, Weddigen and his
fellow officers in the Imperial Navy were quite certain that Britain
would launch her fleet against Germany without the formality of
an ultimatum or a declaration of war. Horatio Nelson had
destroyed the Danish fleet at Copenhagen in just such a way in
1807 while England's Far Eastern ally, Japan, had struck at the
Russian Navy in Port Arthur without warning as recently as 1904,
just ten years ago. And the infamous Lord Fisher, during his
eccentric reign as the Royal Navy's First Sea Lord, was constantly
vowing to do the same to the *Kaiserliche Marine* – a threat which
even King Edward VII, the German Emperor's uncle, had taken
seriously, although he had laughingly told his senior admiral: 'You
must be mad!'

With the sea slapping gently against the bulbous ballast tanks of
the tethered U-boat and the sun sinking slowly towards the rim of
the horizon, Weddigen raised his glasses to his eyes and searched
for the invisible enemy for the umpteenth time that day. A large
Hamburg-Amerika steamer was moving across the Bight with her
lights extinguished and, as he watched the vessel pass in front of
U-9's bows, Weddigen conjectured that she was probably heading
for her war station in mid-Atlantic where she would operate as an
armed raider – a task which, in his opinion, could be better
accomplished by a battle-trained submarine than a converted
passenger liner with a mainly civilian crew.

His gloomy reverie was broken by the sharp crack of the sunset
gun high up on the fortress ramparts of Heligoland – the echoing
boom sent the nesting seagulls screaming skywards in shrill protest
– and, acting upon the signal, the Korting engines of the U-boats
were restarted. Black kerosene smoke rose from the exhaust
trunks abaft the conning-towers and each Commanding Officer
checked that all was clear fore and aft before ordering the men
standing on the bow-casing to slip the mooring cables and cast off
the buoys. Then, joined by their escort and forming up into a long
snaking line behind the flotilla leader, the submarines swung to
starboard in a wide circle and headed back to the shelter of
Wilhelmshaven for the night – an ignominious exit for what was

intended to be Germany's first line of defence against the British Navy.

The spreading glow of the sunset now stretched from one end of the horizon to the other and created a dramatic backcloth to the sparkling wakes of the U-boats as they returned to the mainland. Looking astern, Weddigen stared at the spectacle in silence as though overawed by the magnificence of Nature's artistry. Suddenly, responding to an impulse, he turned to his First Officer who was standing beside him on *U-9*'s diminutive bridge.

'Spiess, you see how red the sky is. The whole world seems bathed in blood. Mark my words – England will declare war on us.'

At 11pm on 4 August his prophecy was fulfilled. The U-boat war had begun and Weddigen was destined to become its first hero.

* * *

Otto Weddigen was twenty-eight years old and an *Oberleutnant* in command of a small gunboat when he decided to transfer to the *Deutsche Unterseeboots Flotille* in the summer of 1910. On 17 January 1911, within months of joining his new profession, he had his first brush with death when *U-3* plunged to the bottom of Kiel Harbour during a routine training exercise that suddenly went disastrously wrong, the submarine having apparently dived with one of its ventilators still open. A telephone buoy was released and the U-boat's captain reported that the vessel was lying in 30 feet of water and was flooding rapidly. In addition, chlorine gas was building up inside the submarine as the result of the salt seawater contaminating the acid in the battery cells. Then the line went dead and contact with the sunken boat was lost.

Discipline inside the cramped and crowded confines of the tiny 421-ton U-boat remained good and, as rescue ships hastened to the scene from the dockyard, Weddigen and the other eight officer-trainees under instruction joined *U-3*'s crew as they struggled for survival in the darkness of the flooded and gas-filled submarine. With the chlorine fumes clawing at their lungs, the trapped men fought for breath while their bruised and bleeding hands searched for the vital valve wheels. They worked with orderly calm until the relevant controls were located. Under the direction of an experienced Petty Officer the main vents were closed and a few seconds later high-pressure air was expelling the water ballast from the for'ard buoyancy tanks. The bows of the U-boat lifted off the bottom and rose swiftly to the surface. Two officers from her flotilla-mate *U-1*, which had been exercising with her, jumped down onto the exposed casing and hammered a morse signal on the steel hull plates, instructing the imprisoned men to open the bow caps so that they could escape through the torpedo tubes.

But the message brought no response and the officers feared that *U-3*'s crew were already dead, killed by the lethal chlorine gas rising up from the battery compartment or perhaps drowned in the flooded interior. But at the third attempt their hammered tattoo brought a frenzied tapping from inside the U-boat. And, as a nearby floating-crane passed a hawser under the projecting stem of the submarine to prevent her from sliding back beneath the surface, the men inside *U-3* managed to locate and operate the switches of the servo-motor controlling the bow caps. Mercifully it still worked and, as the starboard cap swung open, a rope was hastily dropped into the torpedo-tube ready to hoist the first man to freedom.

The diameter of the tube was only 17.7 inches and the long slow haul up its 28-feet length was a terrifying and claustrophobic ordeal in itself. But man after man made the arduous journey, Weddigen among them, and finally a total of twenty-eight survivors lay sprawled on *U-1*'s foredeck coughing, choking and retching from the after-effects of the gas. Only three officers, including the captain, now remained inside the submarine, but, trapped in the conning-tower, they were unable to escape through the torpedo-tube with the others and it was decided to raise the U-boat with the heavy lifting-gear carried by the submarine salvage ship *Vulkan* – equipment specifically designed for just such a contingency as this. But time was against the rescuers. It took an unexpected eighteen hours to raise the U-boat and although the three officers were apparently alive when the conning-tower finally broke surface two were dead when the hatch was opened and a third died on his way to hospital.

It was hardly an encouraging introduction to the U-boat service but Weddigen was undeterred by his ordeal. He passed his final examinations with flying colours and, in due course, after further experience on watch-keeping duties, he was given command of *U-9*, one of Germany's early kerosene-burning submarines.

Like his Royal Navy contemporary Max Horton the young *Oberleutnant* Weddigen established his reputation during a series of peacetime exercises. While taking part in manoeuvres with the High Seas Fleet in May, 1913, he hit three battleships with a salvo of only four practice torpedoes – two from the bow tubes and, after a short interval, two from the stern. Later that year he gained further plaudits, this time for seamanship, when he brought *U-9* safely through an unusually severe storm. On a personal level he won the respect of his crew by jumping into the freezing waters of the North Sea to save a sailor who had fallen overboard, an action that cost him a broken arm when the waves threw him against the steel side of the U-boat while being hauled to safety. Always an innovator, a trait shared by many other great submarine commanders, he perfected the drill for reloading the empty tubes with spare torpedoes while submerged at periscope depth under simulated combat conditions. It was a routine that was to serve him well in the not too distant future.

One of his officers recalled that he 'was the very reverse of a martinet . . . (and) allowed the officers under him the privileges of initiative and freedom of ideas. You did not feel like a subordinate . . . but rather like a younger comrade.' And by 1914 he was acknowledged throughout the fleet as 'an exceedingly capable submarine man'.

The opening days of the war quickly dashed any hopes of instant glory. First came the boredom of static defence with *U-9* moored to a buoy in the middle of the Bight. And then, when Weddigen was finally sent out on his first combat patrol with Germany's other nine operational submarines, engine trouble forced him to turn back and return to harbour after only a few days at sea. *U-9*, however, was luckier than two of her sisters who had left on patrol at the same time. *U-15* was rammed and sunk by the British cruiser *Birmingham*, while *U-13*, living up to the ill-omen of her number, struck a German mine and was lost with all hands.

U-9's mechanical problems kept her in dockyard hands for the next six weeks and, taking advantage of the unscheduled opportunity, Weddigen obtained a short spell of compassionate leave so that he could wed Irma and enjoy a brief honeymoon before returning to duty. His personal happiness was balanced by professional pride when he learned that Hersing's *U-21* had sunk the 2,940-ton British cruiser *Pathfinder* with a single torpedo on 3 September – a feat acclaimed by friend and foe alike as being the first time in history that a warship had been sunk by a submarine.*

After the frustrations of August, Hersing's success gave fresh heart to the U-boat service. And Weddigen felt a new confidence pulsing through his veins when he set off on his next mission even though his operational orders confined him to a patrol area off the Belgian coast where, it was hoped, he might snap up a British troopship on its way to France with reinforcements.

His ambitions were quickly disappointed, however, when *U-9* ran into a violent storm off northern Holland. The shoals and

* See Chapter One. This honour actually belongs to the Confederate States' submarine *Hunley* which sank the Unionist corvette *Housatonic* with a spar torpedo on 17 February, 1864.

30

sandbanks along this stretch of the Dutch coast were a notorious graveyard for submarines* and at nightfall on 20 September, with the weather worsening by the minute, Weddigen altered course westwards to gain sea-room and to escape the angry surf and treacherous shallows on his port hand.

But a compass failure soon made accurate navigation impossible and, despite the gale-force winds and pounding seas, a Petty Officer was sent along the deck to take soundings. The lead showed that they were in 17 fathoms of water. *U-9*'s dead reckoning position on the charts placed her in only 10 fathoms. They were obviously not where they were supposed to be. With heavy storm clouds making it impossible to obtain a star-sight, the *Kapitanleutnant* knew that he was well and truly lost.

The weather was now taking a savage toll of the little submarine but Weddigen obstinately refused to run for shelter or to call off the patrol. Instead, tossed and battered by ten-foot waves, huddled behind the canvas screens in streaming oilskins, and only able to converse with Spiess by shouting at the top of his voice, *U-9*'s captain remained on the exposed conning-tower bridge throughout the night and, by dint of superb seamanship, rode out the storm on the surface.

Dawn brought some relief and improved visibility enabled Weddigen to pin-point the submarine's position by reference to various lighthouses and other navigational marks along the Dutch coast. Having obtained a satisfactory fix, he resumed course towards his assigned patrol area. But once again the weather began to deteriorate and by dusk on the 21st, despite a rise in barometric pressure, the seas had become so wild that he was forced to take *U-9* beneath the surface to escape further punishment.

There was a general feeling of relief as the U-boat's keel gently scraped the pebbles of the seabed and, shutting off the motors to conserve his batteries, Weddigen took on extra water ballast with the intention of spending the rest of the night sitting snugly on the bottom. But it was impossible to escape the storm even at a depth of 100 feet and a vicious undertow rolled *U-9* first one way and then the other in an unpleasant see-saw motion. On occasions she lifted clear of the seabed only to be slammed down hard again a few minutes later. Sleep was impossible and the heavy jolting threatened to damage the U-boat's delicate machinery. Realizing that it would be better to fight the storm on the surface, Weddigen restarted the motors and took *U-9* up to face the elements for the

* The British *E.17* and *H.6* and the German U-boats *UB-6, UB-30,* and *UC-8* were all lost after running aground on the Dutch coast during the First World War.

second night in succession. Shortly after midnight there was a sudden alarm from the lookouts as a group of enemy destroyers was sighted heading northwards. Weddigen was forced to dive again and this time he kept *U-9* on the bottom until daybreak.

At dawn the following morning the submarine was twenty-two miles west-north-west of Scheveningen. The worst of the low pressure system had passed and, although the sea was still running high, the wind had fallen to a breeze and visibility was almost perfect. Squinting through *U-9*'s periscope, Weddigen checked that there were no other ships in the area and told Spiess to bring the U-boat to the surface to recharge her batteries, a procedure which, in normal circumstances, would have been carried out at night.

Some thirty minutes later, while Weddigen was enjoying a hasty breakfast below, Spiess sighted the mast of a warship emerging over the rim of the horizon, followed within seconds by a cloud of heavy black funnel smoke. Bending forward, he put his mouth to the brass voicepipe.

'Captain to the bridge! Smoke on the horizon. All hands to diving stations!'

Weddigen appeared through the upper hatch, hoisted himself up on deck and, still wiping the remains of breakfast from his lips, scanned the horizon with his powerful Zeiss glasses. Spiess was right. They *were* the masts of a warship. And, judging by the volume of black smoke, there was more than one vessel approaching. Perhaps they were the destroyers which had been seen during the night.

'Take her down, *Oberleutnant*. Let's try to have a closer look.'

He waited while Spiess cleared the hatchway and then, having closed and clipped the upper hatch, he slid down the ladder to join him in the brightly lit control-room.

'Ten metres . . . steer zero-two-zero.'

'Bring her level at ten metres, Cox'n. Course zero-two-zero.'

The Petty Officer sitting in front of the hydroplane controls watched the circular dial of the depth-gauge as the red needle swung down.

'Ten metres, sir.'

'Reduce to half-speed. Up periscope.'

Weddigen grabbed the handles of the 'scope as it rose to eye-level, swung the upper lens onto the bearing where the smoke had been observed and quickly estimated the course and speed of the unknown vessels.

'Down periscope.'

It was too early in the game to identify the prey with any degree of certainty but even at this stage Weddigen could not risk an alert lookout spotting the broomstick column of the questing periscope. Having ordered a slight alteration of course, he increased the submarine's speed and waited patiently as *U-9* closed her prospective target. The periscope broke surface again in response to the sharp click of his finger and thumb and this time he spent a full minute carefully surveying the approaching vessels. He carried out his inspection in complete silence and the expression on his face gave no hint of what he could see through the Cyclops eye of his probing lens. And discipline ensured that no one asked.

The servo-motor whined as the periscope slid back into its womb and Weddigen could sense the tension inside the U-boat. He looked around at the anxious faces and allowed himself the luxury of a smile.

'There are three light cruisers – all four-stackers. Probably *Birmingham*-class boats. Perhaps we can avenge *U-15*.' He turned to Spiess. 'Prepare for torpedo attack, *Oberleutnant*. Running depth three metres.'

The orders were acknowledged by the torpedomen serving the submarine's bow and stern tubes. Having adjusted the depth setting of the gleaming Type-G weapons, they opened the valves and flooded the tubes ready for firing.

'Bow tubes flooded . . . standing by!'

'Stern tubes flooded and secured for firing!'

Johann Spiess unscrewed the safety shields that covered the firing buttons and waited. Weddigen, his eye pressed against the monocular lower lens of the periscope, made his final observations of the enemy's course and speed. Unaware that nemesis was lurking in the depths barely 500 yards away the enemy squadron, cruising unescorted in a loose triangular formation, maintained a straight course and a moderate speed.

'Down periscope . . . stand by. Coxswain, watch the trim. I don't want her bobbing to the surface like a demented dolphin when we fire.' He turned to the faithful Spiess and characteristically asked, 'Which tube shall we use, *Oberleutnant*?'

'I suggest Number Two, sir.'

'Very well. Number Two it shall be. Up periscope! Hold her steady . . . watch your depth, Cox'n . . . stand by . . . fire Two! Down periscope! Take her to 15 metres.'

According to the submarine's chronometer it was exactly 7.20 am Central European Time. And thirty-one seconds later *U-9*'s crew heard the muffled thud of an underwater explosion as the torpedo struck the target. The sudden release of tension sent a cheer echoing through the boat. And even Weddigen and Spiess, shrugging aside the constraints of their commissioned rank, slapped each other wildly on the back. As Weddigen had promised – the men of *U-15* had been avenged.

The torpedo hit the *Aboukir* on her starboard beam and she heeled sharply as the sea flooded through the large hole which the Type-G had punched in her hull-plating beneath the waterline. Mistakenly thinking that she had run into a mine, the cruiser's two companions, *Hogue* and *Cressy*, turned and closed their stricken comrade and made ready to give assistance. No one realized that they were standing into mortal danger, for no one suspected the presence of a submarine in the area.

U-9 rose cautiously to periscope depth and Weddigen carried out a rapid survey of the situation. *Aboukir* was going down fast and her two squadron-mates, lying stopped in the water, were lowering boats to rescue the survivors – many of whom were now in the sea and swimming away from the sinking cruiser. Weddigen's face was an expressionless mask as he ordered the periscope to be lowered. Whatever his personal feelings were, he knew what had to be done. He turned to Spiess.

'Reload Number Two tube, *Oberleutnant*. We will make a further attack.'

The exercise drill which he had perfected in Kiel harbour during the happy days of peace was about to reap its dividend. And while the enemy cruisers busied themselves dragging survivors from the water, the U-boat's crew sweated and struggled to slide one of the spare torpedoes into the empty No 2 bow tube. Although *U-9* was still submerged, the surface swell was causing the boat to pitch up and down – 'bumping' as submariners called it in those days – and when the heavy weapon was shifted from the storage rack to the empty tube the transfer of weight upset the vessel's delicate trim. The bows angled down and, with the axis of the submarine tilted, the stern lifted up towards the surface. Blowing the compensating tank had little effect on the boat's equilibrium and, in desperation, Weddigen ordered all hands not engaged in moving the torpedo or controlling the trim, to run to the aft compartment of the boat in a primitive attempt to restore the vessel's balance. For a moment *U-9* steadied herself on an even keel. But the momentum continued and, as the stern began to sink under the extra weight, it was the turn of the bows to rise upwards. Weddigen countermanded the order and brought the men forward into the fore-ends. It was the beginning of a ludicrous, almost surrealist, game of see-saw. But this was no innocent children's pastime. This game was being played for high stakes. For if any part of the submarine broke surface under the guns of the enemy their chances of survival were negligible.

Leaving Spiess to control the trim as best he could, Weddigen concentrated his attention on the attack. His selected target – not a light cruiser as he had originally thought but a 12,000-ton armoured cruiser – was stationary and the range was down to a point-blank 300 yards. It was impossible to miss. But Weddigen was taking no chances and at 7.55 am he fired *both* bow torpedoes at the big four-funnelled ship centred in his sights. *U-9*'s temperamental stability reacted violently to the discharge of the torpedoes and, despite instantly flooding the compensating tanks, the extra buoyancy lifted the upper part of the bows clear of the surface.

Two heavy explosions confirmed that the attack had been successful, but, even as *Hogue* lurched and began to settle, her gunners sighted the U-boat and opened fire. Great spouts of dirty white water fountained around the submarine as the shells exploded, but, fortunately for *U-9*, the gunlayers had over-estimated the range and, by the time they had corrected their sights, the U-boat had already escaped into the safety of the depths.

Hogue remained on an even keel but she was sinking fast and within fifteen minutes she had joined *Aboukir* on the bottom. In less than an hour the Royal Navy had lost two old, but still useful, armoured cruisers. Unable to credit that a single submarine could wreak such destruction unaided, the British convinced themselves that they had been ambushed by a group of U-boats and even accused some innocent Dutch trawlers, who happened to be fishing nearby, of assisting the enemy.

But Weddigen had no need of help – either real or imaginary. The routine of loading the final spare torpedo was repeated, and then, responding to the helm, *U-9* turned her back on the last surviving cruiser so that her stern tubes could claim a share of the action. This time one of the torpedoes missed its target by some twenty feet but the second weapon struck the cruiser's port beam below the waterline, inflicting mortal damage. *Cressy* listed slightly and began to settle in the water, but her gunners bravely remained at their posts. When Weddigen poked his periscope above the waves to assess the extent of the damage he had inflicted, he was met by a barrage of shells from the quick-firers ranged along the boat deck. Submerging rapidly, he swung *U-9* around until she was bows-on to her target and, ignoring the crash of exploding shells, raised the submarine's periscope to take aim. The last torpedo leapt from its tube and a sheet of flame erupted from the cruiser's waterline as it slammed home.

Weddigen watched the death throes of the *Cressy* in silence for nearly half a minute before calling Spiess to the periscope. The

Oberleutnant stared through the periscope. It was, he recalled, 'a fearful picture. The giant with four funnels turned slowly over to port. Men climbed like ants over her side and then, as she turned turtle completely, they ran about on her broad flat keel until, in a few minutes, she disappeared beneath the waves.'

And so, on that fateful September day in 1914, the submarine came of age. *U-9*, a diminutive vessel of only 493 tons in surface trim and crewed by just twenty-eight men, had totally destroyed three armoured cruisers, each displacing some 12,000 tons, and inflicted an horrific 1,460 casualties on the Royal Navy – a figure that sadly included a number of long-service pensioners recalled to the colours and a group of fourteen-year-old cadets who had been sent to sea when war broke out.

Weddigen himself was fulsome in his praise of the British sailors. Of the *Cressy* he wrote: 'Her men stayed at their guns looking for their . . . foes. They were brave (and) true to their country's sea traditions.'

The British, however, were not quite so generous. Having initially insisted that the attack had been carried out by more than one U-boat – *The Times* even quoted an eye-witness who had seen *three* conning-towers – there was more than an element of sour grapes in the Admiralty statement issued after the tragedy. 'The loss of nearly sixty officers and 1400 men would not have been grudged if it had been brought about by gunfire in an open action, but it is particularly distressing under the conditions that prevailed.' No similar crocodile tears had been shed when Max Horton had torpedoed and sunk the cruiser *Hela* in similar circumstances on 13 September with the loss of many lives.

But Weddigen had not yet finished with the British Navy. Leaving Wilhelmshaven on 13 October with Feldkirchner's *U-17* in company, the two submarines crossed the North Sea with the intention of patrolling the approaches to the Grand Fleet's base at Scapa Flow. Two days later, having made landfall on the Scottish coast, Weddigen sighted the 10th Cruiser Squadron off Aberdeen. But the range was too great for a torpedo attack and, despite chasing the ships at maximum speed, he was unable to get into a favourable firing position.

Then, with unbelievable good fortune, he saw the enemy reduce speed and reverse course towards him. *Endymion* was the first vessel to stop and, as a signal flag ran up her foremast, *Hawke* also came to a halt and lowered a cutter, presumably to collect the mail from her companion. It seemed an incredibly stupid thing to do in waters known to be patrolled by enemy submarines, but, despite the loss of the *Aboukir, Hogue* and *Cressy*, the Royal Navy had not

36

yet come to terms with the dangers of underwater warfare – which in any case was regarded as underhand and damned un-English! Weddigen merely thanked his lucky stars and took advantage of his good fortune.

'Bow Number Two stand by . . . fire!'

Having retrieved the mail cutter, the *Hawke* was already moving slowly forward again as the torpedo leapt from its tube. But with the range down to 500 yards, it was impossible to miss and the bronze-bodied Type-G exploded below the cruiser's fore funnel. With no underwater protection it proved to be a fatal wound and within eight minutes the *Hawke* vanished. Mindful of the fate suffered by *Hogue* and *Cressy* when they went to the assistance of *Aboukir*, the cruiser's two companions sheered away and high-tailed for the horizon, leaving the exhausted survivors struggling in the water. Of *Hawke*'s 544-man crew only seventy-three were still alive when rescue ships and destroyers reached the scene.

Weddigen, who had already received the Iron Cross 1st Class for his triple victory in September, was now awarded the coveted *Pour le Merite* – the first German naval officer of the war to be so honoured – the decoration being personally presented to him by Kaiser Wilhelm himself. After a spell of sick leave to recover from a leg injury, he was given command of the submarine *U-29* which, although not a great deal larger than *U-9*, carried 19.7-inch torpedoes instead of the older vessel's 17.7-inch. The larger weapon promised the certain destruction of any warship it struck.

However, when Weddigen left Wilhelmshaven in March, 1915, for his first foray in *U-29*, he found himself chasing different targets. The High Command's decision to impose a submarine blockade on Britain meant that the main thrust of the U-boat attack had moved from naval vessels to merchant ships. And the 'Scourge of the Royal Navy' had to turn his attention to the destruction of unarmed steamers – a task which held little, if any, appeal for him.

Having passed safely through the anti-submarine defences of the Dover Straits and run the gauntlet of the Channel patrols, Weddigen opened his campaign in the vicinity of the Scilly Isles on 11 March. He began by snaring the *Aden-wen* off the Casquet Rocks. Obedient to both the spirit and the letter of International Law, he allowed her crew ten minutes to collect their belongings, abandon ship and take to the boats. His comment that 'We wish no lives to be lost' was reported to Press by the survivors when they came ashore and *The Times* promptly dubbed him the 'polite pirate'. His behaviour on this and many similar occasions was exemplary and he demonstrated a humane consideration for his victims that made nonsense of the often scurrilous propaganda pumped out by British Government hacks in Whitehall. When one member of the *Aden-wen*'s crew fell into the sea while getting into a lifeboat Weddigen personally sent him a suit of dry clothes!

A short while later he stopped and sank the French steamer *August Conseil*, after taking the trouble to apologize to the Master for having to sink the vessel and asking him to 'present his compliments to Lord (sic) Churchill'. The next day, still operating off the Scillies, he stopped four more ships and, having ensured the safety of the crews, sent each to the bottom with a single torpedo. Unlike that other great U-boat ace von Arnauld de la Perière*, Weddigen always sank his victims with a torpedo, despite *U-29*'s two 3.4-inch deck guns – a quirk that restricted the number of vessels he could destroy in the course of a patrol. Having already used six of his limited stock, he headed north in the hope that he could launch his remaining weapons at his favourite target – an enemy warship! Some experts have suggested that Weddigen decided on the northabout route around the top of Scotland because he did not relish tangling with the anti-submarine defences in the Strait of Dover for a second time. But his choice of route was probably determined by an amalgam of both considerations.

Having recharged batteries during the hours of darkness, *U-29* spent a short period resting on the bottom before returning to periscope depth at dawn on the 18th, ready to continue her homeward trek. Suddenly Weddigen found himself staring at the entire British Grand Fleet – a target truly worthy of his skill. Almost unable to believe his luck, the *Kapitanleutnant* took *U-29* deeper and, calling for maximum submerged speed from the electric motors, he steered an interception course which would enable him to attack the dreadnoughts of the 1st Battle Squadron. After an appropriate interval, carefully timed on the stopwatch that hung from a cord around his neck, he brought the submarine back to periscope depth and selected the *Neptune* as his initial target. But the irregular zig-zag pattern being steered by the battleship confused his aim and his first torpedo missed.

The bubbling wake acted as a warning to the other ships that there was a U-boat in the vicinity and the report brought the lookouts to a new peak of alertness as Weddigen swung his sights onto the 4th Battle Squadron. But again, as with the abortive attack on *Neptune*, the intricate weaving movements of the big ships as they steamed towards him at 17 knots made it difficult to

* See Chapter Six

concentrate his aim and, searching for the best target, he failed to see the *Dreadnought* approaching from starboard.

The battleship's Officer-of-the-Watch, Lt-Cdr Piercy, sighted the slim column of *U-29*'s periscope fine on the port bow and Captain Alderson reacted to his warning shout with commendable promptness. *Temeraire*, the next in line, also sighted the U-boat but Alderson, handling the 17,900-ton armoured ship like a fast-moving destroyer, beat his squadron-mate to the draw. *Dreadnought*'s helm spun to port and, almost simultaneously, her ram bow thrust deep into the submarine's side penetrating the steel plating of the pressure hull and sending the sea flooding through the gaping hole with the ferocity of a bursting dam.

U-29 rolled over under the impact and the officers standing on the battleship's bridge had barely time to read the white-painted identification number on her conning-tower before she sank out of sight. The destroyer, *Blanche*, passing over the spot moments later, found only 'much oil and air bubbles on the surface'. But there was no wreckage and no survivors. The bleak emptiness of the sea was all that remained to mark the U-boat's grave.

Otto Weddigen, in challenging the entire might of Jellicoe's Grand Fleet, had died a warrior's death for his temerity. His successes against the *Aboukir, Hogue, Cressy* and *Hawke* had been a latter-day version of the ancient legend of David and Goliath. In the end, however, Goliath – in the shape of the Royal Navy – had won!

—FOUR—

Lieutenant Norman Douglas Holbrook, RN

'A mighty clever piece of work'

The unexpected escape of the German battlecruiser *Goeben* and her consort *Breslau* from the jaws of the British Mediterranean Fleet and their eventual arrival in Constantinople during the opening days of August, 1914, provided the scenario for Turkey's entry into the war nearly three months later.

At that time the Sultan's Navy was little more than a collection of rusting hulks. The major part of the fleet had not been to sea since 1877 and its 8,000 commissioned officers had only 10,000 rank-and-file to command. The ships were obsolete, worm-eaten and of little fighting value. And so, too, were the admirals.

The situation changed dramatically, however, when Kaiser Wilhelm, the self-proclaimed protector of the Moslem world, made a gift of the battlecruiser and its attendant light cruiser to his prospective allies – although, with both ships helplessly trapped inside the Dardanelles, there was little else that the All-Highest could do with them! But the gesture went down well with the Turks who were still smarting from Britain's seizure of two new battleships being built in British yards for the Sultan's government.* And no objections were offered when Rear-Admiral Souchon, the German squadron commander, was appointed C-in-C of the Ottoman Navy and the Kaiser's sailors – among them

---

* The ships in question were subsequently incorporated into the Grand Fleet as the *Agincourt* and *Erin*.

the young signal officer of the *Breslau*, Karl Doenitz – were distributed along the Sultan's ships to instruct their crews, raise morale and generally prepare them for war service.

With the red crescent ensign of the Sublime Porte flying from their mastheads and rejoicing in their new names of *Jawus Sultan Selim* and *Midilli*, the two ex-German ships posed a dangerous threat to the Royal Navy's control of the Eastern Mediterranean. By the middle of August the political situation had become sufficiently tense for the First Lord of the Admiralty, Winston Churchill, to telegraph the Admiral-Superintendent of Malta Dockyard, Vice-Admiral Sackville Carden: 'Assume command of Squadron off Dardanelles; your sole duty is to sink *Goeben* and *Breslau* no matter what flag they fly if they come out of the Dardanelles. We are not at war with the Turks but Admiral Souchon is now C-in-C of the Turkish Navy and the Germans are largely controlling it.' It was a totally illegal order and it was perhaps fortunate that Churchill's bellicosity was never put to the test. For had the British sunk either ship while it was flying the Turkish ensign and nominally under the Sultan's control, her stance of moral indignation against Germany for invading neutral Belgium would have been somewhat difficult to maintain.

While the Royal Navy's battlecruisers and other surface ships took up their blockade stations off the entrance to the Dardanelles, the Malta-based submarines *B.9*, *B.10* and *B.11*, under the overall command of Lt-Cdr P. H. Pownall, were ordered to the port of Mudros on the island of Lemnos where the depot-ship *Hindu Kush* was anchored in mid-harbour to act as the flotilla's headquarters and accommodation ship. Two other boats, *B.6* and *B.7*, were also ordered to Mudros from Gibraltar while the French Admiralty sent the submarines *Faraday*, *Leverrier*, *Coulomb* and *Circe* – the latter boat having acquired an unenviable reputation two months earlier when she had rammed and sunk her sister *Calypso* while exercising off Cape Lardier.

The newly-appointed British C-in-C, Vice-Admiral Carden, sealed off the entrance to the Dardanelles with the blockade squadron as ordered by Churchill, but Souchon and his recently acquired allies maintained a low profile and nothing untoward happened until 28 October when the former *Goeben* and *Breslau*, accompanied by the Turkish *Hamidieh*, sailed forth into the Black Sea and bombarded the Russian ports of Sebastopol, Novorossisk and Odessa. It was an act of war which Enver Pasha made no attempt to deny and his signal to Souchon: 'The Turkish fleet is to win command of the Black Sea' served to confirm his belligerent intention. At midnight on 30 October the Ottoman Empire

41

regularized the situation by declaring war on Britain and France and Carden prepared for a quick blow against his new enemy.

Just two days later the battlecruisers *Indomitable* and *Indefatigable*, supported by a number of British and French warships, carried out a short sharp bombardment of the lower Dardanelles' fortresses. But, although not unsuccessful in material terms, the raid served to warn the Turks that their Gallipoli defences were inadequate, and their resultant reinforcement was to cost the Allies dear when a full-scale land offensive was launched some months later.

Closeted behind guarded doors in *Hindu Kush*'s wardroom, Pownall and his senior commanders, Norman Holbrook, Geoffrey Warburton and Sam Gravener, discussed the possibility of sending submarines into the Dardanelles in search of targets. The *B*-class boats were almost museum pieces even in 1914. Displacing 280 tons on the surface, with narrow steel hulls only 135 feet in length, they relied on the treacherous and still primitive petrol engine for their surface motive power. And their low submerged endurance made it impossible for them to pass right through the Straits into the Sea of Marmora. But the assembled officers were convinced that a demonstration of strength in the Dardanelles itself would be a worthwhile exercise. A French boat had already penetrated above Sedd el Bahr and Holbrook himself had pursued a torpedo-boat four miles into the Straits beyond Kum Kale.

The idea of an underwater raid on Turkish shipping in the Chanak area was rapidly converted into an operational plan and submitted to Carden who gave it his tentative approval in early December. But, despite the short distances involved, the attack was to be no easy task. The Turks had a number of solidly-built coastal forts along both shores of the Dardanelles and the fortress guns were supported by mobile howitzer batteries and searchlights. In addition, five lines of mines stretched across the Straits below Kephez Point while another field had been laid further north in the vicinity of the Narrows. The threat posed by the guns and searchlights meant that the chosen submarine would have to remain submerged throughout the entire mission. And although the boat could pass safely beneath the minefields – which had been laid with the intention of catching surface ships – the mooring cables represented a serious hazard to an unwary submarine if they snagged around the hydroplanes or fouled the propellers.

Naturally every submarine commander in Mudros was anxious to carry out the raid and both British and French officers vied for selection. But the French boats were not a practical proposition because their externally mounted torpedo-tubes limited their maximum diving depth while, of the five British vessels available, only *B.11* possessed the necessary underwater endurance thanks to her new and recently fitted battery. And so for entirely technical reasons Pownall assigned the operation to Holbrook.

The first task was to prevent the submarine from snagging the mooring cables of the mines and, benefiting from the experiences gained by the 8th Flotilla in the North Sea, the engineers from the *Blenheim* quickly extemporised tubular steel guards which they fitted over the fore and aft hydroplanes. A stout steel jumping wire running from the stem to the stern served to protect the conning-tower, compass binnacle and other awkward projections. Without the convenience of dry-dock facilities it was difficult work but by dint of carefully flooding the ballast tanks and altering the trim of the boat, first the bows and then the stern of the submarine were brought out of the water so that the improvised hydroplane guards could be bolted into place.

The Turks, however, were not totally reliant on their mine-fields –or even their forts, shore batteries or searchlights. For the vagaries of the four-knot current that swept through the narrow strait of the Dardanelles constituted a formidable obstacle in its own right and was a valuable natural support to their man-made defences. In addition, some ten fathoms down, there was a stratum of fresh water which, because of its differing density, made submarine depth-keeping extremely difficult. The practical problem posed by these natural hazards, however, lay in the future. So far as Pownall and Holbrook were concerned the strong current merely reinforced the necessity of a new battery so that an adequate underwater speed could be maintained. For the early submarines suffered the same problem as the biplanes battling against headwinds over the Western Front – if you didn't have enough power you were likely to go backwards!

B.11 cast off from the *Hindu Kush* at 3.00 am on the morning of 13 December and by 4.15 am Holbrook was some three miles from the entrance to the Straits in the vicinity of Cape Helles. He had been given no specific instructions or targets. His mission was to penetrate as far up the Dardanelles as possible and sink any enemy ships encountered. It was a *carte-blanche* for mayhem and he intended to exploit his operational freedom to the utmost. Turkish searchlights were sweeping the narrow waters that lay ahead as *B.11* approached the entrance and, although they were too far away to cause any immediate alarm, Holbrook cautiously shut off his main engines. Routine observation of enemy procedures had revealed that the Turks habitually switched off their searchlights *before* dawn. And Holbrook planned to enter the straits during this brief period of absolute darkness that preceded sunrise.

The submarine rolled gently in the swell as the lieutenant waited. But his patience was rewarded and, at around 5.00 am, the questing searchlight beams were extinguished one by one until only the blackness of the night remained. Taking advantage of the darkness that had settled over the entrance to the straits, Holbrook brought *B.11* to within a mile of Cape Helles and scanned the northern shore of the Gallipoli peninsula through his glasses. The clutches were already disengaged and the submarine was running on her electric motors so that the burbling exhausts of the petrol engine did not attract the attention of a keen-eared lookout.

'Stand by to dive, Number One . . . take her down.'

Waiting below in the cramped control room Lieutenant Winn rapped out the familiar routine orders:

'Hands to diving stations . . . open vents. Flood Q . . . flood main ballast. 'Planes hard a-dive!'

As *B.11* sank quietly and obediently beneath the surface Holbrook closed the hatch, intoned the ritual 'Hatch shut and clipped', and clattered down the steel ladder to join Winn.

'Steer zero-five-zero, Number One. Trim level at 20 feet. Maximum speed.'

'Grouper up! Level at 20, coxswain!'

'Steady on zero-five-zero, sir.'

'Up periscope.'

Despite Holbrook's demand for full power the swirling current racing down the straits kept *B.11*'s speed down to a funereal two knots as she battled upstream, but her commander was content with their progress as he watched the shoreline through the periscope. All was apparently well except for an intermittent vibration that kept shaking the hull at regular intervals. Clearly something had worked loose. But what? It was not an easy decision but Holbrook made it without hesitation.

'Take her up, Number One.'

'Aye, aye, sir. Stand by to surface. Close all vents. Blow main ballast. Fore planes hard-a-rise. And keep her level, cox'n.'

Although *B.11* had surfaced in enemy waters, Holbrook showed a bold disregard for the inherent danger of the situation and, accompanied by an Engine Room Artificer, he climbed out through the hatchway to inspect the outer casing of the hull. The cause of the vibration was soon located – the bolts of the forward port hydroplane guard had sheered and the entire contraption was hanging loose. On Holbrook's instructions Winn flooded the stern ballast tanks in order to raise the bows higher while the ERA and another man set to work to clear the wreckage. It was a difficult task and the two sailors, working up to their thighs in water, had to be secured to the boat with life-lines as they sweated and strained to release the damaged guard. Dawn was due to break within minutes and there was the ever-present danger that an alert enemy sentry would spot the surfaced submarine and raise the alarm. But, as is so often the case, fortune favoured the brave. The twisted remains of the guard suddenly came away and, as it splashed over the side, Holbrook ordered the men back inside the boat and told Winn to submerge. In less than a minute *B.11* was once again safely under the waves and moving upstream.

At 8.30 am Holbrook glimpsed the mouth of the Suandere River over the port bow and knew that they were approaching the Kephez minefield – the first major hazard to be encountered on their passage up the Straits. The men had, by this time, eaten breakfast in relays and even Holbrook had found time to consume half a lobster thoughtfully presented to him by the disappointed French captains he had left behind at Mudros. That anyone should want to eat in such a situation may seem surprising, but sub-mariners have always claimed that there is something about the interior atmosphere of a submarine that encourages the appetite!

At 8.40 am Holbrook ordered the coxswain to take *B.11* down to 80 feet in readiness for the run through the minefields and, as the vessel nosed into the depths, officers and men alike braced themselves for the nerve-racking hours that lay ahead. The submarine would now be sailing blind and with its notoriously unreliable compass system navigation was very much a matter of 'by guess and by God'. To make the tension worse the crew could hear the mooring wires of the explosive mines scraping down the hull as *B.11* pushed aside the taut steel cables. Without the protection of the port hydroplane guard there was now a serious risk of snagging one of the lines – a situation that would force the submarine to the surface in full view of the Turkish shore batteries.

After running blind for an hour *B.11* was brought cautiously to periscope depth so that Holbrook could fix their position. He found the submarine well over on the European side of the Straits as anticipated, but was surprised to find that they were consider-ably further upstream than expected. In fact the huddled houses and minarets of Chanak on the Asiatic shore were only just over a mile away on the starboard bow and the entrance to the Narrows was clearly visible. The Turkish lookouts, not expecting to find an Allied submarine in their midst, failed to spot the stalk of *B.11*'s periscope. Taking advantage of his good luck, Holbrook con-tinued to search the scene through the eye-piece of his periscope.

45

After examining the shipping off Chanak he turned his attention towards Sari Siglar Bay, a sheltered anchorage nestling in the lee of Kephez Point to the south-west of Chanak.

Moored in the bay was a large twin-funnel warship with a single mast and heavy-calibre guns in turrets at bow and stern. Holbrook recognized her as the Turkish battleship *Messoudieh* – a veteran ironclad built as long ago as 1874 but modernized and rebuilt in 1902 by the Italians. According to the reference books *Messoudieh* displaced 10,000 tons and was armed with two 9.2-inch, twelve 6-inch and fourteen 3-inch guns. But the reference books did not truly reflect the parlous state of the Sultan's navy in 1914. The barrels of the 9.2-inch weapons jutting agressively from the single turrets fore and aft *were made of wood*!

The enemy warship was at least a mile away – a range too great for the doubtful accuracy of the puny 18-inch torpedoes carried by the *B*-class boats. In addition the attack angle was too narrow to guarantee success – and *B.11*'s captain had not come all this way to fail. Having digested the situation, Holbrook lowered the periscope, ordered the helmsman to steer four points to starboard and allowed the current to carry him downstream towards his unsuspecting target. The next time he made a periscope observation *B.11* was less than 800 yards from the anchored battleship and a little abaft its beam. A slight alteration in course brought the submarine's bows in line with the forward section of the Turkish vessel.

'Flood both tubes and stand by.'

Holbrook made a series of estimates and passed the results of his mental arithmetic to the Torpedo Gunner's Mate in the bows:

'Deflection angle zero. Running depth 10 feet.' He paused for confirmation of his instructions and watched the torpedo sight of the periscope centre on the dove-grey hull of the *Messoudieh*. 'Fire one! Fire two!'

The submarine lurched as the torpedoes shot from the tubes and the coxswain flooded the compensating tank to balance the decrease in weight in the fore-ends. Holbrook watched the twin wakes speeding towards the enemy but, at the vital moment, a sudden eddy in the current swung the boat sideways. The upper lens of the periscope dipped beneath the water and the coxswain swore under his breath as he restored the trim and brought the boat level once again. The unmistakable thump of a torpedo exploding echoed through the submarine and by the time Holbrook was able to get a clear sight through his periscope, the warship was settling by the stern with an enormous cloud of black smoke mushrooming from her shattered hull. Sharp spurts of flame along the side of her armoured central citadel showed that the Turkish gunners were still at their posts, and a barrage of exploding shells churned the water to white foam as they brought all weapons to bear on *B.11*'s exposed periscope.

They were still bravely serving the guns when the *Messoudieh* capsized ten minutes later, trapping many of them inside the armour-plated hull. But Allah looked kindly upon his sailors. The following day holes were cut through the upturned keel of the sunken battleship and most of the imprisoned crew were able to make their escape.

Holbrook, however, had little time to savour his historic victory. The shore batteries were remarkably accurate and, ordering the submarine down to 50 feet – the maximum depth of water shown on the chart – he swung the boat around so that her bows were pointed down the open Straits. Then, suddenly, in their very moment of triumph, *B.11*'s luck ran out!

In the early submarines the compass was housed on deck so that it was not affected by the various magnetic influences inside the hull. A system of tubes and prisms threw a picture of the compass card onto a frosted glass screen situated just in front of the helmsman. It was a primitive way of doing things and its fundamental weakness was exposed at that precise moment when sea water leaked into the optical system and the dim image faded from sight. The helmsman, unable to steer an accurate course, reported that the compass had flooded and Holbrook had to rise to periscope depth again in order to pilot the submarine out of trouble. As the lens broke through the water he was horrified to discover that the current had swept them deeper into Sari Siglar Bay. Towering cliffs seemed to be surrounding the submarine on all sides. And, to make matters worse, a torpedo-boat and some other vessels were hurrying out from the shore intent on ramming. He ordered the boat down to 50 feet again. But the bay was shelving rapidly and at 38 feet *B.11* struck bottom!

The life of every man aboard the submarine now depended on the skill and judgement of its 26-year-old skipper. Holbrook ordered maximum speed in the hope that the motors would pull them clear. His ploy met with immediate success as the boat lurched clumsily off the mudbank. But moments later her bows lifted sharply as she slid onto another. Unlike more modern designs, *B.11*'s conning-tower was not sealed off from the hull and, as Holbrook stood in the control-room, he could see the sunlight streaming in through the circular glass ports. And *that* could mean only one thing: the conning-tower was sticking up above the surface and standing clear of the water like a rock exposed by the tide. As if to confirm his prognosis the Turkish shore batteries opened fire again.

'I put the helm hard a'port,' Holbrook wrote in his official report, 'and went on to full speed, the submarine frequently touching bottom from 10.10 to 10.20 am, when we got into deeper water.'

Those fateful ten minutes seem of little consequence in the laconic phrasing of Holbrook's report, but to the men involved they must have been an eternity. Inside *B.11* the electric motors were pushed to their limits and the ammeter needles swung into the discharge segments of the dials as the propellers churned to maximum revolutions. The ancient hull groaned and creaked under the strain of full power and, taking up position in the conning-tower, Holbrook peered out through the tiny glass ports while he calmly conned the boat through the shallows. The submarine shuddered violently each time the keel struck the bottom but, grinning to himself as if he was enjoying the bumpy ride, he maintained course as exploding shells threw up fountains of dirty water all around the exposed conning-tower.

They finally reached deep water at 10.20 am and *B.11* was taken thankfully to periscope depth so that Holbrook could survey the situation on the surface. Only the upturned keel of the *Messoudieh* remained visible and there was clear water on the port hand. Keeping the bows pointing towards the European shore for a few more yards, he waited until they were in mid-channel before he dared to alter course downstream. The long run at maximum speed had drained the batteries to danger point. And although the interior lights were already abnormally dim the security of the open sea still lay some 16 miles ahead. Holbrook knew that he must husband his remaining amp-hours if they were to reach safety and, curbing his impatience, took *B.11* down the Straits at slow speed with her motors grouped down for economy. She was barely making 1½ knots but, fortunately, the current was now behind her and her relative speed began to gradually increase without any additional demands on the batteries.

Because of the compass malfunction, it was not safe to go deep and dive beneath the minefields at Kephez Point as they had done on the way upstream. On the return trip Holbrook had to thread his way through the mines at periscope depth so that he could keep a continuous check on the boat's position. There were five lines of mines for the submarine to pass through and no one dared to breathe until they reached the mouth of the Suandere River and knew that they had run clear. But they still faced the hazards of the shore batteries and fortress guns and Holbrook was forced to submerge for another ten miles during which time the men took their dinner in relays while their skipper finished off his lobster. By way of celebrating their survival Holbrook ordered a tot of rum to be issued to every member of the crew.

Finally, at 2.10 pm, when some two miles west of Cape Helles, *B.11* was brought to the surface. The hatch was thrown open and a cloud of greenish-yellow poisoned air billowed out through the narrow circular hatchway. The submarine had been almost continuously submerged for eight hours – an incredibly long period for such an early design – and conditions were so bad that it was half an hour before sufficient oxygen had accumulated inside the boat for the petrol engines to start!

Norman Holbrook was awarded a well-deserved Victoria Cross – the first member of the Royal Navy to be so decorated in the 1914–18 war and also the first submariner ever to win the honour. His second-in-command, Lieutenant Sydney Thornhill Winn, was made a Companion of the Distinguished Service Order and every man of *B.11*'s crew received either the Distinguished Service or the Distinguished Conduct medal for his part in the attack. They also received a more tangible reward under Section 42 of the Naval Prize Act 1864 following an Order in Council by King George V on 2 March 1915.

Prize bounties, once known as blood or head money, dated back to the time of Henry VIII and were first regularized by statute in 1649. In the words of the Prize Act of 1708: 'If in any action any ship of war or privateer shall be taken from the enemy, five pounds shall be granted to the captors for every man which was living on board such ship . . . at the beginning of the engagement between them.' In 1805 the rules were amended from 'taken', i.e. captured, to the 'taking, sinking, burning or otherwise destroying' of an enemy man-of-war.

The rules were complex and flag officers present during the action normally took the lion's share. Other recipients were granted portions of the bounty in accordance with their rank or rating. In the case of the *Messoudieh* a total bounty of £3,000 was awarded by the Prize Court of which £601.10s.6d went to Holbrook while, at the other end of the scale, the submarine's Able Seamen each received £120.6s.1d – a sizeable sum of money in those days and equal to the average factory worker's wages for a full year. *B.11*'s crew were not the only beneficiaries of the Prize system – Horton's *E.9* was awarded £1,500 for sinking the cruiser *Hela* in 1914 and Goodhart's *E.8* received £3,500 for the destruction of the *Prinz Adalbert*.

As a matter of historical interest the prize system was not finally scrapped until December, 1945, and of the £5¼ million accumulated during World War Two £1¼ million was handed to the RAF for its part in the destruction of enemy shipping. The final individual bounties paid to members of the Royal Navy and Royal Marines in 1947 ranged between £60 for senior officers and £6 for an Ordinary Seaman – a far cry from the £125,000 paid to Admiral Anson following his four-year rampage around the world which ended in 1744!

Holbrook's destruction of the *Messoudieh* was a great day for the Royal Navy and its infant submarine service. The French Commander-in-Chief sent a signal to Vice-Admiral Carden: 'Please accept my warmest congratulations for the glorious deed of the submarine *B.11*' and, not to be outdone, the Admiralty telegraphed: 'Communicate to the officers and men of *B.11* Their Lordship's high appreciation of the daring and skilfulness which have achieved this exploit.'

The submariners preferred to celebrate in their own way and before official news of Holbrook's Victoria Cross was received in Mudros a group of his flotilla colleagues presented him with a giant cardboard Iron Cross in an hilarious ceremony on the quarter-deck of the battlecruiser *Indefatigable*. And in his *Smoke on the Horizon* Vice-Admiral Usborne summed up the enemy's reaction to Holbrook's daring exploit.

'The Turks were so astonished at the feat that they hardly knew what to say. That a British submarine . . . could walk up, in broad daylight, right through their minefields with four miles of shore batteries on either side, torpedo a ship at its very heart, and get away with it, filled them with consternation.'

With hindsight it may seem strange that a totally obsolete warship of little fighting value and with a main armament of dummy wooden guns should be regarded as such a valuable prize. In fact, the British public was led to believe that the *Messoudieh* was a powerful modern dreadnought. But it was a matter of means rather than ends. Holbrook's gallant foray into enemy-controlled waters in an outdated boat demonstrated that the Straits were not impenetrable. There seemed little doubt that Britain's more modern submarines would be able to enter the Sea of Marmora itself and play havoc with the enemy's sea communications and even threaten Constantinople with bombardment.

As a result, when Vice-Admiral Carden – urged on by his Chief-of-Staff Roger Keyes the former Commodor (S) in charge of the Harwich submarines at the beginning of the war – sent an urgent signal to the Admiralty asking for a flotilla of the Royal Navy's latest E-class boats to be sent out to the Dardanelles his request was granted without delay or argument. Their arrival at Mudros marked the beginning of one of the most glorious chapters in British naval history and in the campaign that followed three submarine commanders were to win the Victoria Cross: Martin Eric Nasmith, Edward Courtney Boyle and, posthumously, Geoffrey Saxton White.

Perhaps the last word on Holbrook's destruction of the *Messoudieh* should rest with the enemy. On being asked what he thought of *B.11*'s achievement the local German commander, Vice-Admiral Merten, smilingly admitted, 'It was a mighty clever piece of work'.

—FIVE—

Kapitanleutnant Adolf Karl Georg Edgar Freiherr Von Spiegel Von Und Zu Peckelsheim

'I was told it was so'

Unlike Britain's Max Horton who regarded 13 as a symbol of personal good fortune, *Kapitanleutnant* Baron von Spiegel had a healthy respect for the aura of ill-omen that surrounded that notoriously unlucky number and he would take almost any steps to avoid being associated with it. His apparently irrational fears were proved to be more than justified in the light of subsequent events – especially when that fateful numeral appeared in combination with equally unlucky Friday. In his experience any venture scheduled to start on Friday the 13th was doomed to irreparable disaster before it had even begun.

Although von Spiegel was a pre-war submariner and had taken part in combat operations from the very first day of the conflict, he dated the origin of his superstition to Friday 13 January, 1915, when three U-boats – *U-22* skippered by *Kapitanleutnant* Bruno Hoppe, *U-31* under the command of *Oberleutnant* Siegfried Wachendorff, and the Baron's own boat *U-32* – had left Wilhelmshaven for a routine North Sea patrol. The weather was appalling and the wild seas and shrieking winds threw the submarines about like matchboxes tossed into a storm-drain. The rolling thunder clouds, stinging ice-cold spray and torrential rain soon reduced visibility to nil and within hours the three boats had separated and lost contact with each other.

Von Spiegel drove northwards towards his patrol area but *U-32* was barely controllable in the Force 11 winds and mountainous waves and the lookouts on the exposed conning-tower bridge had to be strapped to the periscope columns to save them from being swept into the raging waters. Conditions below were, if anything, even worse. With the hatches battened down to keep out the sea the interior stank of diesel oil, human sweat, sour cabbages and vomit. The pitching movement of the submarine threw the men about like rag dolls. Mechanics slithered on the steel deck of the engine room as they struggled to lubricate the machinery and the spilt oil only served to add a further hazard for the unwary. Off-duty seamen were thrown bodily from their bunks while others were hurled headlong down the full length of the boat – their progress only arrested when they were brought to a halt by something hard and unyielding. Every few hours a fresh victim would be helped into the control room to report a gashed head or a broken limb and, without a doctor or proper medical facilities, it fell to an inadequately trained Warrant Officer to staunch the bleeding cuts and to improvise splints to hold the fractured arms and legs. In cases of severe pain the First Officer was authorized to give the injured man a few hours of oblivion with the aid of a hypodermic syringe filled with morphia. But he was inexpert and clumsy with the needle and many chose to suffer rather than call for his help.

The Baron fought the weather for more than a week, but, finally giving best to the Nordic storm gods, he decided to turn back. No ships had been sighted and, in these conditions, none were likely to be encountered. *U-32* still had her full complement of torpedoes aboard as her battered salt-encrusted bows slid thankfully into the calm of the U-boat basin. Von Spiegel light-heartedly blamed Friday the 13th and gave the matter no further thought, but his carefree attitude changed when *U-22* nosed her way into harbour nine days later. Her captain, Bruno Hoppe, was pale and grim-faced as he stepped off the gangway onto the quay and, without speaking a word to his friends who had come down to greet him, he hurried to the flotilla commander's office.

'I have to report that I have torpedoed *U-7*,' he announced in a broken voice. 'There is only one survivor.'

The error in identification was the result of bad staff work and faulty intelligence at U-boat headquarters in Kiel. Hoppe had not been warned that another U-boat was operating in his patrol area and, when he encountered an unidentified submarine which failed to respond to his recognition signals, he naturally assumed the vessel to be hostile and had sent it to the bottom with a single torpedo.* The tragedy was heightened by the fact that Hoppe and *U-7*'s captain, Georg Koenig, were close friends and inseparable companions. 'They ate together, drank together, and what belonged to one belonged also to the other,' a fellow officer recalled. It was, indeed, a bitter blow for the flotilla.

But the malevolent evil of Friday the 13th had not yet exhausted its venom. Another week passed and concern mounted when the third member of the ill-fated trio failed to return and was provisionally listed as 'overdue'. The U-boatmen at Wilhelmshaven waited anxiously on the quayside for their shipmates and optimistically told each other that the submarine had probably suffered an engine failure and was, even now, crawling back to the Fatherland in a crippled condition. But they were finally forced to face the truth when the *Reichsmarineamt* in Berlin posted *U-31* as 'missing and presumed lost'. Her ultimate fate was never established and it is thought that, like so many other submarines that went missing in the North Sea, she had struck a mine and gone down with all hands. Von Spiegel often related a story that the lost U-boat had run ashore on the English coast and that her crew were found lying in their bunks dead – presumably poisoned by escaping gas from the batteries while the vessel was submerged. It was an excellent tale told with all the detailed embroidery of a skilled raconteur and in the post-war years the Baron dined out on the strength of it many times. But, as official records show, there was unfortunately not a shred of truth in it from beginning to end.

These two disasters, however, had a profound effect on von Spiegel and he swore a solemn oath never to go to sea again on Friday the 13th. It was a vow which he ultimately failed to honour, and the failure nearly cost him his life.

U-32 was soon back on patrol again and the Baron was kept too busy to waste time thinking about his lost comrades Wachendorff and Koenig. In March, 1915, he chased and stopped a British merchantman in the North Sea and, having ordered its crew to abandon the vessel and take to the boats, he sank the ship with a single well-placed torpedo. He then took the three lifeboats in tow and only cast them free when they were within easy rowing distance of the coast. And as a final gesture he presented the survivors with three bottles of red wine.

The hours that followed this particular attack proved to be a

* An identical error occurred on 10 September, 1939, when the British submarine *Triton* sank her flotilla-mate *Oxley* off Norway.

1. (*Left*) Lieutenant Richard Sandford of *C.3* and Zeebrugge fame.
2. (*Right*) Lieutenant Norman Holbrook. The Royal Navy's first submarine VC.

3. Commander Max Horton (centre in fur hat) enjoys a joke with *E.9's* Russian liaison officer.

4. Lieutenant Frederick Halahan. His rewards for destroying a Chinese pirate gang – the Distinguished Service Cross and a writ for damages!

5. Commander Howard Gilmore, the captain who gave his life to save his boat.

nightmare of alarms and narrow escapes. Soon after dark two British patrol boats were observed signalling to each other and, warned by their flashing lights, von Spiegel was able to guide *U-32* out of danger. He then retired to his bunk leaving the customary instruction that he was to be called if anything untoward was sighted. Between 10 pm and 5 am he was summoned to the bridge no less than six times and on the final occasion found the U-boat perilously close to a British destroyer. Slamming the hatch shut he ordered an emergency dive. But *U-32* had already been spotted by the enemy lookouts and the destroyer's guns opened fire before she was safely beneath the surface. A submarine is at its most vulnerable at moments like this and every member of von Spiegel's crew knew that they were balanced on the very edge of eternity. But on this occasion the gods were in a merciful mood and the U-boat escaped into the depths without damage. Faced by such stresses, it is not surprising that von Spiegel should have written: 'Nerves are the all-important feature in submarine officers in time of peace and much more so in time of war. Resolution, strength, endurance, and will-power are all dependant upon the condition of our nerves. Nerves are precious possessions and the most import-ant thing on a voyage is to keep them in good order.'

On another occasion the Baron encountered a group of sixteen steam and sail drifters peacefully working their nets in the middle of the North Sea. With characteristic caution he remained submerged at periscope depth while he checked for the presence of decoy ships and hidden weapons, and then, satisfied that the boats were harmless, he surfaced in the centre of the unsuspecting fishing fleet. Grasping a German ensign in one hand and holding a megaphone in the other he called for the captain of the nearest steam drifter to identify himself. There was a brief pause and then a fisherman in a crumpled peak cap emerged from the dimunuitive wheelhouse and showed himself on the bridge.

'I mustered my best English,' von Spiegel recalled, 'and informed the red-nosed individual that all the fishing boats round about would be sunk before sunset. I told him, further, that I had detailed him to collect all the other crews on board his drifter and that he must . . . follow me at a distance of 500 metres.' He added that if the man did not obey he would blow his boat out of the water.

With the steam trawler trailing obediently behind and with the signal *Abandon ship immediately* flying from the conning-tower mast, von Spiegel cruised slowly through the flotilla and, as the boats were emptied of their crews, he despatched them one by one with gunfire. Soon only two sailing drifters and the steam-powered rescue vessel remained. But at this point *U-32*'s Executive Officer reminded the Baron that the steam drifter would get back to England more quickly than the sailing boats and that this might give the Royal Navy a chance to catch up with and possibly attack the submarine. Von Spiegel appreciated the logic of the argument and, having transferred the grumbling fishermen into one of the remaining sailing vessels, he promptly sank its smaller companion and then destroyed the steam drifter before proceeding on his way. It was scarcely a glorious victory by comparison with the exploits of Weddigen, Hersing or von Arnauld, but it clearly pleased von Spiegel and the chapter in his book which describes this one-sided action is headed: *A Great Prize*.

In their efforts to stop the U-boats from attacking the busy shipping lanes of the Western Approaches and to force them to proceed northabout Scotland – a diversion which reduced the number of days they could spend in their Atlantic patrol areas – the British had laid two large minefields in the Strait of Dover which were backed by a system of explosive nets patrolled by armed trawlers and other small craft. The Royal Navy called it the Dover Barrage; the German Navy knew it as the Witches' Cauldron. But, whatever the name, its purpose was crystal clear: German U-boats were to be prevented from passing through the Dover Strait and into the Channel.

The first flag-officer to command the Dover Patrol was Rear-Admiral Horace Hood. But, despite his good work in making the defences more effective, he did not enjoy the confidence of the First Lord, Winston Churchill, and in April, 1915, he was superseded by Rear-Admiral Reginald Bacon, the Royal Navy's first Inspecting Captain of Submarines and an expert in under-water warfare. Bacon continued to strengthen the barrage and soon both he and the Admiralty were convinced that the improved minefields had made the Straits too hazardous for German U-boats to tackle. While this was true if the submarine was submerged, Bacon and the Board had overlooked the fact that the *unterseeboots* could still get through at night on the surface, although, admittedly, as von Spiegel was to discover, the passage could be a terrifying experience.

U-32 surfaced some distance from the barrage and, with the aid of a chart, the Baron explained his intentions to the helmsman. 'It is exactly 22 miles from here to the first minefield. From there to the second minefield is 14 miles – making a total of 36 miles. We must time ourselves to reach the first minefield shortly before low-water, on the last of the ebb tide, as the mines are only visible from a little before to a little after low-water. It is six-thirty now and low-water is at ten o'clock. We can therefore proceed comfortably at half-speed and have plenty of time to recharge the batteries.'

The U-boat reached the edge of the first minefield an hour before low water as planned and two officers joined von Spiegel on the exposed conning-tower bridge. There was a heavy sea running and all three, plus the helmsman, were swathed in thick oilskins. The gleaming black canisters were partially awash and clearly visible despite the weather conditions and the darkness. Von Spiegel was 'overwhelmed by the quantity of mines' and found that their irregular pattern made steering difficult. But Lomann, the helmsman, excelled himself. And so expertly did he pilot *U-32* through the deadly maze that the Baron was content to leave the steering entirely in his capable hands.

They passed clear in ten minutes and, as they gathered speed towards the second field, von Spiegel estimated that they had passed through no less than 800 mines. Yet, despite the tension of weaving through the closely packed minefield, it had been a relatively easy task and the Baron was in good spirits as *U-32* sped towards the second barrier. A British destroyer was sighted on patrol on the far side of this next minefield and von Spiegel prudently took the U-boat to periscope depth to avoid detection. The thought of proceeding submerged through the minefield was, in his own words, 'highly disagreeable', but there seemed no alternative. And, peering through the lens of the submarine's periscope, the *Kapitanleutnant* could feel the adrenalin pumping through his veins as he watched the sinister black spheres through the eyepiece and passed steering instructions to Lomann. On one terrifying occasion a mine actually struck the column of the periscope with a loud metallic clang and von Spiegel thought his final moment had come. But, by incredible luck, the sensitive detonator horns did not make contact and the lethal canister swept safely astern.

But there were other hazards to be faced and surmounted. They were now in an area of shoals and, to avoid running aground, von Spiegel needed to locate a particular marker buoy and to pass it on his port hand. But the worsening weather conditions were making things difficult. On returning to periscope depth after diving deep to avoid detection by the patrolling destroyer the Baron found that the heavy rain had reduced visibility to zero. The chart showed the submarine to be some 2½ miles from the French coast but the strength of the flood tide was an unknown factor and it was highly probable that they were closer inshore than intended. As they ran clear of the squall, visibility momentarily improved and von Spiegel caught a glimpse of the vital marker. But to his horror the buoy was in the wrong place – it was on the submarine's *starboard* side. That meant they were running into danger!

'Hard a'port! Full astern both!'

But it was too late. Before the order could be obeyed *U-32* ploughed full-tilt into a sandbank. To make matters worse she came to a stop lying at an angle with her bows partially exposed and the sea crashing against the conning-tower which was standing clear of the water like a half-submerged rock. Not wishing to be spotted by the enemy destroyer which was still dutifully moving up and down the western edge of the minefield von Spiegel flooded the main ballast tanks to prevent the stranded boat from rising up any further while he considered the situation with his Executive Officer.

Periscope observation showed that the destroyer's patrol line extended to five or six miles and that she was at least three miles away when she turned at the end of her run to the north. It was a dark night and the scudding storm clouds and heavy rain squalls frequently reduced visibility to no more than 500 yards. If he timed his escape attempt to coincide with the destroyer's *outward* leg when she was her greatest distance from the U-boat *and* still steaming north they might, with luck, break free unobserved.

Von Spiegel watched the enemy vessel fade into the darkness and then, blowing *U-32*'s ballast tanks and running full astern on the motors, he attempted to pull the stranded submarine off the sandbank and into deep water before the destroyer reversed course and approached them again. It called for fine judgement and a generous helping of luck, and on this occasion the Baron had both in good measure. *U-32* slid clear and von Spiegel, wiping the sweat from his brow, took her to periscope depth and once again headed westwards. Having passed through the two minefields, and with the shallows safely astern, the Baron felt sure he had now successfully broken through the barrage. But, in fact, worse problems lay ahead. Continuing down-Channel he sighted a group of trawlers towing a steel anti-submarine hawser and, once again, *U-32* went deep. But von Spiegel was rapidly getting to the end of his tether. He knew that the shore was still uncomfortably close and yet, unable to surface to obtain an accurate fix because of the enemy patrols, he had no precise knowledge of where he was. Bringing the boat back to periscope depth in the hope of sighting a helpful landmark he found, instead, a modern French destroyer only 500 yards off the starboard bow.

U-32 dived quickly but, only moments later, a violent explosion kicked the submarine sideways and blew the fuses, plunging the U-boat into darkness. There was no doubt that a mine had detonated close by, but, miraculously, as the emergency lighting glowed to life, no leaks could be found and the hull seemed undamaged. But before von Spiegel had time to congratulate himself on their lucky escape the First Coxswain reported that the boat was not responding to the hydroplanes. There could be only one explanation. The U-boat had become enmeshed in an anti-submarine net. And, judging by the explosion, one to which mines had been secured!

U-32 was fitted with a net cutter above her bows and, by moving the vessel backwards and forwards like a gigantic saw, the serrated steel teeth of the device could be used to tear a hole through the steel links of the mesh – a process that entailed considerable risk for there was a constant danger of accidently triggering the other mines. But there was no other way out of the trap and von Spiegel gave the necessary orders. Moving rapidly from full ahead to full astern *U-32* began to cut a ragged hole in the net. The struggle continued to more than ten minutes – each an eternity in itself – until finally, to the cheers of the crew, the U-boat tore free and ran clear.

But the nightmare was not over yet. Only moments later the Chief Engineer reported that something was fouling the propellers and that *U-32* was consuming twice her normal amperage in order to maintain speed. At this rate, he pointed out, the battery would be exhausted within hours. But ill-luck continued to dog them. No matter how much he varied the speed or altered the course of the U-boat von Spiegel found the French patrol boats waiting to pounce every time he rose to periscope depth. The cat-and-mouse game continued throughout the whole of the following day and the Baron only finally succeeded in outwitting the hunters when darkness fell.

Rising cautiously to the surface, he discovered the reason for the enemy's uncannily accurate assessment of his submerged position. What remained of the net was still clinging to the submarine but, more seriously, the serpentine float that was used to suspend it in the water had become tangled with the débris and, resting on the surface, it had mirrored every movement of the submerged U-boat and had shown the enemy *exactly* where *U-32* was lurking! Once rid of these tell-tale encumbrances, the Baron continued on his way and reached his patrol area in the Western Approaches without further trouble.

It was apparent that the Dover defences were now virtually impregnable and von Spiegel, unwilling to tempt fate twice, returned to Germany by the northern route via the Orkney and Shetland Islands. His signal to U-boat Headquarters warning of the hazards of the Witches' Cauldron led to all U-boats being re-routed around the north of Scotland in future. Churchill had been wrong about the efficiency of Hood's barrage, and when he learned of the amended sailing instructions he showed his contrition by appointing the sacked Rear-Admiral to command the 3rd Battlecruiser Squadron – an altruistic gesture that was to unfortunately cost Hood his life when his flagship blew up at the Battle of Jutland in 1916.

* * *

Although in after-years von Spiegel claimed that he spent part of 1916 in hospital receiving treatment for a heart condition it seems fairly clear that he suffered a nervous breakdown – probably, and not surprisingly, as a result of his experiences in the Dover Barrage. He admitted to American Journalist Lowell Thomas in 1928 that 'submarine men were likely to break down with nerve strain of some kind or other and were constantly being sent away to recuperate'. His own writings confirm an abnormal concern with 'nerves'.

The Baron took advantage of his enforced rest to write a book about the war beneath the waves which he entitled *U-Boat 202*. There is little doubt that the majority of the incidents described in the text relate to his own experiences in *U-32* although he took care to alter names, dates and places for security reasons. It is apparent, too, that unscrupulous officials interfered with both the author and the book with the result that it contained a number of crude anti-British passages which reflected contemporary German propaganda and which were clearly aimed at influencing American public opinion.

One chapter: *England's Respect for the Red Cross*, was pure poison. In it von Spiegel accused Britain of using her hospital ships as troop transports. He recounted meeting up with a large twin-funnel steamer in the Channel. Her hull and upperworks were pure white in colour with broad green bands interspersed with large red crosses painted along her sides. In addition she was flying Red Cross flags from her mastheads. Von Spiegel watched the vessel through his periscope. 'The ship with the sacred flag of purity and human mercy was laden with guns fore and aft, and an army of soldiers and horses was packed between the guns and their mountings. Under the protection of the colours and flags thus shamelessly misused, the transport-hospital ship was proceeding towards the scene of war in the full light of day and without any escort.'

It was dangerous material to have circulating in a neutral

country where the word of a German – and a Baron at that – was no less believable than the word of an Englishman, and British Intelligence spent many weeks trying to kill the story without success. In England the First Lord and the Admiralty fumed with impotent rage but there was little they could do. At most they could only hope to send the author of *U-Boat 202* to the bottom the next time he encountered British warships. But this was only the satisfaction of vengeance. It would do nothing to disprove the dangerous lies which the Baron had disseminated.

On his discharge from hospital von Spiegel was given command of the *U-93*, a brand-new boat, slightly larger in size than *U-32* and displacing around a thousand tons in submerged trim. Armed with six 19.7-inch torpedo tubes and two 10.5 cm deck guns, she was 235½ feet in length and could steam at more than 16 knots on the surface. But her first war cruise got off to an unfortunate start when the Baron was ordered to put to sea on Friday 13 April, 1917. He pleaded with the authorities to delay the U-boat's departure by twenty-four hours, but, unable to understand his fears, the request was refused and in obedience to orders von Spiegel steamed out of Emden's submarine basin on the appointed and ill-omened date. But the Baron was a determined man and, on the flimsiest of pretexts, he put into Heligoland a few hours later and remained in the island's harbour until the following morning. He then proceeded to convince himself and his crew that *U-93* was, in fact, starting her maiden patrol on Saturday the 14th!

The first day of the mission was beset by bad weather with a Force 10 south-westerly making conditions so bad that von Spiegel was forced to run submerged. But on the 15th, when the weather moderated, he intercepted a small Danish freighter carrying British coal which he sank by gunfire after first giving the crew time to abandon ship. Three days later, west of the Shetlands, he found a large British-owned vessel and, having once again ensured the safety of the crew, sent it to the bottom with a single torpedo. These two successes quickly raised morale and most of the crew were now prepared to admit that the Captain had outwitted the hoodoo of Friday the 13th by his overnight sojourn at Heligoland.

But it was not all plain sailing. These two sinkings were followed by an irritating shortage of targets and, in addition, the gyro was giving trouble. Spirits were depressed further when von Spiegel failed to cut off a large steamer which had the speed to outrun him. But, finally, the gyro was repaired and when, a few days later, contact was made with *U-60, U-67* and Juerst's *U-43*, everyone began to cheer up.

29 April, however, began with disappointment when two

steamers were unsuccessfully attacked, but two more were destroyed later in the day – the first blowing up with considerable loss of life. The other was sunk in a more leisurely fashion and, having seen the crew safely into their boats, von Spiegel seized the Captain and the ship's two gunners and took them aboard the U-boat as prisoners of war. It was a perfectly legitimate thing to do and several U-boat commanders made a practice of capturing experienced officers and taking them back to Germany for internment in order to deny their valuable services to the Allies. But to British and American propagandists it was just one more Hun atrocity and a certain Captain Pennewell of Philadelphia declaimed that: 'German submarine captains have added kid-napping to their other crimes!' In point of fact these prisoners were often considerably better off than the unfortunate survivors who were cast adrift in open boats and left to die of exposure by the more callous U-boat commanders.

Von Spiegel certainly did not fall within this latter category, and when he sank the steamer *Horsa* the following day he showed a commendable compassion for his victims. Finding a group of survivors clinging to an overturned lifeboat which was drifting helplessly before the wind, he brought *U-93* alongside so that the injured men could be transferred to the submarine. Several had broken limbs sustained when the torpedo exploded and the German U-boatmen provided splints and drugs from the sub-marine's medical chest to ease their suffering. 'My men were naturally kind-hearted,' von Spiegel recalled, 'and the sight of those poor fellows lying battered and broken on our deck touched them deeply.' While this Samaritan work was in progress a sharped-eared German sailor heard knocking coming from inside the upturned lifeboat and, diving underneath the boat to investi-gate, he found two more survivors who were hurriedly taken below and cared for with the others.

The crew of their next victim was less fortunate. The ship, a 3,200-ton Italian ammunition carrier, blew up in an awe-inspiring sheet of flame when the U-boat's torpedo detonated her cargo of high explosives and, on this occasion, there were no survivors. On the following morning, 30 April, von Spiegel surfaced to inspect a Swedish sailing vessel only to find it already under attack by Hersing's *U-21*. Leaving his flotilla mate to sink his victim, the Baron set off in pursuit of the lifeboats. The Swedes, familiar with British newspaper atrocity stories, thought that the U-boat intended to machine-gun them to death and they cowered in terror as the conning-tower hatch opened. But they had nothing to fear. Von Spiegel came alongside and, assisted by the gentle hands of the U-boatmen, the injured survivors from the *Horsa* were transferred into the lifeboats and placed in the care of the Swedish sailors. Then, having given them a course to steer, the Baron waved a cheery farewell to his former guests and *U-93* sank quietly beneath the waves in search of fresh prey.

But the next target proved a considerably tougher nut to crack. Armed with six guns, she gave the U-boat as good as she received and von Spiegel was forced to break off the action and submerge. A few hours later he caught up with and sank the Greek freighter *Phaleron*. It had been a busy if not overly successful day and with only two torpedoes left in his tubes von Spiegel decided to move northwards in anticipation of the final leg of his homeward passage. There was, however, another and more personal reason for wishing to return to the Fatherland without undue delay. The Baron had two horses running in the Berlin races during the second week of May!

At 8.35 pm that evening an innocent-looking three-masted topsail schooner was sighted. It was steering a north-westerly course and making a laborious two knots, despite having all sails set. *U-93*'s maiden patrol had already yielded eleven victims and von Spiegel was anxious to raise his score to a round dozen. Bringing the submarine to the surface, he signalled the sailing ship to stop. The schooner obediently turned into wind and her crew scrambled into the boats with more haste than speed and the Baron could not restrain a chuckle as he watched their frantic efforts to escape. But there was no time to enjoy the impromptu entertainment. The sun was already slipping towards the western horizon and, anxious to finish off his victim before darkness made it impossible to shoot accurately, he ordered the gun crews to open fire – and to aim at the waterline for a quick result.

The German gunners pounded the sturdy little vessel mercilessly for some twenty minutes and von Spiegel was quite certain that the schooner had been abandoned for nothing and nobody would be able to withstand such punishment without revealing themselves. Growing bolder, he closed the range. But a sudden shift in the wind had swung the sailing-boat into a more advantageous position and her captain, Lieutenant William Edward Sanders, a New Zealand-born Reserve officer, knew that his chance had come. The shrill blast of a whistle sounded on the schooner, a large White Ensign was run up her mainmast and various pieces of superstructure hinged down to reveal machine guns and the long barrels of naval quick-firers. Von Spiegel had made a fatal mistake. The innocent-looking sailing vessel was one of the Royal Navy's dreaded decoy ships: *HMS Prize* alias *Q-21*. The Baron was about to face a battle to the death!

63

The Q-ship's shooting was superbly accurate and within minutes the U-boat had been struck several times. Von Spiegel tried to ram the schooner but she was too close and, with shells exploding all around the ambushed submarine, he ordered the helm to be put hard a'port in an attempt to steer out of trouble. A shell passed through the base of the periscope and this, plus raking machine-gun fire, forced von Spiegel and his companions to evacuate the bridge with indecent haste. Ziegner, *U-93*'s Executive Officer, took refuge in the lee of the conning-tower while the Chief Engineer slid smartly down the ladder into the control room. The Baron, however, made his way aft to encourage the men fighting the after-deck gun. But the steel plating was slippery and, startled by the explosion of a shell only yards away from the boat, he lost his footing and nearly fell. The stumble probably saved his life. Another shell struck the barrel of the Krupp 10.5 cm gun with a searing yellow flash and exploded in the crew's faces. The gunlayer's head was blown off and von Spiegel staggered back, stunned and blinded by the blast.

U-93's forward gun continued in action for several minutes, during which time it inflicted further damage on the schooner but, ultimately, it too was silenced. With her ballast tanks holed, oil leaking from the ruptured fuel bunkers and a 14° list to starboard, the U-boat was barely under control. It was difficult for Ziegner to see what was happening through the smoke and spray as they ran the gauntlet of shells and bullets and, as the wounded were being helped below, the submarine staggered under the impact of another direct hit.

Thrown into the water by the blast, but under the impression that *U-93* had sunk beneath his feet, von Spiegel swam for his life. A man shouted in the darkness, then another. Moving cautiously to his left the Baron found the submarine's Warrant Officer Navigator, Knappe, and a Machinist's Mate, struggling to keep afloat, both equally certain that *U-93* had gone down. The sea was cold and von Spiegel was hampered by his leather topcoat and heavy sea boots. But fortunately *Prize*'s boat was close at hand and within minutes they were being dragged out of the water by their enemies.

Once aboard the Q-ship they were well treated and, in fact, Knappe used his medical training to help various wounded members of *Prize*'s crew. But, like *U-93*, the Q-ship had been seriously damaged in the fight and, leaking like a colander, she was in imminent danger of sinking.

Left alone in Sanders' cabin, von Spiegel lapsed into dark depression. 'I couldn't forget my crew, my friends going down out there, drowned like rats in a trap, with some perhaps left to die of slow suffocation.' While the Baron was occupied with his gloomy thoughts, the Q-ship's crew were busy trying to quench a fire in the auxiliary diesel engine. They managed to extinguish the flames but found themselves unable to restart the motor and, in a moment of almost farcical irony, they turned to the U-boat survivors for help. Deppe, the Machinist's Mate, was an expert on diesels and, with the aid of borrowed tools, the assistance of his captors and rude comments on the Royal Navy's obsolete machinery, he finally persuaded the motor back to life. Nevertheless the *Prize* had to be towed the last few miles into Queenstown where she and her prisoners arrived two days later.

Lieutenant Sanders' calm fortitude under fire was rewarded with the Victoria Cross and every man of the schooner's crew was decorated for bravery. But they did not survive long to enjoy their glory. Three months later, on 13 August, *Prize* was torpedoed by Steinbauer's *UB-48* and was lost with all hands.

One of the first persons to greet von Spiegel as he stepped ashore at Queenstown was the Captain of the *Horsa* who grasped him by the hand saying, 'I have wanted to meet the man who rescued and took care of my crew as your men did'. But there were other, less well-disposed persons who also wanted to meet the Baron. Admiral Sir Reginald Hall, the Head of British Naval Intelligence, for example, was very anxious to speak to the author of *The War Cruise of U-Boat 202*!

Before the interrogation took place, however, there was another twist to the remarkable story of *U-93*. For, contrary to von Spiegel's impression and Sanders' observations, the submarine had, in fact, survived her ordeal and was, at that very moment, crawling painfully back to Germany under the command of her First Officer, *Oberleutnant* Wilhelm Ziegner.

The deepening dusk had saved the U-boat, for the darkness had provided a protective shield against further attack when the Q-ship's gunners had lost sight of their target. Both deck guns had been destroyed, the conning tower damaged and the periscopes smashed. Five men were wounded, one of whom died during that same night. Fuel was short, there was no fresh water and *U-93* was too badly crippled to submerge, but, listing to starboard with her bows raised and her stern awash, the submarine remained afloat and, taking a longer route north of the Arctic Circle to the east of Iceland to avoid enemy patrols, Ziegner succeeded in coaxing his boat safely back to Germany after a nine-day voyage that deserves to be ranked as one of the great epics of submarine history.

After a short rest the Baron was brought to the Admiralty in

London where he was shown into the presence of a small, white-haired admiral with piercing eyes and a rather disconcerting habit of blinking rapidly. He was Rear-Admiral Reginald Hall, Britain's brilliant wartime Head of Naval Intelligence. He showed his visitor to a chair close to a window looking out over the Horse Guards Parade and offered him a cigar. Then Hall produced a copy of *U-Boat 202*.*

'You know this book, I think?'

Von Spiegel nodded.

The Admiral turned the pages. He explained that he had found it interesting although it contained little that the British did not know already. He spread the book open at the relevant page.

'This chapter about the hospital ship with the guns and troops on board. Now, do you know, we cannot trace this particular occasion. Perhaps you could help us?'

The Baron remained silent. He wondered what this was all about.

'You say you saw this incident yourself?' Hall prompted.

Von Spiegel nodded.

'When did you see it?'

U-93's captain made no reply so his interrogator repeated the question.

'When and where did you see it? What was the date?' Hall peered at the Baron through his horn-rimmed glasses. When there was still no answer he continued, 'But it is here, in print, in your native tongue, in a book published under *your* name. Did you write it?'

'Yes.'

'Is it true or untrue?'

Von Spiegel was sweating slightly. 'I did not see it myself,' he admitted reluctantly.

His interrogator pounced quickly. 'I see – then your second-in-command, this man Groning, *he* saw it and reported it to you?'

'No.'

'Then why did you say it?'

'I was told it was so.'

'On that particular day?'

'No. On several occasions.'

'But, you never saw, with your own eyes, British hospital ships carrying troops and guns?'

There was a long pause. Baron von Spiegel got up from his chair

* Details of the interrogation are quoted from *Strange Intelligence* by Hector Bywater and H. C. Ferraby, Constable & Co. 1931.

and stared down at the Horse Guards Parade. He finally turned to face Hall.

'I did not see it personally,' he admitted. 'I was told it was so.'

An Admiralty stenographer, hidden behind screens, had taken down every word of the questions and answers. And the accuracy of her verbatim transcript was confirmed by other discreet concealed witnesses. A few hours later a triumphant 'Blinker' Hall issued von Spiegel's confession to the Press and the lie that had damaged Britain's credibility throughout the world was nailed, once and for all, from the very lips of the author himself.

Slightly bemused by the circumstances of his interrogation and the nature of the questions asked, Adolf Karl Georg Edgar *Freiherr* von Spiegel von und zu Peckelsheim, returned to his prison camp at Donnington Hall. For him the war was over. And, had he but known it, he had just lost his final battle with the enemy.

—SIX—

Lieutenant Richard Douglas Sandford, RN

'Well done Uncle Baldy'

In the words of Winston Churchill the Zeebrugge raid was 'the finest feat of arms in the Great War and certainly, as an episode, unsurpassed in the history of the Royal Navy'. And it was in the course of this desperate assault from the sea that Lieutenant Dick Sandford broke the mould of tradition. For, instead of sinking enemy ships like his contemporaries, he deliberately blew up his own submarine. And he won the Victoria Cross for doing so!

Known to his friends as Uncle Baldy because, despite his youthful 27 years, he frequently affected a mock-humorous old-man pose, Sandford was one of the elite band of heroes who took part in the Zeebrugge raid. Operating as part of *Unit K*, under the command of his elder brother Francis, he was given the task of ramming an explosive-laden submarine, *C.3* against the piers of the viaduct that connected the harbour's concrete mole to the mainland and then blowing it up. All this, of course, under heavy enemy fire and with little direct naval support, for most of the British effort was directed towards backing the military assault on the mole and ensuring that the three blockships were sunk in the mouth of the canal. And it was the unspoken understanding of the planning staff that neither he nor his five-man crew were likely to survive the attack.

Having occupied Bruges during the early months of the war, the Germans had developed the inland port into an advanced base for the repair and servicing of destroyers and small U-boats of the *UB*

68

and *UC* types. Other units were berthed in a second part of the complex – the well-equipped cross-Channel harbour at Ostend. Protected by shore guns and AA weapons, and ringed by fighter airfields, Bruges was well defended against British sea or air attack and the concrete pens which had been constructed to house the U-boats guaranteed almost total protection from bombs or long-range naval bombardment guns. Although more than six miles from the sea, the vessels stationed in Bruges were able to make their way to the coast by means of a fine modern waterway that linked the ancient city-port to Zeebrugge – an artificial harbour which the Belgians had built at the western end of the Ship Canal.

Detailed planning for the raid commenced within days of Vice-Admiral Roger Keyes taking over command of the Dover Patrol on 1 January, 1918. The key objective of the operation was to seal off the entrance to both Ostend Harbour and the Zeebrugge canal with blockships, thus bottling up the U-boats in Bruges and preventing the German Navy from using the city's facilities for many months. The two main targets were heavily defended by shore batteries, strong-points, machine-guns, entrenched troops, barbed wire and a system of carefully contrived underwater nets and buoys. Of the two it was clear that Zeebrugge would be the tougher nut to crack. The mole and its extension measured some 1½ miles in length from the shore to the lighthouse at its extreme eastern tip and, in addition to a permanent garrison of 1,000 soldiers protected behind barbed wire and armed with machine-guns and anti-aircraft weapons, the mole extension housed nine 3.9-inch guns in concrete emplacements skilfully sited to give each piece a 360° arc of fire.

The navigational hazards posed equally formidable problems. Both harbours were approached through a maze of shoals and shallows – the former constantly shifting with the scouring effect of wind and tide and so variable that it was impossible to maintain accurate charts. These difficulties were compounded by strong cross-currents of up to 3 knots closer inshore. The timetable also allowed for little operational flexibility as the blockships would only have sufficient depth of water to negotiate the entrance to the canal successfully during a period of just 90 minutes on either side of high water.

The planners unanimously agreed that the attack must be carried out during the hours of darkness, preferably on a moonless night, and that supporting ships should withdraw out of range before daylight. Yet, despite these rigid Staff requirements, it remained impossible to guarantee total surprise. For the distance between Dover and Zeebrugge, coupled with the slow speed of the

69

assault convoy, meant that the early stages of the voyage would have to be made in daylight. This would expose the force to the danger of being sighted by enemy submarines or aircraft.

Finally, and to ensure that the blockships would be able to penetrate the harbour without being blasted out of the water by the batteries on the mole, Keyes planned to land a storming party on the great concrete breakwater to destroy both the infantry garrison and the guns. To prevent the German Army from rushing reinforcements and mobile artillery teams on to the mole, the connecting viaduct was to be blown up, a task which was assigned to *Unit K*'s two veteran submarines, *C.1* and *C.3*

Such, then, was the essence of the plan. As Keyes' biographer, Cecil Aspinall-Oglander, has written: 'The intended operation [called] not only for professional skill, but also for courage, faith and self-confidence of the highest possible order.' Unfortunately the grand panorama of the raid falls outside the scope of this narrative and the events of that historic night must be restricted to the saga of *Unit K*. Nevertheless it remains a story worth telling.

In its original form, the plan envisaged floating wooden rafts laden with explosives against the piers of the viaduct – a scheme dangerously dependent upon the vagaries of the tidal currents and fraught with uncertainties as to direction and timing. The idea of substituting a submarine steered by human hand and running under its own power came from Dick's brother, Francis Sandford, a Lieutenant-Commander serving on the Dover Patrol staff. He suggested that Keyes should obtain an obsolete submarine and pack five tons of Amatol explosives into its bows. Then, towing two small motor-skiffs astern, he planned to have the submarine taken to within a few hundred yards of the viaduct, at which point, and at a safe distance from the target, the vessel was to be switched over to an automatic gyro steering system. Having lit the delayed action fuses of the detonators, he then intended the crew to abandon the submarine and retire seawards in the skiffs. Just in case these latter craft were damaged, or some other mishap prevented their use, the submarine was to carry a pair of scaling ladders. The survivors were intended to use these to climb up on to the viaduct where they could make their way along the mole and join forces with the naval landing parties. This particular refinement seemed a trifle fanciful and unrealistic, but the scheme, as a whole, appeared to be sound.

Keyes liked the idea, but promptly decided that *two* submarines were needed. His vast experience of combat operations, especially at Gallipoli, warned him that things *could* go wrong with even the best laid of plans and that a back-up unit was a necessary precaution. On the same premise he ruled that both submarines must be crewed by *unmarried* men – a decision which indicated that the Admiral did not give much for their chances of survival. In fact, Captain Carpenter, who was to lead the force into action, observed that, 'We little thought that we should ever see these heroic attackers of the viaduct again'.

Bulldozing all objections aside, Keyes obtained two old petrol-engined boats, *C.1* and *C.3*, from the 6th Submarine Flotilla at Portsmouth and work was immediately started to rig them out for their suicide mission. The Commanding Officer of *C.1*, Lieutenant Aubrey Newbold, was a bachelor, so his appointment raised no problems. But the captain of *C.3* was married and, despite his pleas to remain in command, Keyes insisted that he must stand down and another officer found as a replacement.

Lieutenant Richard Sandford was the seventh son of the Archdeacon of Exeter. He had joined the Navy as a thirteen-year-old cadet in 1904 and had transferred to the Submarine Branch in 1914. The beginning of 1918 found him serving on one of the Royal Navy's gargantuan steam submarines of the ill-fated K-class, *K.6*. Only a few weeks before Keyes arrived in Dover to begin planning the Zeebrugge raid, Richard Sandford was on duty as Officer-of-the-Watch when two groups of K-boats collided disastrously off May Island in the Firth of Forth.

The submarines were taking part in an operational exercise, *EC 1*, with the Battlecruiser Force of the Grand Fleet, when an unexpected night encounter with some minesweepers, plus a jammed helm, led to *K.22* ramming her sister, *K.14*. Although both vessels were seriously damaged, they remained afloat and when Captain Ernest Leir, the commander of the 13th Flotilla, learned of the accident he immediately reversed course and led the remaining submarines back to the scene to render assistance.

Utter chaos followed when the two flotillas met head-on in the darkness. The cruiser *Fearless*, leading the 12th Flotilla, smashed into *K.17* and sent her to the bottom, while the other K-boats weaved and twisted in a series of hair-raising near-misses. *K.3* almost rammed *K.4* and only a last-minute alteration of the helm by *K.3*'s captain, Herbert Shove, avoided a further disaster. Sandford, on the bridge of *K.6*, handled the giant submarine with cool-headed aplomb as he skilfully steered through the surrounding confusion. His prompt reactions narrowly averted a head-on collision between *K.6* and *K.12* of the 13th Flotilla, the boats brushing past each other at high speed with only inches to spare. In the excitement of the moment, the men on the bridge lost sight of *K.3*, the submarine next ahead in the line, but within seconds

Sandford spotted a white light in the darkness and, bringing *K.6* around, he took station on what he thought was *K.3*'s stern.

Aroused by the commotion on the bridge, the yelping cacophony of sirens, and the rapid alterations of helm, *K.6*'s captain, Commander Geoffrey Layton, hurriedly climbed the conning-tower ladder to find out what was happening. Sandford explained the situation and indicated the white light which he was now following. Layton agreed that it must belong to *K.3*, but his experienced eye warned him that the mysterious submarine was lying broadside across *K.6*'s path and was not end-on as Sandford had supposed. Calling for full-speed astern, Layton ordered the helm to be put hard a'port, but a collision was unavoidable and it was now only within his power to minimize the force of the impact. With *K.6* travelling at 18 knots the inertia of her massive 1,800 tons made it impossible to stop within such a short distance and her stout steel bows sliced into the other submarine, virtually cutting it in half. The two giants remained locked together for more than 30 seconds but as *K.6* reversed away the sea rushed into the gaping wound which she had punched into her victim's side and the other submarine sank with all hands. Only later was it discovered that *K.6* had sunk *K.4* and not *K.3* as Layton and Sandford had thought.

It had been a night of disaster unparalleled in submarine history, with two boats lost and three others seriously damaged. Tragically, 103 officers and men had died. After such a traumatic experience, it was hardly surprising that Sandford, on learning of his brother's involvement in the planning and preparation of a top-secret operation, volunteered for a role in it. After all, he reasoned, nothing could be more dangerous than life in the K-boat flotillas. Realizing that Richard was the perfect choice, Francis formally submitted his younger brother's name to Keyes with the suggestion that he should be given command of the leaderless *C.3* and the Admiral minuted his approval without hesitation.

Now that the matter of the captaincy had been settled, both boats were brought up to Dover from Portsmouth and notices were posted in all submarine flotilla bases in home waters calling for 'stout-hearted and enterprising men' to volunteer 'for an undertaking of real danger', the nature of which was not disclosed to volunteers even after they had been accepted. Hundreds of eager submariners answered the call and Sandford had to spend several days sorting through the applications and interviewing likely candidates. His final selection comprised: Lieutenant John Howell-Price DSC, RNR, to act as navigator and second-in-command, Petty Officer Walter Harner as Coxswain, Leading

Seaman William Cleaver, Engine Room Artificer Allan Roxburgh and Stoker Henry Bindall.

When the detailed plans of the viaduct were received from the Belgians, it was discovered that, by a piece of fortuitous good luck, its construction was ideally suited for the method of destruction already envisaged. The steel framework of the viaduct supported a 'road' of heavy oak planking on which was laid a double-tracked railway line. And the whole edifice was carried across the water on a series of tubular iron piers, six deep and 16½ feet apart, cross-braced to each other with steel ties like the rigging wires of an old biplane. The plans also revealed a horizontal girder running lengthways between the piers and lying some ten feet below the surface at high water.

The design was almost tailor-made for destruction. The bows of the submarine would clear the submerged girder and smash a path through the maze of cross-bracings. Then, as the girth of the hull increased amidships, the girder would force the keel to ride up so that the bows became enmeshed in the tangled mass of broken steel ties and iron piers beneath the viaduct. Finally, the height of the conning-tower would act as a wedge and would prevent the vessel from plunging straight through and out the other side.

The two submarines and the rest of the seventy-five ships making up the expedition were ready by the end of March and expectations rose to fever pitch, as the dates for the most favourable tides grew nearer. But weather conditions, especially wind direction, also had to be suitable, for the final plan now included an ambitious smoke-screen which was to be laid by an armada of small boats which would go in ahead of the main force. This screen was to be put down on both sides of the harbour, with the intention of blinding the enemy's coastal batteries. But in order not to impede the accurate navigation of the blockships, the harbour itself had to be kept clear of smoke. It was a somewhat impractical refinement, but Keyes was adamant.

The first attempt to launch the raid proved a bitter disappointment. Having sailed from Dover during the afternoon of 11 April, the convoy had to turn back when it was only thirteen miles from Zeebrugge after an unexpected shift in wind direction threatened to play havoc with the smoke-screen. A further attempt, made two days later, fared no better. Worsening weather forced Keyes to abandon the operation for a second time when it was realized that the rising seas would make it impossible to bring the assault ships alongside the mole.

It was a frustrating time for all concerned but, as far as *Unit K* was concerned, it was not all waste, for the two abortive trips had shown that the skiffs could not be towed behind the submarines without suffering severe damage and the respite gave the Sandford brothers time to rig wooden sponsons from the conning-towers so that the escape boats could be carried inboard.

The operation was given the go-ahead for the third time on 22 April and at 2 pm *Unit K* formed up and joined the starboard wing of the assault convoy which was steaming in three separate columns headed by *Vindictive*. *C.3* was being towed by the destroyer *Trident; Mansfield* was immediately astern with *C.1*, while *Phoebe* and Francis Sandford's picket-boat brought up the rear. Before leaving Dover, the Admiral's wife, Eva, had pointed out to her husband that the morrow, 23 April, was St George's Day, and spirits were raised when Roger Keyes semaphored 'St George for England' from the bridge of the destroyer *Warwick* – a signal which inspired Captain Carpenter of *Vindictive* to respond: 'May we give the dragon's tail a damned good twist!'

At 10.30 pm the starboard column swung away from the convoy and began to move inshore, while motor launches and coastal motor-boats sped ahead to lay down the smokescreen preparatory to the main assault. All appeared to be going well, although *Unit K* was having more than its fair share of trouble. The picket-boat had been misbehaving ever since they had left Dover and, having nearly capsized on several occasions, it finally snapped its tow-line. Fortunately Francis Sandford was able to flash up the boiler and steer it towards the viaduct under its own power but the reduction in speed meant that, despite all the careful planning, he would be fifteen minutes late in reaching his rendezvous.

C.1 was beset by even worse problems. At one point she had actually been fired upon by her escorting destroyer, *Mansfield*, who had mistaken her for a prowling U-boat and, soon after passing 'C' buoy, she too broke her tow-line. Newbold, however, shrugged the mishap aside and, starting the submarine's petrol engines, continued on course at a steady 8½ knots. But *C.1* soon encountered more trouble when the remains of her towing hawser threatened to foul the propellers and Newbold was forced to stop engines and investigate. Lieutenant Beyford, the second-in-command, was sent down to the stern but lost his footing on the slippery casing and was washed overboard. Dragging himself back onto the submarine, apparently none the worse for his ducking, Beyford cut away the remains of the tow-line and *C.1* was able to continue on her way, although, like the picket boat, she too was now well behind schedule.

Dick Sandford, at the head of the column, knew nothing of the dramas taking place astern of *C.3*. It was unpleasantly damp on

74

the conning-tower bridge of the submarine and a fine drizzle soaked him to the skin as he peered through the thickening mist that threatened to upset all their carefully laid plans yet again. The first diversionary raids and bombardments were timed to begin at 11.20 pm, but the monitors lying off-shore in the darkness were finding it difficult to lay their guns in the worsening visibility and, despite the rigidly implacable timetable, their weapons remained silent. Back in England the mist had turned to fog and the aircraft that had been given the task of bombing the German defences were grounded.

Unperturbed by the failure of the diversionary attacks, Sandford continued to keep a wary eye on the tow-line and at 11.26 pm, exactly as laid down in the operational plan, *Trident*'s shaded signal lamp flashed a brief code group and, in response to Sandford's quietly spoken order, Leading Seaman Cleaver, standing balanced on the fore-casing, slipped the tow. The timetable, shaved to the last second to ensure that the vital blockships arrived in position during the final minutes before high water, imposed an 11.30 deadline on *Unit-K*'s three boats to join up with each other and concentrate for the last leg of their hazardous journey. But when neither *C.1* nor his brother's picket-boat appeared through the swirling mist within the requisite four minutes allowed in the plan, Dick Sandford told Roxburgh to start the engines and, calling down for a speed of 8½ knots, he ordered Howell-Price to steer for the viaduct.

The monitors straddling the seaward horizon had finally come into action by now and the flickering sparkle of flame from the massive 15-inch guns of *Erebus* and *Terror* provided a small crumb of comfort for the six submariners who were now irreversibly committed to their lone suicide mission. The enemy, however, remained blissfully unaware of the vast armada of ships closing in on Zeebrugge and the German commander dismissed the monitors as being part of the normal bombardment routine to which the Royal Navy subjected them at regular intervals.

C.3 was exactly half-way to her objective when the enemy's shore guns opened fire but, fortunately for Sandford and the rest of the raiding force, the first shells were directed at the distant monitors and whistled harmlessly overhead. At 11.51 pm *C.3* increased speed to 9½ knots and Howell-Price altered course to port. Four minutes later a change of wind rolled back the smoke-screen and the defenders suddenly woke up to the fact that some sort of raid was in progress. The alarm sirens wailed and, almost immediately, tracer bullets and starshells lit the night sky, while the thud of the shore batteries and the rattle of machine-guns from the mole reverberated and echoed across the sea. With incredible bravery Carpenter drove *Vindictive* through the gauntlet of the German guns and made a valiant attempt to run alongside the mole at exactly midnight – the zero hour laid down in the operational timetable. But the change in wind direction had now swept the protective smoke away to seaward and the assault ship was exposed to the full blast of the Zeebrugge defences. Hit time and time again, she sustained terrible casualties before Captain Carpenter was able to bring her hard up against the towering wall of the breakwater and release the storming-parties on which the success of the venture depended. To his credit *Vindictive* arrived at the mole just one minute behind schedule!

The unexpected change of wind also had its effect on *C.3*. Driving against the current, she was still nearly one and a half miles from the viaduct – a matter of ten minutes steaming instead of the two to three minutes anticipated by the planners – and as the smoke drifted away the submarine was clearly visible to the defenders. Shells were already beginning to splash into the water around the vessel and the glare of the two searchlights stationed on top of the viaduct was blinding in its intensity. In an attempt to obtain some cover from the merciless shelling Sandford told Cleaver to turn on *C.3*'s own smoke-making apparatus but the wind quickly snatched away what little protection it afforded and the submarine was once more nakedly exposed to the enemy. As a realist, Sandford knew that nothing could survive the holocaust of red-hot shell splinters and bullets that lay ahead. Only a miracle could save them. And that miracle was granted. The searchlights were suddenly and inexplicably extinguished and, as the barrage faded away, *C.3* was able to proceed unhindered towards her target which was, by now, only half a mile away.

'It was a silent and nervy business,' Stoker Bindall recalled. And there was certainly an eerie contrast between the quiet calm that surrounded the submarine as she approached the gaunt outline of the viaduct and the noisy battle raging on the mole. Not surprisingly, Sandford was equally uneasy about the lack of opposition. And in case the enemy had an unexpected surprise in store for them, he decided not to use the gyro steering mechanism but to retain full manual control of the submarine right up to the moment of impact. Calling the crew on deck to ensure that no one would be trapped below during the final moments he offered up a silent prayer that the 12-minute delay fuse would allow sufficient time for them to make their escape in the motorised skiffs.

With only two hundred yards to go, the British sailors could hear the soldiers laughing and talking as the submarine closed its target.

76

Every now and again a searchlight flashed out of the darkness to settle on *C.3* but, having apparently satisfied themselves that the boat was still heading for the viaduct, the defenders promptly switched it off again. It all seemed very odd. Then Sandford realized the explanation for the enemy's strange behaviour. The Germans were obviously under the impression that the submarine had lost its way and that, by holding fire, they were luring the unsuspecting vessel to its doom against the unyielding iron piers that formed the base of the viaduct. Sandford's conclusions were confirmed when a peal of sardonic laughter greeted the shrieking clatter of torn steel as *C.3* smashed through the cross-bracing like a battering ram, rode up over the horizontal girder and thrust her bruised and dented bows through the far side of the latticed framework.

'She was going full tilt when we hit the viaduct,' Stoker Bindall said later. 'It was a good jolt but you can stand up to a lot when you hang on tight. I do not think anyone said a word except: "Hold on tight – we're here!" '

Sandford ordered the men to lower the starboard skiff, its companion on the port side of the conning-tower having been smashed to pieces by the impact, and stooped to light the fuse to the detonator. A searchlight stabbed through the darkness and, as it picked out the stranded submarine, the German defenders realized their mistake. Within seconds they let fly with every weapon in their armoury: rifles, machine guns, pom-poms and, somewhat optimistically, pistols. The skiff was hit several times while it was being let down into the water.

Roxburgh started the engine and Sandford leapt aboard at the last moment as Cleaver pushed the tiny boat away from *C.3*'s side. But the gods of war who had shielded them from danger this far now chose to desert them. The fierce current surging beneath the viaduct threw the skiff bodily against the submarine and the engine coughed to an abrupt stop as the propeller shaft was torn from its mountings by *C.3*'s exhaust pipe. Bindall and Petty Officer Harner grabbed the oars lying in the bottom of the boat and tried to row out of trouble but a fusillade of rifle bullets swept the cockleshell craft and the stoker collapsed over his oar with blood pouring from an ugly wound in his chest. Sandford moved forward to help but fell back almost immediately as a machine-gun bullet shattered his hand. As Leading Seaman Cleaver took Bindall's place another burst from a heavy-calibre Spandau mounted high up on the parapet of the viaduct raked the skiff and hit Walter Harner. Roxburgh pushed the Petty Officer to one side, seized the oar and pulled hard. But the tide was running against them and progress was pitifully slow. Ignoring the pain of his injured hand Sandford wedged himself into the stern of the boat and took over the tiller, while Howell-Price dragged the two wounded men into the bows where the bulwarks offered some small protection.

The gunners on the viaduct were firing over open sights at point-blank range and the flares hanging in the sky 'made the darkness just like daylight'. Bullets splattered the sea around the overloaded skiff and, every now and again, a burst from one of the chattering Spandaus scythed across the boat forcing the men at the oars to duck for their lives as hot lead whined and screamed on all sides. The staccato bark of the pom-poms, the sharp crack of the Mauser rifles and the heavy thud of the coastal defence guns added to the din of battle. While the British sailors were struggling to pull clear, the Torpex fuse which Sandford had ignited was hissing towards the detonator under the piled sacks of Amatol in *C.3*'s bows.

Aware that the submarine would blow up within the next two to three minutes, Sandford urged the oarsmen to pull harder. If their distance from *C.3* was not increased rapidly they would all go up with the viaduct when the explosives were detonated and the pessimism of the planners would prove to have been justified. The two oarsmen, Roxburgh and Cleaver, were drenched with freezing water as the cannon shells from the pom-poms exploded around the boat. Another burst of machine-gun fire raked the skiff and Sandford jerked sideways as a bullet smashed his thigh. Howell-Price hurried aft and, pushing the captain aside, seized the tiller and brought the boat back on course.

Lying in the bottom of the boat, Dick Sandford continued to encourage his men until another bullet momentarily silenced him. Bindall was also unconscious by now and Harner had dragged his bleeding body into a corner so that he would not impede the efforts of his shipmates. The bilges of the skiff were awash with blood and as the suction pump laboured to keep them clear the sea surrounding the boat was stained a bright red.

But their agony ended when the burning fuse reached the detonator. A sheet of white flame leapt skywards and an ear-splitting thunderclap of sound echoed across the waters – its deafening intensity momentarily swamping the noise of battle as the landing-parties stormed the German defences on the mole. Captain Carpenter, on the bridge of *Vindictive*, recalled the moment: 'I never saw such a flame. It seemed a mile high!'

The viaduct disappeared in the blast of the explosion and with it went the enemy infantrymen, the searchlight operators, the machine guns and the pom-poms. All that remained was a smoking gap some forty yards in length. The Zeebrugge mole was now completely cut off from the mainland – an island of concrete surrounded by water. Without the viaduct the defenders were denied all hope of reinforcement. Sandford and his men had succeeded beyond their wildest dreams!

Lieutenant Newbold in *C.1*, still chugging through the night to give support to Sandford, saw the massive explosion, but, strangely, did not hear it. Uncertain whether *C.3* had carried out her mission or had been sunk at the last minute, he decided to investigate further. He brought *C.1* closer inshore but, sighting *Vindictive* limping back towards Dover, he realized that the raid was over and, turning seawards, he joined the other ships that were heading westwards.

C.3's self-immolation gave the exhausted men in the skiff a much-needed respite, though Cleaver and Roxburgh continued to row as hard as they could in case the Germans brought up a mobile battery or sent ships in pursuit. The picket-boat, which had been steaming steadily for the Belgian coast ever since it had parted company with the *Phoebe* some hours earlier, arrived on the scene just ten minutes after the explosion. They spotted the skiff a few hundred yards off the mole and, having closed it, Francis Sandford and his men gently lifted the survivors to safety. The three wounded submariners were in a bad state and their injuries needed expert medical attention, something which the rescuers could not provide. So Francis Sandford went off in search of the destroyer *Phoebe*, which he knew had a surgeon aboard, and, having found her, brought the picket-boat alongside to transfer the survivors to his care.

Dick Sandford's version of events was characteristically modest. As he told a *Daily Mail* reporter: 'We were lucky in being picked up by the picket-boat afterwards. The firing from the shore was a bit severe at 200 yards and only the fact that the sea was a bit rough and we went up and down a good deal saved us. The crew did their duty – every man.'

Captain Carpenter was more forthright in his appraisal. 'The execution of this most difficult submarine operation was beyond all praise; it was, indeed, a miracle that the crew of *C.3* lived to witness the unqualified success of their efforts.'

King George V personally approved the award of the Victoria Cross to Richard Sandford for his valour in bringing the submarine through the jaws of death to successfully destroy the viaduct. Lieutenant Howell-Price was decorated with the Distinguished Service Order, while the four crew members, Walter Harner, William Cleaver, Allan Roxburgh and Henry Bindall, were each

79

given the Conspicuous Gallantry Medal in recognition of their heroism. But what pleased Dick Sandford more than the medals and honours was the telegram he received from a former shipmate while he was recovering in Haslar Hospital. It was brief, laconic and to the point. It read: 'Well done Uncle Baldy'.

* * *

Sadly Richard Sandford did not live long to enjoy the glory of his deeds. Having recovered from his wounds he was appointed to command the submarine *G.11* but was taken ill and had to be relieved. Naval doctors examined him and he was rushed to Grangetown Hospital in Middlesborough with typhoid fever. He died on 23 November, 1918 – less than a fortnight after the Armistice had been signed.

—SEVEN—

Korvettenkapitan Lothar Von Arnauld De La Perière

'It was just ordinary routine'

The Vienna-Pola express was already running five hours late and its unpunctuality did nothing to improve the temper of the young naval officer sitting in the corner of a cold and otherwise empty first-class compartment. It was midwinter, the train's heating system had failed, and wartime regulations meant that no hot food or drink was available from the dining-car. Snow swirled like confetti as the locomotive groaned up the long gradient leading to the Baca Pass where the railway crossed the Julian Alps and frozen signals added a further thirty minute delay before it started on the slow descent to Gorizia and its final run through Trieste and into Pola.

It was a journey that could have been shortened to a matter of a few hours by a Zeppelin airship, a fact that only added to *Kapitanleutnant* Lothar von Arnauld de la Perière's gloom as he stared out of the frosty window at the stark mountains and the drab January sky. Even the knowledge that he was to take command of a U-boat did little to restore his spirits. His original ambition to become a naval aviator and to follow in the footsteps of his brother Friedrich had been frustrated by the powers-that-be and service in the *Deutsche Unterseeboot's Flotille* was very much a matter of second choice – and a poor one at that. Yet, when the conflict ended in November, 1918, this reluctant hero of the underwater

81

war had become the acknowledged Ace of Aces and had sunk no fewer than 194 merchant ships grossing 453,716 BRT – a record that has remained unbeaten by any other submarine commander through two World Wars!

Von Arnauld de la Perière's ancestry, as his name suggests, was part French and part German. His great-grandfather had been an officer in the army of Louis XIV but had offered his services to Frederick the Great after a disagreement with his military superior, the Duke of Bourbon. Finding the aristocratic life of Prussia to his liking he had settled in Germany and started a family. For more than a century the von Arnauld dynasty raised sons for service in the Prussian army, but, following the creation of the Imperial German Navy in 1870 several, including Lothar and Friedrich, broke the family tradition and sought, instead, a career at sea as professional sailors.

After cadet training at the Naval Acadamy in Kiel and service in various ships of the Kaiser's fast-growing fleet, Lothar gradually progressed in rank as he gained experience, and by 1910 he was the torpedo officer of the brand-new cruiser *Emden* – a ship which was to enjoy a war career of distinction under *Kapitan zur See* Karl von Muller. But Lothar gave up this promising sea-going appointment to become an aide-de-camp to the aging but still influential Grand Admiral von Tirpitz. Obviously being groomed for the career of a Staff Officer, the up-and-coming *Leutnant zur See* von Arnauld was serving at the *Reichsmarineamt* in Berlin as Naval Assistant to Admiral von Pohl when war started on 1 August, 1914.

But desk work held no appeal for an ambitious young officer eager to gain honour and glory in the roar of the cannon's mouth and, realizing that Germany's naval policy would offer little opportunity for action if he volunteered for watch-keeping duties with the battle-wagons of the High Seas Fleet, von Arnauld requested a transfer to the Airship Section for training as a Zeppelin officer. His application was turned down on the grounds that the German Navy had insufficient airships in commission to merit training any more aviators for the Zeppelin Service, so Lothar promptly amended his request and applied, instead, for training as a submarine captain at Kiel's Periscope School, the nursery of such famous U-boat commanders as Weddigen, Hersing and von Spiegel. If he could not fly above the sea in a Zeppelin then he would go under the sea in a submarine. Either was preferable to the boring routine of a junior officer's life with the battle fleet swinging permanently from its mooring buoys in the Jade River.

U-35, the submarine he was about to join at Pola, had served in the Mediterranean for nearly six months and her commander, *Kapitanleutnant* Waldemar Kophamel, who had brought the U-boat safely into the Adriatic following a long and hazardous voyage from Germany via the Straits of Gibraltar in August, 1915, had enjoyed an impressive run of success. Operating off Salonika, where he sank the 7,000-ton troopship *Marquette*, and along the coast of North Africa, Kophamel had not only demonstrated his prowess as a submarine commander but had, on one occasion, gained brief notoriety by bringing two camels back to Cattaro as a gift to the Kaiser from a wealthy Senussi admirer. Legend has it that the smell of the animals was so vile that *U-35*'s crewmen were banned from the mess in the U-boat barracks until they had been issued with new uniforms.

Kophamel's successes were rewarded by promotion to *Korvettenkapitan* and appointment as the flotilla captain at Cattaro. In December, 1915, von Arnauld was sent post-haste to the Adriatic by train to take over Kophamel's old boat. It was a less than heroic way in which to arrive and, aware that their new skipper lacked combat experience and had come straight from a comfortable desk-job in Berlin, *U-35*'s battle-hardened veterans wondered how he would shape up when he met the enemy. They did not have long to wait before they found out.

Unlike the majority of submarine commanders von Arnauld preferred to surface and sink his victim by gunfire rather than to remain submerged and waste one of his valuable torpedoes. It was a technique that, when perfected, enabled him to run up a record tally of enemy tonnage for a submarine carries a relatively large number of shells but very few torpedoes. By exposing himself on the surface so that he could use his deck guns he was, of course, putting his submarine at risk in the event of a counter-attack by the enemy, but von Arnauld seemed unworried by the danger. And it is clear that his apparent bravado was a matter of brains rather than bluff when he took care to select a crack gunlayer from the High Seas Fleet to control *U-35*'s 4.1-inch quick-firer.

At this stage, however, untested by practical experience, the new technique remained no more than a theory. When he proceeded to put the theory into practice on his first combat patrol from Cattaro he nearly brought his promising career to an untimely end before it had even started!

The morning of 17 January, 1916, dawned bright and clear over an empty sea and von Arnauld, patrolling the shipping lanes to the east of Malta, cursed his luck as the hours ticked past without sighting a potential victim. Suddenly, shortly after 9 am, his gloomy reverie was broken by the shout of the starboard lookout:

'Smoke bearing Red-Zero–Twenty!'

Having confirmed that the tell-tale smudge of black on the starboard horizon was the smoke of an approaching ship von Arnauld ordered the deck party below and, having closed the upper hatch, he followed them down the steel ladder into the control room where the First Officer, Lauenberg, was waiting expectantly.

'Take her down to ten metres, *Oberleutnant*. Course Starboard 15.' He grinned widely. 'It seems that our luck is in after all.'

Ten minutes later *U-35* rose cautiously to periscope depth and von Arnauld carried out a detailed examination of his unsuspecting victim from a safe distance. She appeared innocent enough. But Lothar knew it was impossible to be too careful, for the British were now deploying their deadly Q-ships in the Mediterranean – merchant vessels manned by naval personnel and converted to carry concealed guns whose sole purpose was to trap and destroy U-boats. The *Baron Napier* looked harmless enough, however, and von Arnauld decided to come to the surface, give the crew time to take to the boats and then sink her by gunfire at his leisure.

As a procedure it had two advantages. It meant that the destruction of the freighter would be carried out in accordance with the requirements of International Law. *And* it meant that von Arnauld could put his theories into practice. But even the best laid plans can go awry. As *U-35*'s deck-gun fired the first warning shot across the bows of the lumbering freighter ordering her to heave-to, the *Baron Napier*'s Marconi wireless operator tapped out an urgent SOS that the ship was being shelled by a U-boat.

His cry for help was picked up by the Q-ship *Margit* steaming some eight miles to the north en route for Malta. Lt-Cdr G. L. Hodson altered course immediately and, as *Margit* hurried south at maximum speed, the Dutch ensign was hoisted at her mainmast – a *ruse-de-guerre* permissable under the Rules of War provided that the vessel did not fire its guns while flying false colours. Surprised by the unexpected arrival of the Dutchman as he appeared over the horizon, von Arnauld did not stop to wonder whether the approaching ship was, in reality, one of the Royal Navy's dreaded trap-ships. Instead, anticipating another easy victory, he ordered *U-35*'s gunners to shift fire to this new target.

By doing so he played into Hodson's hands. For, taking advantage of the situation and displaying all the expected symptoms of genuine panic, the 'neutral' vessel blew off steam and ran up the International Code flags for *I am stopped*. Then, as part of a well-rehearsed charade, Sub-Lieutenant McClure lowered a lifeboat and, with the 'panic' crew aboard, rowed hastily away from the endangered ship. Hiding themselves out of sight, Hodson and two officers remained behind on the Q-ship with the rest of the crew waiting to use their concealed guns as soon as the opportunity arose. The fact that the ship might be torpedoed before they could bring their weapons into action was one of the routine risks of their dangerous calling.

Some innate sixth sense, however, warned von Arnauld that the *Margit* posed a threat and, to Hodson's dismay, *U-35* suddenly stopped firing, dipped beneath the surface and vanished. Fifteen minutes later the U-boat's periscope poked through the water some 800 yards off the *Margit*'s bows and, showing commendable caution for someone so inexperienced, von Arnauld proceeded to circle the vessel while he examined every detail of her hull and superstructure from end to end. Apparently satisfied, he brought *U-35* back to the surface some 1,000 yards to starboard. Then, having raised the German ensign to confirm his identity, he began steering towards *Margit*'s lifeboat, reasoning, no doubt, that if the steamer *was* a Q-ship she would not dare to open fire for fear of hitting her own men.

But Hodson quickly anticipated von Arnauld's cynical tactics. A shrill blast from a whistle on the bridge sent the White Ensign scurrying up *Margit*'s halyards as the Dutch flag was hauled down and the screens and false upper-works hiding the guns fell away. Flames flickered down the starboard side of the warship as the quick-firers opened up and, realizing that he had fallen into a trap, von Arnauld ordered the deck crew below and put *U-35* into a steep dive. The British claimed to have scored a hit on the submarine just abaft the conning tower but no damage was reported by the German authorities nor was any mentioned by von Arnauld in post-war interviews.

The young *Kapitanleutnant* did, however, admit to one frightening moment during the encounter. *U-35* was already beginning to submerge when one of the crew reported that the Watch Officer, *Oberleutnant* Lauenberg, was still on deck. Ignoring the danger – for *Margit*'s gunners still had the range and shells were exploding all around the U-boat – von Arnauld returned to the surface without hesitation. The upper hatch was thrown open and a bedraggled Lauenberg tumbled down the ladder into the control room. The hatch was slammed shut again and in a single smooth movement *U-35* sank beneath the waves, descending so quickly that she reached 180 feet before the dive could be checked and the vessel trimmed onto an even keel.

Unaware of the true situation, *Margit*'s officers were misled by the U-boat's unexpected reappearance. 'The submarine showed her conning-tower 70 yards off (the starboard beam) and was apparently in difficulties. The Q-ship therefore opened fire once more but the enemy again submerged.' This British report of the action thus agrees that the *U-35 did* return to the surface to rescue the unfortunate Lauenberg and served to confirm that von Arnauld's story was not, as might have been imagined, an exaggerated account of mock heroics.

This narrow escape, however, did not deter von Arnauld from pursuing his policy of sinking ships by gunfire whenever such a course of action was possible. 'I very rarely torpedoed a ship even when it was authorized,' he explained after the war. 'I much preferred the method of giving warning and doing my sinking by gunfire or by placing explosive charges aboard the enemy vessel.' It was a technique that also produced other benefits for the leisurely killing of the victim enabled von Arnauld to identify his target beyond any doubt and this meant that he received full credit for his victories. As he shrewdly pointed out: 'Many officers sank more tonnage than appeared on their records because of their inability to produce names and verifications.'

U-35's second patrol under her new captain produced the sort of success that quickly established the reputation of a submarine commander. On 26 February he intercepted the 13,753-ton armed transport *Provence II* and sent her to the bottom with a single well-placed torpedo. The doomed vessel went down in five minutes and a total of 990 French soldiers en route for the trenches of Salonika were drowned in the disaster. The submarine's 35-man crew had inflicted as many casualties on the French army in a few brief minutes as one of von Molkte's divisions could achieve in the course of a week's hard fighting on the Western Front. Such, indeed, was the military value of the U-boat campaign.

Three days later, patrolling off Port Said, von Arnauld torpedoed the British sloop *Primula*. The weapon struck the enemy warship in the bows, bringing down its foremast but, underterred by the calamity, the sloop's captain reversed engines and attempted to ram the U-boat by going astern. *U-35* twisted away under full helm to escape the assault and replied with two torpedoes – both of which missed. But the British skipper, undismayed by the counter-attack, continued to chase the U-boat by steaming backwards and it took a fourth torpedo to put an end to the somewhat ludicrous proceedings. 'Four torpedoes to sink one tiny wasp,' von Arnauld grumbled on his return to Cattaro. 'I don't want to come up against any more *Primulas*.'

In April he took *U-35* on a five-week cruise which included a venture through the Straits of Gibraltar and out into the Atlantic

6. Lieutenant-Commander Malcolm Wanklyn VC (left, with beard) with fellow submarine officers at Malta.

7. (*Left*) *Korvettenkapitan* Lothar von Arnauld de la Perière, the world's most successful submarine commander.

8. (*Right*) Commander Richard O'Kane, the captain of *Tang*, the submarine that torpedoed itself. One of the United States Navy's greatest heroes.

9. HMS *Seal* is towed back to Kiel after her captain's surrender to a German seaplane.

shipping lanes where he destroyed another seventeen vessels. On his way back to the Adriatic he tangled with a French seaplane but managed to dive out of danger before the pilot could make an attack and by the time he returned to his flotilla base at Cattaro at the end of his foray he had added a further 65,000 tons of enemy shipping to his tally.

Another patrol in June, 1916, afforded von Arnauld further publicity when, on the 21st, he sailed into Cartagena harbour to deliver a signed letter from the Kaiser to King Alfonso thanking him for the welcome given to German refugees from the Cameroons on their arrival in the neighbouring colony of Spanish Guinea. With carefully orchestrated effrontery, Lothar drew supplies from an interned German steamer, the *Roma*, before leaving Spanish waters in search of fresh victims.

British Intelligence sources subsequently claimed that the Kaiser's letter was only part of an elaborate cover and that the true purpose of *U-35*'s visit to Cartagena was to deliver two phials of anthrax and glanders germ cultures for use by German agents in Spain. The true story behind this early example of bacteriological warfare has never been revealed but it is an established fact that von Arnauld picked up *Leutnant zur See* Wilhelm Canaris – the head of Hitler's *Abwehr* in World War Two – some four months later in Spanish waters and that, after he had left *U-35*, she had landed two secret agents off Cartagena on 14 February, 1918. Aside from such cloak-and-dagger missions, the June cruise proved to be very successful and a further thirty-nine merchant ships totalling 56,818 tons had been added to von Arnauld's impressive tally of victims by the time it was over. This was in addition to the French armed steamer *Herault* which he had torpedoed soon after leaving Spain's territorial waters.

U-35's next war patrol lasted only twenty-four days but it proved to be an all-time record in terms of sinkings. When von Arnauld finally steamed triumphantly into Cattaro on 20 August he had claimed another fifty-four ships grossing 90,150 tons. 'Yet we encountered no spectacular adventures,' he explained at a later date. 'It was just ordinary routine. We examined ship's papers, gave sailing instructions to the nearest land, and sank the captured prizes.' Von Arnaud's statement was not entirely true for they had, at one point, encountered the Italian Q-ship *Citta di Sassari* but had dived, under fire, and escaped. Of equal interest, however, was the submarine's tally of ammunition expended during the record-breaking cruise – 900 4.1-inch shells and only *four* torpedoes. The *Kapitanleutnant* obviously believed in giving the Kaiser value for money!

Another astonishing patrol followed when, between 13 September and 9 October, he accounted for a further twenty-one ships of 70,413 tons which brought his bag in this four-month period to an incredible 114 merchantmen. No other submarine commander has even approached, let alone surpassed, such figures and von Arnauld stands supreme as the Ace of Aces.

It was during this patrol that he was responsible for one of France's greatest naval disasters when, on 4 October, he sighted the 14,966-ton auxiliary cruiser *Gallia* south of Sardinia en route for the Salonika battlefront with more than 3,000 French and Serbian troops aboard. Steaming at 18 knots and steering an irregular zig-zag course, she offered a difficult target and von Arnauld's skill was taxed to the utmost as he strove to bring the U-boat into a suitable attack position. With only one *Type G-7* left in his tubes he could not afford to make a mistake. But the *Kapitanleutnant*'s luck was in. *Gallia* turned unexpectedly and, although the range was a daunting 900 yards and her squat hull still presented an awkward firing-angle, von Arnold knew it was now or never.

'*Torpedo los!*'

The weapon streaked from the stern tube and Lauenberg gave the order to flood the compensating tank to maintain the boat's trim as they waited for the torpedo to strike home. Eighty seconds of uncertainty passed before they heard the echoes of a large explosion and von Arnauld brought the submarine up to periscope depth to confirm his victory. The horror of the scene that met his eyes remained etched in his memory for the rest of his life and was only erased by his premature death in a flying accident in 1940 while serving as a senior Staff Officer. The troopship was already listing heavily and her decks were a scene of panic and confusion. Lifeboats were being lowered far too quickly, causing them either to jam in the falls or overturn on hitting the water. With discipline in tatters, hundreds of terrified soldiers were jumping into the sea and a mass of bobbing heads surrounded the sinking transport. In von Arnauld's own words: 'The sea became a terrible litter of overturned lifeboats, overcrowded and swamped lifeboats, and struggling men.'

Members of *U-35*'s crew were allowed to view the carnage through the periscope and they were equally shocked by what they saw. As one sailor wrote to a friend in Kiel: 'It was like looking through a peephole into hell.' Von Arnauld claimed that he had to leave the scene because rescue ships were arriving, but this is contradicted by the official French report of the disaster which stated that the rafts and lifeboats were not found until the following day. But whatever the truth, there was nothing that von Arnauld could have done to help. He had once again inflicted horrendous casualties on the French army – 1,852 officers and men were lost in the tragedy – but, as he confessed many years later, 'After what I had seen I did not feel elated'.

The destruction of the *Gallia* was perfectly permissible under International Law, for a troopship shared the same status as a belligerent warship and von Arnauld had no cause to reproach himself for what he had done. In his dealings with merchant seamen he consistently showed a punctiliously correct adherence to the rules of war and exhibited a sympathetic humanity to his victims that was matched by few other U-boat commanders.

During the early weeks of 1917, in the course of a patrol that took *U-35* far out into the Atlantic, von Arnauld sank the *Parkgate, India, Stromboli,* and *Patagonia* together with several other vessels. In every case the crews were given time to get clear of the ships in their boats and von Arnauld ensured that they were given the correct course for the nearest land. On occasions the Master of an attacked vessel was taken aboard the submarine as a prisoner-of-war on the grounds that his experience and knowledge rendered him too valuable a prize to return home with the other survivors. Yet even in the heat of war, and in circumstances that were hardly likely to endear a prisoner to his captor, von Arnauld's consideration was appreciated and acknowledged by his involuntary guests. On 6 May, 1917, William Hunter, the Master of the *Patagonia* wrote this letter to the captain of U-35:

I cannot leave your submarine without just expressing my gratitude for the kind and courteous treatment I have received at the hands of you, your officers, and in fact the whole of your crew during the 23 days I have been a prisoner-of-war on your vessel.

Von Arnauld continued his depredations on Allied shipping in the Mediterranean throughout the remainder of 1917, but the introduction of convoys, tighter defensive measures, and an improved system of centralized command reduced the number of his successes and he had to work harder for his later victims. Nevertheless, when he was finally recalled to Germany to take over command of the cruiser-submarine *U-139* early in 1918, his total bag with *U-35* had risen to three warships, five transports, and 187 merchant vessels – the latter figure including sixty-two sailing ships. It was a handsome reward for two years' work.

His new submarine *U-139* was one of a special class of large U-boats intended for long-range operations along the eastern seaboard of the United States and down the coast of Africa as far south as the Cape of Good Hope. Its surface displacement of 1,930 tons made the 685-ton *U-35* seem like a midget by comparison. What interested von Arnauld most, however, was not the sheer size of his new boat but its deck armament of two 5.9-inch weapons – a far cry from *U.35*'s single 4.1-inch pop-gun. It meant that *U-139* could fight it out on the surface with any vessel smaller than a cruiser. That suited von Arnauld's tactical book admirably.

But conditions in the Atlantic were not comparable with those in the Mediterranean and the newly promoted *Korvettenkapitan* found it difficult to repeat the success he had enjoyed in *U-35*. The new boat was large and unwieldy. Diving exercises and gunnery training took up a good deal of time, while the larger crew created its own problems. Weather conditions in northern Europe were atrocious during the initial shake-down cruise and training was frequently interrupted when raging blizzards swept the Baltic. There was little improvement when *U-139* finally proceeded on her first combat mission. Fierce storms and heavy seas played havoc with patrol routines and the Allied convoy system in the Atlantic made it difficult to find safe targets.

But von Arnauld was not alone in his misery. The first of the cruiser submarines, *U-151*, under the command of *Korvetten-kapitan* von Nostitz und Jackendorff, returned to Germany on 20 July, 1918, with a bag of twenty-three ships totalling 61,000 tons after a successful cruise along America's Atlantic seaboard, but those that followed were not so lucky. Von Arnauld's former flotilla commander, Waldemar Kophamel, took *U-140* on a similar mission, but, despite spending nearly three months at sea, he only sank a disappointing 30,000 tons. Richard Feldt and *U-156* were even more unlucky. Having laid a belt of mines along the eastern coast of the United States, his boat was sunk with all hands in the minefields of the Northern Barrage west of Bergen on 25 September. He died without knowing that his final mission had been crowned with success. On 19 July the US cruiser *San Diego* had fallen victim to one of *U-156*'s mines off Fire Island, New York, and had gone down virtually within sight of the American mainland.

During the month of October, as the war situation continued to deteriorate, the other U-cruisers operating off the New England coast were recalled to Germany. *U-155* and *U-152* arrived in Kiel after the Armistice had been signed, while Max Valentiner, in *U-157*, shrewdly put into Trondheim where he was interned by the neutral Norwegians, thus avoiding the War Crime charges which Britain and America were waiting to lay before him.

Only *U-139* was left and, while cruising off Cape Finisterre, von Arnauld sighted a ten-ship convoy escorted by two armed merchant cruisers and some patrol vessels. His initial submerged attack failed when the torpedo missed and he decided to come to the surface and engage the enemy with his big 5.9-inch guns. By ill-chance *U-139* emerged in the centre of the convoy and was greeted with a far from friendly barrage of shells that quickly persuaded von Arnauld to dive again. A depth-charge attack followed but the submarine was too deep to be in any serious danger and, as the rumble of the explosions died away, he returned to periscope depth to renew the attack.

He found the convoy steaming hard for the northern horizon, so, coming to the surface, he used the submarine's powerful diesels to catch up with the fleeing freighters. Bringing his deck guns into action, he damaged two of the enemy merchantmen but was forced to break off the battle and dive when an escort ship tried to ram him. Another and even fiercer depth-charge attack followed. *U-139* was rocked and buffeted by the underwater explosions, but, apart from a few smashed light bulbs, she withstood the attack well and as soon as the enemy abandoned the hunt von Arnauld brought his boat back to periscope depth in search of a victim.

It is impossible not to admire von Arnauld's perseverence and determination – not to mention courage. The U-boat had been subjected to two heavy depth-charge attacks and had only narrowly escaped being rammed. In addition he knew that he was completely out-gunned by the convoy's escorts. Yet, despite the odds ranged against him, he renewed the assault for the fourth time.

One of the vessels he had damaged earlier was now stationary and was listing sharply to starboard. Anxious to obtain a kill, von Arnauld circled his crippled prey as he prepared to launch a torpedo attack, but the lookouts on the escorts spotted the stalk of the periscope and *U-139* was forced deep again, although on this occasion her crew was spared another barrage of depth-charges. It was nightfall before he dared to return to periscope depth but, by a stroke of good fortune, he found his intended target lying square in his sights and, not daring to waste time, he loosed a snap shot at the vessel before diving for cover. This time, however, he maintained course towards his victim, instead of turning away, on the assumption that this was the last place the escorts would expect to find him.

U-139's crew exchanged congratulatory grins as the thud of the detonating torpedo echoed through the submarine's brightly lit interior. But the triumphant smiles quickly faded into expressions of alarm as a strange noise reverberated against the hull plating. Suddenly the lights went out, leaving the U-boat in total darkness.

The gurgle of water flooding into an empty compartment was clearly audible while the rasping noise of metal against metal added to their terror as the U-boat rolled violently to starboard sending loose equipment crashing to the deck.

The voice of the First Coxswain came through the darkness reporting that he could obtain no response from the hydroplanes and, as the emergency lighting system came to life, the Second Officer, stationed by the diving panel and depth-gauges, warned that the boat was sinking fast. The mystery deepened when a quick inspection of the hull revealed no evidence of damage or leaks. Yet *U-139* was still going down. It was as if some unseen hand was forcing them into the depths. The explanation for the predicament was, however, rather more mundane. By a million-to-one chance the sinking freighter had tangled with the submarine as she passed underneath and now, grappling her assailant in a lethal embrace, she was dragging the U-boat to its death on the ocean floor 3,000 feet below! It was an unnerving situation that demanded an immediate response and von Arnauld acted without hesitation.

'Close main vents – blow all tanks! Group up! Full ahead motors! Up planes – hard a'rise!'

The submarine lurched as the compressed air screamed into the main ballast tanks and she bucked like a young horse in her efforts to struggle free from the clutch of her former victim. Suddenly the U-boat came onto an even keel and, almost at once, she began rising to the surface. Von Arnauld tried to slow the rate of ascent but *U-139* seemed possessed of a mind of her own and she shot to the surface like a cork.

The submarine's deck was a shambles of crushed and broken fittings where the sinking ship had smashed against her. The conning-tower was badly dented and all three periscopes had been bent and twisted out of recognition. It was obvious that *U-139* was in no condition to renew the fight, but as von Arnauld took her down again, she came under another fierce depth-charge attack from the escorts. This time he was forced to give best to the enemy and, rigging the boat for silent running, he stole away from the scene on the electric motors and, by skilful manoeuvring, gave his attackers the slip.

Once clear of trouble von Arnauld set course for the Azores and, as *U-139* plunged into the Atlantic swell, her crew repaired the damaged hull with cement. The action against the convoy, however, proved to be *Korvettenkapitan* von Arnauld de la Perière's final clash with the enemy. As the submarine approached the Portuguese-owned islands the wireless operator picked up an urgent transmission from Berlin repeating the High Command's general recall signal of 21 October which had ordered all attacks on merchant shipping to cease. Von Arnauld took the message to his cabin to examine. Having satisfied himself that it was genuine, he returned to the control room and, with disciplined obedience, he ordered the navigating officer to set course for Germany. Five minutes later *U-139* turned north-eastwards and blue diesel smoke belched from her exhausts as she increased speed. But not even the thought of returning home could erase the expression of weary gloom from the faces of her officers and men. Even the once-proud Imperial Ensign at her stern seemed to droop disconsolately with the indignity of defeat.

But a worse humiliation awaited the *Fregattenkapitan* when he arrived at Kiel on 14 November, three days after the Armistice had been signed. The entire dockyard was in a state of open mutiny. Groups of armed sailors roamed the wharves and barracks in search of loot, red flags fluttered from masts and windows, and the ships of the Kaiser's navy – no longer smartly painted but dirty and unkempt – lay at the mercy of the victorious Allies. Kiel itself had been under the control of a Bolshevik-inspired Sailor's Council since the beginning of the month and Brunsbuttel, Wilhelmshaven, Hamburg and Bremen were in the hands of the mutineers by the 7th. Only the men of the U-boat flotillas remained loyal to their officers.

Paragraph 22 of the Armistice required Germany 'to surrender at the ports specified by the Allies and the United States all submarines at present in existence (including all cruiser-submarines and minelayers) with armaments and equipment complete'.

Such an abject capitulation was more than von Arnauld could stomach and, leaving a young Lieutenant aboard the *U-139* to complete the formalities, he decided to go ashore in order to escape this final humiliation. But not even this could be done with dignity. The mutineers were arresting, and in some cases shooting, any officers they found upon the streets without proper authority from the Sailors' Council. To avoid being recognised he was forced to leave his submarine in civilian clothes like a fugitive on the run from justice.

Thus did the German Navy bid farewell to its most successful U-boat commander.

—EIGHT—

Lieutenant Frederick J. C. Halahan, RN

'The go under water war junk.'

Unlike their more colourful forebears who roamed the Spanish Main in well-gunned galleons and ravaged the Barbary Coast with fast-oared galleys, the latter-day pirates of the China Seas were frequently forced to hijack their victims because they had no vessels of their own. With little knowledge of seamanship, they would have been incapable of sailing a ship even had they possessed one. The traditional pirate vessel was, in fact, something of a rarity in Chinese waters and its absence made the task of the authorities charged with suppressing the activities of these sea brigands that much more difficult.

Like modern political terrorists, their methods were brutally simple. Having selected a promising target, the pirates, disguised as coolies, with weapons hidden in their bed-rolls or inside their clothing, would board the chosen ship as deck passengers at a busy port such as Shanghai or Amoy, confident that the milling mob on the quayside would make their detection difficult. Once at sea, in response to a pre-arranged signal from their leader – often a well-dressed businessman travelling first-class – they would seize the vessel, overwhelm and sometimes murder the European officers, and take the hijacked ship to a desolate bay where they could loot the cargo and plunder the passenger's valuables without disturbance. On occasion hostages would be taken for ransom. Sometimes the ship itself would be destroyed, but usually both ship and passengers would be released unharmed once the pirates had removed everything of value. It was a lucrative trade with only a minimum of risk for those involved. And there was no dearth of eager volunteers for these cut-throat expeditions.

Less adventurous criminals organized protection rackets and threatened action against ships whose owners refused to pay them for the guarantee of a safe passage. The demand notes, written in pidgeon English, were deadly in intention but frequently hilarious in style:

'To the Hang Lee's illustrious junk to peruse. We have to write this few words to you and beg lend us $10,000 in foreign banknotes as protection expenses and to deliver to our Tong at an early date before starting otherwise torpedo would be used to fight against your junk, and don't blame on us for no liberality as well – with compliments.'

Others, like this warning sent to a purser working for Butterfield & Swire, were more chilling: 'We understand your company frequently ships silver dollars from Shanghai to Hankow. You are requested to let us know how much is on the way and other particulars of shipment, such as the name of the steamer, port of shipment, date of departure, amount of shipment, and probable date of arrival. If you found of having witheld information on purpose we will mete out proper treatments to you and you must not say you are not forewarned. . . . We have placed the word 'Death' before us. If there be any damage to us and if there is no reply and if you are indiscreet about the matter we shall shoot to kill.'

Thousands of pirates also operated on the great rivers of mainland China, and the more important commercial waterways, such as the Yangtse, were policed by a multi-national force of gunboats flying a variety of flags, although the majority of the vessels belonged to either Britain, the United States or Japan – Britain taking the lion's share of the responsibility with a fleet that out-numbered all the other gunboats added together. But it was impossible to protect every stretch of open water or to probe each island and creek and, despite the intervention of these small but well-armed warships, the waterfront gangs carried on their murderous trade with little hindrance from the authorities.

Strictly speaking, the river pirates of China should be described as bandits for, under International Law, an act of piracy can only take place on the 'open sea' – a term applicable solely to salt water. Thus raiders and hijackers operating on fresh-water rivers, however piratical their methods and intentions, are not, in the strict legal meaning of the word, pirates. So far as their victims are concerned it is a somewhat academic distinction!

The unsettled political situation that followed the death of Sun Yat-sen in 1925 and the subsequent opening of Chiang Kai-shek's offensive against the northern war-lords and the Communist forces under Mao Tse-tung provided a perfect scenario for the growing power of the pirates, whether they plied their trade along the Yangtse and its tributaries or on the open waters of the South China Sea. And incidents were reported almost daily by the English-language newspapers in Hong Kong and Shanghai.

In August, 1927, the steamship *Man On* was stopped by the Chinese Navy's gunboat *Kong Ko* in the lower reaches of the Pearl River. A party of uniformed seamen came aboard and demanded the right to inspect the vessel's armoury – a locked case containing rifles, pistols and ammunition situated in the chart-house. But when the key was produced the naval boarding-party disclosed their true colours by promptly seizing the guns and turning them on the *Man On*'s crew. Emulating the buccaneers of the eighteenth century, the gunboat's seamen had apparently mutinied against the constraints of naval discipline, murdered their officers and seized the little paddle-powered warship with the intention of earning their fortunes from piracy. The steamer was taken under the lee of a nearby island and, after off-loading the cargo and seizing the Master and twenty-four passengers for ransom, the riverine pirates allowed the vessel to continue on its way. A few days later the would-be pirates were ambushed by government forces and the gunboat was recaptured.

A more serious incident occurred in early September when the 500-ton Hong Kong-registered, and therefore British-protected, *Kochow* was hi-jacked on the Si-Kiang a few miles below Samshui while on passage from Hong Kong to Wuchow. The pirates had come aboard the steamer in the customary manner disguised as coolies and, just before nightfall, they stormed the bridge and the saloon simultaneously. The Captain, at dinner in the saloon, was shot in the stomach and the Chief Engineer was gunned down as he ran out into a corridor brandishing a revolver. Heaving his body overboard without ceremony, the pirates kept the frightened passengers covered with their guns while other members of the gang who had stormed the bridge forced the Chief Officer and helmsman to reverse course and proceed down-river.

A short while later the terrified Chinese coxswain was ordered to bring the *Kochow* alongside a small wooden pier at the village of Taipinghu and, as soon as the steamer was tied up, a fresh horde of pirates stormed aboard to strip the vessel of its cargo and to herd the Purser and 160 passengers ashore as potential hostages. Quite by chance a British steamer had observed the Kochow moving *down*stream and her alert captain, realizing that something was amiss, reported his suspicions to the British river gunboat *Moth* which found the abandoned steamer at dawn the following morning, but the pirates and their hostages had vanished. After medical assistance had been given to the wounded Master and other members of the crew, the plundered vessel was escorted back to Hong Kong.

Four days later, with the approval of the local Chinese Admiral, Chan Chak, three Royal Navy gunboats, the *Cicala*, the *Moth* and the *Moorhen*, proceeded to Taipinghu and, having given the villagers time to leave their houses, opened fire on the little township and proceeded to bombard it with their 6-inch guns until the entire waterfront area had been destroyed. Then, forming up in line ahead with their battle flags streaming, the three gunboats moved up-river to Shekki, another notorious pirate stronghold, and subjected it to a similar bombardment. It was a punitive expedition redolent of nineteenth century imperialism, but it was the only way to exterminate piracy in a country whose leaders were too busy fighting with each other to worry about such matters as brigandry and murder.

The Colonial authorities in Hong Kong were equally worried about the growing number of attacks on British ships which were taking place in the South China Sea and Intelligence Officers had established that the Chinese hijackers were taking captured vessels into Bias Bay, a notorious pirate lair on the coast of Kwantung Province to the north-east of Hong Kong. Several cruisers and sloops were despatched to patrol the general area of the South China Sea and it was decided to send a submarine to cover Bias Bay itself, possibly the first and only time in history that a submersible has been used against pirates.

The boats of the 4th Submarine Flotilla, which was based at Hong Kong, fascinated the Chinese. After all, most of *their* efforts were aimed at keeping their frail vessels afloat. Yet here were the English deliberately allowing their ships to sink beneath the water and return to the surface none the worse for the experience. To the superstitious Chinese the 'Go-under-water war junk' was the most frightening weapon in Britain's naval armoury – its joss exceeding even that of the aeroplane. Many looked upon it as being almost divine in origin – for who other than the Sun God could produce a boat that was able to sink to the bottom of the sea without drowning its crew?

L.4, the 'go-under-water war junk' selected for the Bias Bay patrol, had been completed in 1918 and was one of the submarines built by Vickers under the Emergency War Programme. An

97

enlarged and improved version of the famous wartime *E-class*, they served the British Navy well during the immediate post-war period, pending the arrival of the new *Oberon* boats in the late 'twenties and, in fact, a few even survived into the Second World War. Displacing 890 tons in surface trim with a ballast capacity of 180 tons, *L.4* measured 231 feet in overall length with a maximum beam of 23½ feet. Her Vickers-built diesel engines produced 2,400 hp, giving the submarine a top speed of 17½ knots on the surface, while her electric motors could push her along at a submerged speed of 10½ knots for short periods. Armed with six 18-inch torpedo tubes and a single 4-inch deck gun carried in a shielded emplacement forward of the conning-tower, the *L.4* was a formidable vessel for her time and her 36-man crew had every confidence in their boat – and in their captain, Lieutenant Halahan.

Frederick Halahan had graduated from the Dartmouth Naval College in 1919 and his confidential report for that year described him as being 'distinctly clever and a nice fellow'. The following year Martin Nasmith, who had won the VC for his exploits in the Sea of Marmora with *E.11* in 1915, found the young Sub-Lieutenant to be 'energetic, keen, and reliable'. In a report dated 31 December, 1921, his new Commanding Officer noted him to be 'hard-working, keen, and absolutely reliable. His ability is most marked, being well in advance of his years . . . and in every way a most promising officer'; an opinion readily endorsed by his Flotilla Captain, C. P. Talbot, a wartime veteran who had sunk the German destroyer *V.188* and the U-boat *U-6* while in command of *E.16* in 1915.

In 1922, during the post-war economy drive to reduce the inflated number of junior officers serving with the Fleet, Lieutenant Halahan was one of those whose name was considered for an involuntary and premature return to civilian life. But a glowing report by his Commanding Officer, Gordon Hine, backed to the hilt by Max Horton – by this time Chief of Staff to the Rear-Admiral (Submarines) – saved the day: 'A valuable submarine officer. I consider that it would be detrimental to the interests of the Service if this officer's services were dispensed with.' Thanks to their unstinting support, Halahan also escaped falling victim to the notorious 'Geddes Axe', a redundancy measure introduced by the former First Lord, and now the Chairman of the Committee on National Expenditure, Sir Eric Geddes, under which some 200 Lieutenants agreed to voluntary retirement while a further 350 were 'selected' for virtual dismissal.

After the obligatory period of big-ship duty and further underwater experience as Second-in-Command, Halahan was selected for the 'perisher' course at *HMS Dolphin* from which, after weeks of intensive training, he emerged as a qualified submarine captain. Graduation was quickly followed by a posting to the 4th Flotilla in Hong Kong and appointment in command of the *L.4*. Halahan's arrival in China triggered a love affair with the Far East that was to endure throughout his life. After service as an acting Captain during the Second World War, he returned to the Orient in 1948 to serve as a Commander at the Hong Kong shore establishment *HMS Tamar*, an appointment which he retained until his retirement.

The China Station was popular with officers and men alike. Between 1919 and 1939 it offered an ambitious officer the opportunity of action as well as a chance to demonstrate gallantry under fire, a traditional short-cut to promotion in the Royal Navy. But such incidents tended to be monopolized by the gunboats, although, on rare occasions, the destroyers and sloops also had a taste of action. Submarines were unsuitable for punitive expeditions. Their duty was to protect the Colony and British interests in mainland China in the event of a major war. Their officers could only watch with envy as their gunboat compatriots earned the glory.

But the outbreak of piracy which erupted in the wake of the Civil War in 1927 was far more serious than anything the British Navy had experienced in the past and new tactics had to be evolved to combat the menace that now threatened the busy and lucrative trade routes of the China Seas. The decision to use submerged submarines to patrol areas favoured by the hijackers broke new ground in the war against the pirates and it was welcomed by the Commanding Officers of the 4th Flotilla. The submarines were in the front line at last, and no one was keener to get to grips with the pirates than the newest member of the flotilla, Lieutenant Frederick Halahan.

Bias Bay proved to be empty when *L.4* arrived to start her patrol on 14 October and, in obedience to orders, Halahan remained at periscope depth throughout the day watching and waiting. But no ships appeared and, as darkness fell, he brought the submarine to the surface to charge her depleted batteries while the cook began preparing the evening meal. Halahan had been instructed to maintain a strict blackout and *L.4* was not even burning her red and green running lights as she rolled gently in the swell. But, ignoring the demands of security, he allowed the ship's company to come up on deck in small groups to enjoy a quick cigarette and a breath of fresh air.

The ensuing days found the submarine following the same monotonous routine. Breakfast for the crew thirty minutes before dawn and then, with the Duty Watch closed up for diving stations and all hatches closed, *L.4* nosed beneath the water as the sun rose. It was hot and humid inside the submarine and droplets of moisture shimmered on the arched steel ribs of the curving deckhead. The men dozed fitfully as *L.4* quartered the entrance to the Bay and her officers took turns to maintain a continuous periscope watch over the sea.

But although Bias Bay itself was quiet, a number of things were happening further up the coast, things that were to bring His Majesty's submarine *L.4* and Lieutenant Halahan into the headlines within the next 96 hours.

On 17 October the China Merchants Steam Navigation Company's ship *Irene* left Shanghai laden with cargo and deck passengers bound for Hong Kong. She was flying the colours of the Chinese Republic but her Master, Captain J. H. Jahnsen, was a Norwegian, and all five officers were Europeans – three being British. She put into Amoy during the early hours of Wednesday, 19 October, where she embarked further cargo and more passengers. It was here that the pirates apparently boarded their victim disguised as coolies with their weapons carefully concealed inside their bed-rolls. The Shipping Agents and the vessel's officers made no attempt to search the passengers as they came up the gangways despite the recent spate of attacks and, passing into the ship unchallenged, the gang of cut-throats quickly disappeared into the swarming mass that crowded the decks of the small steamer. Their plans had been worked out in detail several days earlier and they waited eagerly for their leader's signal as the *Irene* backed away from the quayside at Amoy, swung her bows to port and, with white water churning from her stern, set course southwest for Hong Kong.

Captain Jahnsen, his Second Officer, and the Second Engineer were having breakfast in the officers' saloon on the boat deck when, at 8 o'clock precisely, the pirates burst into the cabin and, in the mêlée that followed, shot the Chinese steward in the chest. Unarmed and outnumbered, the three European officers were quickly overpowered and, having been bound and gagged, were locked inside the pantry adjacent to the saloon together with the unfortunate steward. Leaving two armed men to guard the prisoners, the rest of the gang proceeded to rob and plunder the terrified Chinese passengers as they huddled on the open deck.

A separate party made for the bridge and, holding a loaded pistol to the head of the First Officer, they ordered him to maintain course for Hong Kong so that the suspicions of passing ships were not aroused – a precaution that showed they were well aware of the mistake made by the *Man On*'s hijackers when they reversed course and thus drew attention to their crime. The intelligence network that served the pirate fraternity of the China Seas and the Yangtse River was clearly of a high order. A third group descended into the bowels of the ship and occupied the engine and boiler rooms to ensure that the stokers kept the furnaces fed with coal and to forestall any attempts by the *Irene*'s Chief Engineer to sabotage the machinery. Once again everything went according to plan and the sea bandits were now in complete control of the vessel. It had taken just five minutes!

The pirate's attention to detail was so complete that, when the hi-jacked steamship encountered and passed a British warship, they politely dipped *Irene*'s ensign in salute; a bluff that indicated an unexpected degree of sophistication among their leaders.

With the ship's officers either locked inside guarded cabins or carrying out their duties at gunpoint, it was not difficult to quell the cowed and frightened passengers or the Chinese seamen who made up the steamer's crew and the pirates passed their time eating, drinking and gambling for the loot they had acquired. As the drink took effect, the women passengers were dragged screaming into the upper-deck cabins where they were stripped and raped.

The nightmare voyage continued through the hours of darkness and into the heat of the following day until, during the late afternoon, *Irene* altered course towards Bias Bay and Captain Jahnsen, who had been brought to the bridge under guard, was ordered to regulate the vessel's speed so that she would arrive off the entrance at nightfall. Everything had gone smoothly so far and the pirates were jubilant at the success of the hijack. All that now remained was to bring the steamer alongside the landing-stage so that their waiting comrades could start off-loading the cargo. Captain Jahnsen's hands were sweating as he guided the helmsman towards the entrance to the pirate's lair.

'Starboard 10 . . . half speed . . . midship's helm . . . steady as she goes.' He surveyed the darkness through his glasses. An area of shadow lay off the bow. He peered at it carefully but decided that his eyes were playing tricks. He turned to the Chinaman standing at his side in an attempt to distract his attention.

'I need to take soundings to make sure we have enough depth of water to pass over the bar.'

The pirate's understanding of English was somewhat limited. He scowled and shook his head. 'No talk. You go in bay!'

Irene's captain shrugged. He wanted to take another look at that long low shape lying off to starboard but dared not use his glasses again in case the guard smelled a rat.

Suddenly a white light flashed out of the darkness. Dash-dot-dash . . . Dash-dot-dash. Jahnsen recognized it as the morse symbols for the letter 'K' – the International Code meaning: *You should stop your vessel immediately*. It was brief and imperative. There was little doubt that the signal was coming from a warship. Taking his cue Captain Jahnsen reached for the handle of the engine-room telegraph and rang down an order to stop engines. The pirate raised his pistol and cocked the hammer.

'You no stop! Full speed!'

Jahnsen had no choice. His hand moved back to the telegraph and moved the indicator to *Full Ahead*.

Halahan, on the bridge of the surfaced *L.4*, heard the tinkle of the telegraph's repeater bell and, guessing what had happened, ordered the submarine's searchlight to be switched on. *Irene* was already gathering speed and a white wisp of spray was rising from her bows as the beam settled on the steamer's upperworks amidships.

'Put a shot across her bows, Guns!'

'Aye, aye, sir.' The Gunnery Officer moved forward. 'With one round blank . . . load! Fire!'

Irene ignored the traditional warning. Smoke poured from her single funnel and the bow wave rose higher as she built up speed. A second blank charge cracked from the submarine's deck gun, but again it had no effect. To emphasize their determination to run clear, the pirates lined the rails of the steamer and opened fire with an assortment of rifles and pistols. They were poor shots and their bullets posed no immediate threat to the submarine, but their response was a clear warning that bloodshed would certainly follow if any attempt was made to put a boarding party on the hijacked ship.

Halahan's operational orders were clear and unambiguous. He was to stop and search *every* ship attempting to enter Bias Bay. *Irene*'s refusal to stop in response to his warning signals, plus the fusillade of gunfire from the men lining the vessel's side, suggested that the steamship was already in the hands of pirates. If this was the situation, International Law gave him *carte-blanche* to respond in any way he considered suitable. It was an unenviable decision for a young Lieutenant to make, and the fact that the *Irene* was flying Chinese colours did not make the problem any easier. Should his assumption be wrong he could find himself being held responsible for creating an international incident. Coming down in favour of a compromise, he told the Gunnery Officer to load with live shell but to aim the shot well clear of the steamship's bows.

L.4's quick-firer swung towards the target. Moments later a towering geyser of dirty water rose into the air some 20 yards ahead of the *Irene*. But even this failed to impress the pirates, who clearly thought that the British submarine would not dare to fire at the ship for fear of killing or wounding its passengers. They decided to bluff it out; holding the passengers as trumps, they considered that they had nothing to fear.

But Halahan's patience was running out. Summoning his First Lieutenant and Gunnery Officer to a council-of-war on the submarine's bridge, he discussed his options in a low voice. It was agreed that a shot fired low-down at the steamer's hull would minimize casualties as the passengers appeared to be confined to the upper deck. There was always the chance of a lucky shot knocking out the engines and bringing the vessel to a halt by disabling the boilers or propulsion machinery. It would also show the pirates that the Royal Navy meant business.

The submarine's 4-inch gun swung to starboard and the barrel was lowered to maximum depression as the gun-layer brought his sights amidships roughly in line with the funnel. *Irene* was only a few hundred yards away and the range, by naval standards, was point blank. A flash of flame lit *L.4*'s conning-tower as the gun fired and the 31-pound shell slammed into the target with a muzzle velocity of 3,000 foot-seconds. Almost before the hydraulic recuperating system had fully dampened the weapon's recoil the roaring crash of the explosion echoed across the waters of the bay. Scalding steam hissed from ruptured pipes and flames flickered from the splintered woodwork inside the engine-room. The pistons ground to a standstill as they lost pressure and, as the engines came to a stop, the crippled ship drifted helplessly before the current. The shell had caused only one casualty. The pirate holding a gun at the head of the Chief Engineer had, by some quirk of poetic justice, been struck down and killed by a fragment of red-hot steel.

Not surprisingly, the exploding shell caused immediate panic on the steamship. Terrified passengers ran shrieking and screaming in every direction. Taking advantage of the confusion, the imprisoned officers had broken free and, helped by some Chinese crewmen, tried to lower *Irene*'s lifeboats, but the pirates drove them away from the davits at gunpoint and snatched two boats to make good their own escape. Some passengers, braver than the rest, climbed up on to the rails and leapt into the water as the flames from the burning engine-room began to engulf the entire ship.

Halahan ran *L.4* alongside and, while some of the British sailors helped the terrified passengers to climb over the rails and jump down on to the submarine's narrow deck, others dived into the cold waters searching for survivors – a courageous act that was to win the Royal Humane Society's Silver Medal for three of them: ERA Thomas Duckworth, Able Seaman Harry Patterson and Stoker Edward Wright. The citation to the awards credited them with saving at least thirty lives.

A radio signal from the submarine informed the Hong Kong authorities of the situation and the destroyer *Stormcloud* and the sloop *Magnolia* were immediately despatched to give assistance. The cruiser *Delhi*, which was lying at anchor in a nearby bay, was also alerted and, responding promptly to the emergency, she arrived in time to save a further twelve passengers.

'It was sheer hell,' one eye-witness told newspaper reporters on his return to Hong Kong. 'Women and children were screaming. Men were jumping into the sea to escape from the flames. And in the midst of the chaos the pirates who had failed to get away in the ship's boats with the others were shooting indiscriminately in all directions.'

Some of the Chinese women who were dragged out of the water were completely naked – a problem which was quickly solved by the First Lieutenant who retrieved two bales of looted silk from the sea and used it to wind around the hysterical females before they were hurried below for a hot cup of tea. According to local newspaper reports, the *Irene*'s six European officers were among the first to be rescued and there was an implication that they had done little to help the passengers. But it seems that their efforts were directed towards saving the wounded crew-members, especially the steward, who were in need of urgent medical attention.

The heavy swell and a freshening off-shore wind demanded seamanship of the highest order from Halahan as he held the submarine close alongside the burning steamer and by 10 o'clock he had 222 survivors aboard *L.4*. The helpless mass of humanity posed problems of security, however, for, although many of the pirates had escaped in the boats, there was little doubt that some remained on board and it was suspected that they had resumed their coolie disguises and intermingled with the passengers to avoid detection. Halahan took the precaution of having everyone searched for concealed weapons before they were allowed below. But needless to say no guns were found, for the pirates had thrown them overboard as soon as they realized that the game was up.

With the tide carrying the *Irene* towards the shore, Halahan put a salvage party on board with orders to drop anchor to save the vessel from running aground and to fight the fire. But with the steering-gear destroyed, the mechanical pumps out of action, and the majority of the manual pumps burned and useless there was little the British sailors could do to extinguish the flames and they were finally forced to abandon the blazing ship and return to the submarine. Having been informed by radio that a Royal Navy tug was on its way from Hong Kong, *L.4*'s captain reluctantly gave best to the inferno and, at 3 am on Friday morning, he backed the submarine away from the burning wreck. Once clear of danger, both clutches were engaged and black oil smoke erupted from the exhausts as the diesel engines rumbled to life. Moments later the 'go-under-water war junk' was heading twards the open sea with new fewer than 258 persons aboard!

Despite Halahan's efforts to minimize casualties, there was, inevitably in the circumstances, some loss of civilian life as a result of the submarine's attack, although it was not as serious as some Chinese political sources tried to pretend. According to Captain Jahnsen the *Irene* had left Amoy with 258 passengers and crew aboard. Taking into account the twelve survivors picked up by the cruiser *Delhi*, a total of 234 persons were rescued – a figure that included the wounded steward and three passengers suffering from burns. This left twenty-four civilians unaccounted for. But, as Captain Jahnsen's total would have included the pirates who had boarded the ships at Amoy – for they would have been counted with the passengers – it is probable that the majority of those presumed missing were, in fact, members of the hijack gang, many of whom had escaped in the ship's boats or had jumped over the side and swum to the shore. It is likely, therefore, that only a handful of innocent civilians perished as a result of the incident – depending on the number of pirates involved in the attack, possibly none at all.

But the submarine's triumphant return to Hong Kong was not the end of the story so far as Halahan was concerned. The smouldering wreck of the unfortunate *Irene* had foundered while she was under tow by the tug which the Navy had despatched to Bias Bay. And, mindful that the fire had originally been triggered by the submarine's shell exploding inside the vessel's engine-room, her owners, the China Merchants Steam Navigation Company, promptly sued *L.4*'s captain for £53,000 as damages for the 'wrongful sinking' of their ship.

That the boat was eventually destroyed by the fire was not disputed, but it was hardly Halahan's fault. The shell had only started a small conflagration which, in normal circumstances, could have been easily contained and extinguished by the crew.

But the presence of the pirates had prevented any prompt emergency action being taken and by the time the officers and crew were free to fight the flames the blaze had taken too great a hold and the pumps, hoses and other fire-fighting equipment were either damaged or inadequate. In addition, Halahan had acted in accordance with superior orders and, further, he was fully authorized to use force by International Law.

The *Irene*'s owners obviously did not agree and, after consultation with their lawyers, they submitted a supplementary claim of £100 per day in respect of lost profits occasioned by the destruction of the ship – a sum that had accumulated to more than £48,000 by the time the case finally came before the High Court in Hong Kong some fifteen months later. But their legal manoeuvres proved to be in vain. The Defence contended that the loss of the *Irene* was due to an 'Act of State' – a view accepted by the judicature. The plaintiffs' claim was dismissed with costs and Halahan was exonerated of all blame.

A few of the pirates were subsequently captured, tried and executed by Chinese Government soldiers and it is probable that several others had been killed during the attack on the steamship. But the majority of the buccaneers who had boarded the *Irene*, and the faceless men ashore who had organized the assault, were never brought to justice. Their lawless days, however, were nearly over. When Japan took advantage of China's internal turmoil to launch her invasion of Manchuria in 1931 the pirates found themselves swept up in the general conflict. The Japanese Navy soon gained control of the entire coastal area of mainland China and, with brutal efficiency and scant regard for the law, stamped out the brigands and bandits who had threatened the shipping lanes of the South China Sea from time immemorial. Ironically, on odd occasions when the pirates struck back at their new adversaries, they found themselves being honoured by the Chinese Government as patriotic guerrillas fighting for the freedom of the Republic. Political necessity had turned the once-feared sea bandits into national folk heroes!

Although not similarly elevated to the status of a demi-god, Lieutenant Halahan did not go unrewarded for his part in the incident. He had gained a well-deserved place in the annals of the Royal Navy as the first submarine commander to battle with, and defeat, a gang of pirates on the High Seas. When the furore of the court hearing had died down he was awarded the Distinguished Service Cross. It was a signal honour for the captain of a 'go-underwater war junk'!

—NINE—

Kapitan* Jan Grudzinski

'Good luck and God bless you.'

Operation *Fall Weiss*, planned to begin at 4.45 am on 1 September, 1939, was both the prelude and the overture to the Second World War. When Hitler's panzer divisions rumbled over the Polish border at dawn that Friday morning the roar of their exhausts heralded the start of a global conflict that was, during the ensuing six years of bloody combat, to result in the destruction of no fewer than 1,280 submarines from twelve different nations: the United States, Britain, France, Germany, Greece, Italy, Holland, Japan, Norway, Poland, Soviet Russia and, even though she was neutral, Sweden.

The submarines of the Polish Navy's undersea flotilla – *Sep (Vulture)*, *Zbik (Wild Cat)*, *Rys (Lynx)*, *Wilk (Wolf)* and *Orzel (Eagle)* – were berthed at Gydnia on the western side of the Gulf of Gdansk and, not surprisingly, the base was an early target for Goering's dive-bombers. The torpedo-boat *Mazur* and several smaller surface craft were sunk during the first series of attacks but, miraculously, the five submarines escaped unscathed. Minutes after the sirens began wailing the *All Clear* they had cast off their moorings and were heading for the open sea to defend their homeland.

The Polish army, despite having thirty divisions in the field and a further 2,500,000 trained conscripts available for mobilization,

* *Kapitan* = Lieutenant Commander.

107

could offer little cohesive resistance to the advancing German troops. Without armoured units, and with their military strength measured in terms of antiquated cavalry brigades, the gallant Poles quickly found themselves out-numbered and out-gunned on all fronts. Their obsolete *PZL P-11* fighters, and the general inadequacy of the country's anti-aircraft defences, could achieve little against the might of the massed Stuka, Dornier and Heinkel squadrons ranged against them. Although 120 German machines were shot out of the sky during the brief campaign, their destruction was due to the heroism of the Polish pilots rather than to any superiority of their aircraft.

Within twenty-four hours Warsaw lay in ruins and, although the men of the White Eagle fought valiantly, they knew they had no real hope of success against the overwhelming power of Hitler's war machine. And when Stalin's Red Army crossed the Republic's eastern frontier on 17 September in support of their Nazi ally, Poland's doom was sealed.

At sea the Navy's task was to cut German communications and to protect the coast against any enemy attempts to land troops and tanks. It was confidently anticipated that German heavy ships would move eastwards into the Baltic to guard the seaward flank of von Bock's advancing Army Group North and that these would be the prime targets of the five submarines which were ordered to Puck's Bay to cover the vital seaward approaches to Gdansk. But the Polish admirals had guessed wrong. Realizing that Britain would probably declare war in support of Poland, even though there was little she could do to help her Eastern European ally by direct means, Hitler and Admiral Raeder had decided to keep the main strength of the *Kriegsmarine* in the North Sea for operations against the Royal Navy and to send only their older and smaller warships into the Baltic. In fact, only three of Doenitz's twenty-one operational submarines were retained east of Kiel – the remaining eighteen being allocated to patrol areas in the North Sea and along the coasts of the British Isles. And of Germany's three pocket-battleships two were already en route to their war stations in the North and South Atlantic several weeks before the *Wehrmacht* marched against Poland.

Nevertheless some major surface ships assisted the Army by taking part in bombardment operations and the former battleships *Schlesien* and *Schleswig-Holstein* shelled the fortresses of Hel – Poland's Gibraltar at the head of the Gulf of Gdansk – and Westerplatte. The destroyer *Wicher* and the minelayer *Gryf* were sent to engage the German inshore squadron but in a running battle with dive-bombers and surface ships both vessels were sent to the bottom. Total confusion reigned as the Luftwaffe pounded the naval bases and gun emplacements along the Baltic coast and, warming to their task, the German bombers soon turned their attentions on any Polish warship they could find.

The survey ship *Pomorzanin*, together with eight minesweepers and five auxiliaries, were sunk by the Luftwaffe. The Polish Navy's three remaining destroyers, *Blyskawica, Burza,* and *Grom*, were forced to leave the Baltic and escape to Britain following the surrender of Westerplatte on the 7th and the evacuation of Gdynia five days later. Only the five submarines remained to continue the war at sea and within days they, too, found themselves faced with an impossible task.

Deprived of worthwhile targets by Raeder's decision to keep his major units out of the Baltic, the submarines were left with no operational objectives. When they ventured to the surface they were pounced upon by Luftwaffe bombers during the hours of daylight and naval anti-submarine patrols at night. *Sep* was roughly handled by German aircraft while covering the approaches to Gdynia. Thirty-five bombs were dropped and she suffered considerable damage not only to her conning-tower and upperworks but, more importantly, also to the pressure-hull where a number of seams were opened by the concussion of the exploding weapons.

Unable to return to Gdynia, the crew had to carry out makeshift repairs at sea in order to keep the crippled submarine on patrol. But, by 15 September, with two compartments completely flooded and the boat virtually unmanageable, there was only one course open to her captain and, reluctantly, *Sep* headed for Stockholm and internment.

Rys fared little better. She was attacked on 4 September and, trapped in shallow inshore waters, was unable to dive to safety when a Stuka Ju-87 appeared overhead. The aircraft was soon joined by others and fifty-three bombs were aimed at the submarine before the enemy finally withdrew. Like *Sep*, running repairs had to be carried out at sea. Thirteen days later, on the very day that the Russians stabbed Poland in the back and all organized military resistance collapsed, *Rys* crawled into Swedish territorial waters and gave herself and her crew up to internment. *Zbik* suffered a similar fate, although she succeeded in remaining on patrol until 25 September. But two days later the Polish capital, Warsaw, surrendered to the German army and on 29 September von Ribbentrop and Molotov, the Foreign Ministers of the Third Reich and the USSR, signed an agreement to divide the twenty-year old republic between the two victors, a document that was to spell the end of Polish independence for several generations. Despite the final victory of the Allies over Nazi Germany in 1945, the Polish nation never regained its freedom and has now been a satellite and vassal-state of the Soviet Union for more than forty years.

The *Orzel*, captained by Commander Kloczkowski, left Gdynia with the other submarines on the morning of 1 September and headed for Puck's Bay in accordance with her war orders. No targets were sighted but there was a considerable amount of air activity and she was forced to go deep on a number of occasions to escape the attention of enemy bombers. But, luckier than her sisters, *Orzel* avoided attack and, suffering no damage at the hands of the Luftwaffe, remained fully operational. Kloczkowski quickly realized that his war orders were based on a false appreciation of German intentions and, after discussing the situation with the submarine's Executive Officer, Jan Grudzinski, he took *Orzel* eastwards across the Gulf to lay a defensive minefield in the seaward approaches to Gdansk.

While engaged on this particular operation, Kloczkowski received a distress signal from an unidentified submarine reporting that she was under attack by enemy E-boats and, having completed the minefield, he immediately steered to the assistance of his comrade. But the message proved to be a carefully contrived German trap and, on arriving at the indicated position, *Orzel* found herself under depth-charge attack by an anti-submarine patrol which was lying in ambush for its unsuspecting victim. With shoaling water on three sides Kloczkowski had only one avenue of escape – and that was back through the minefield which he had only just finished laying! It was a frightening experience, especially when, on two occasions, the mooring cables of the mines grazed along the side of the submarine. But, as one member of the crew put it: 'Our Lady, the Queen of Poland, was watching after us. And she protected us from harm'. For the deeply religious Poles faith was of far more importance than mere luck.

Enemy air and surface patrols were increasing in strength and intensity with every passing day and *Orzel* spent the next forty-eight hours playing cat-and-mouse with the Germans. On one occasion Kloczkowski was forced to go deep and remain on the bottom for more than two hours during which time at least ten depth-charges were heard to explode in the submarine's immediate vicinity. But finally, on 5 September, *Orzel*'s captain received radio orders to quit the Gulf of Gdansk and make for the open waters of the Baltic. The move gave the exhausted officers and crew a much-needed respite from attack but the new patrol area proved to be disappointingly unrewarding and for the next six days not a single warship – friendly, enemy, or even neutral – was sighted. In addition, the news from home was growing steadily worse and communications with the submarine's home base of Gdynia ceased on 12 September. But worse was to follow. A few hours later *Orzel*'s hydraulic system broke down and, hard on the heels of this disaster, Commander Kloczkowski fell seriously ill. Although the captain continued in nominal command and, in fact, insisted on trying to carry out his watch-keeping duties, responsibility for running the boat now devolved on *Orzel*'s Executive Officer, Lt-Cdr Jan Grudzinski.

A Council-of-War comprising all but the most junior officers was called in the wardroom and it was unanimously agreed that the hydraulic failure could only be rectified with the full facilities of a properly equipped dockyard. In addition, despite Kloczkowski's personal dissension, it was agreed that their Captain must be landed for immediate hospital treatment. Having examined the charts, Grudzinski decided to make for Tallinn, the capital of neutral Estonia, and to claim his belligerent rights under International Law to remain in harbour for 24 hours to carry out urgent repairs.

Orzel arrived at Tallinn the following morning, 13 September, and was met by Government officials accompanied by two patrol vessels. Grudzinski's request was received with broad smiles and friendly handshakes and, an hour later, the submarine was escorted into the inner harbour in which was anchored the German freighter *Talassa*. On seeing the Polish ensign fluttering proudly from *Orzel*'s conning-tower jackstaff, the enemy seamen promptly hauled down their Swastika colours and made themselves scarce. Despite the protection offered by the neutral harbour, they clearly did not relish a confrontation with the Poles whom they knew to be thirsting for their blood. Berthing the submarine in the farthest and most inaccessible basin available, and having moored the boat with her stern towards the entrance to prevent a rapid escape, the Estonian officials reopened their parley with Grudzinski. Satisfied that the submarine was genuinely in need of urgent repairs they agreed to allow a stay of 24 hours and they also arranged for an ambulance to come alongside to take Kloczkowski and a Petty Officer who was also ill to hospital for treatment. Then, after another flurry of salutes, handshakes, and good wishes, the officials withdrew and the work of refuelling, reprovisioning and repairing the submarine began, while the crew, taking advantage of the brief break from routine, went ashore to pay a much-needed visit to the municipal baths.

But the official smiles of welcome were merely a façade. Along with her neighbours, Latvia and Lithuania, the tiny republic of Estonia was in a difficult diplomatic position. Cut off from the rest of Europe, the three Baltic states were at the mercy of the Russians – with whom they shared a common border – and their Nazi allies. One false move, one ill-advised action, and their precarious independence would vanish overnight. And, whatever the niceties of International Law, the presence of the *Orzel* was an embarrassment which the Estonian authorities could well do without. Discreet enquiries were made at the respective embassies and, as the day progressed, the telegraph lines linking Tallin with Berlin and Moscow chattered urgently.

Work on the *Orzel* had gone well. The hydraulic failure had been traced and sorted out by the dockyard's experts, all stores were aboard, and the fuel bunkers were full. By evening, and well inside the 24-hour time limit, the submarine was ready to sail. But, suddenly and unexpectedly, there was a hitch. An Estonian soldier came aboard and informed Grudzinski that he was required to attend the Port Commandant's office immediately. Leaving Lieutenant Andzej Piasecki, *Orzel*'s new Executive Officer, in temporary command, Grudzinski put on his cap and followed the soldier to a squat concrete building in the heart of the dockyard.

Here he was informed that the German freighter was about to leave harbour and that, in accordance with International Law, there must be a six-hour interval between the sailing of belligerent ships. *Orzel*'s departure must therefore be put back by six hours and no doubt the Captain would understand the reason for the delay. The Estonian Commodore spread his hands in a gesture of apology. He was, he explained, merely observing the requirements of the Hague Convention.

Despite the Commodore's explanation, the *Talassa* showed no sign of an immediate departure and Grudzinski fumed impotently as the hours slipped by. Finally, towards midnight, the German vessel weighed anchor and moved slowly out into the dredged channel. A few minutes later Grudzinski's thoughts were interrupted by the arrival of an Estonian officer who informed him that, in accordance with an Agreement signed by the three Baltic states at the beginning of September, any submarine or other warship found in their territorial waters was to be disarmed and interned. It was a transparent piece of fiction, but, despite Grudzinski's protests that he had not been warned of this new situation when he had first arrived at Tallin, his objections were ignored. Before any counter-action could be taken by the Poles a party of armed soldiers was placed on board the vessel, while naval officers supervised the removal of the submarine's charts and navigational instruments, together with the breech-blocks of her deck guns.

As soon as the officer had departed Grudzinski again summoned *Orzel*'s officers to the wardroom and, having informed them of this new and dramatic turn of events, promised that the submarine would be taken to sea as soon as circumstances permitted. Once an escape plan had been drawn up, it was his intention to make a break for freedom even if the attempt resulted in bloodshed – a sentiment strongly supported by his fellow-officers who had little love for the treacherous Estonians. That same night the submarine's confidential papers and code books were destroyed and *Orzel*'s officers visited the various messes and crew spaces to explain the situation. A few hotheads wanted to take immediate and precipitate action but they were ultimately persuaded that, for the moment, it would be to everyone's advantage to help the Estonians to demilitarize the vessel. It was an essential part of the plot to lull the Estonian authoritfiies into a false sense of security if Grudzinski's daring escape plan was to work.

Early the following morning the Naval Attaché from the British Embassy drove to the dockyard to pay his respects to the Polish captain, but the armed guards on the quayside would not allow him to go aboard and, taking a visiting card from his wallet, he wrote a few words on the back. Then, attracting the attention of a seaman standing on the bow casing while the guards were not looking in his direction, he gestured to him to take it.

Unable to read English, but realizing that the message might be important, the Polish sailor hurried below and handed the card to Grudzinski who was sitting in the wardroom studying some papers. The Lieutenant-Commander glanced at the printed pasteboard and, turning it over, read the scribbled note on the reverse: *Good luck and God bless you*. It was a heartening reminder that they still had some friends in the world. Those five simple words did much to raise morale when news of the message filtered down to the mess deck.

An hour or so later more soldiers arrived to reinforce the men standing guard over the submarine and a group of civilian dockyard workers drove a low-loading truck on to the quayside ready to hoist out the torpedoes. In the midst of all this activity one of the *Orzel*'s senior Warrant Officers borrowed a dinghy and rowed out into the harbour to enjoy a quiet bit of fishing. But it was not quite so innocent as it seemed to the casual onlooker, for his lines were carefully knotted at fathom intervals and were intended for another and rather more serious purpose than the simple snaring of fish. Casting the line over the side, the Warrant Officer lowered it into the water until he felt the lead weights touch bottom. Then, hauling it back into the boat, he counted off the knots and noted the depth on a scrap of paper. Within the space of a few hours he had surveyed the entire length of the submarine's projected escape route and, as he rowed back to the *Orzel*, he showed no resentment when the watching guards jeered at his empty basket.

Everyone contrived to look busy throughout the morning and the Estonian officer in charge of the soldiers was so impressed that he personally thanked Grudzinski for the crew's helpful assistance in demilitarizing the submarine. But again, everything was not quite as it seemed. *Orzel*'s coxswain, for example, had smuggled a saw from the dockyard stores and, unobserved by the guards, had partially cut through the mooring hawsers so that they would part as soon as they came under strain. And the Chief Petty Officer Telegraphist, who had dismantled the submarine's radio equipment during the morning, bluffed the soldiers into helping him put it back together again in the afternoon by short-circuiting some wires and causing a minor electrical fire. This, he explained to a gullible sergeant, meant that he would have to reassemble the apparatus in order to trace and rectify the fault – a story which the Estonian guards accepted without question.

By noon on the 14th sixteen of *Orzel*'s torpedoes had been hoisted up through the forehatch and were lying stacked on a lorry with their detonators removed. Only a piece of bare-faced sabotage could prevent the final six from being unloaded and, seizing an opportune moment, Grudzinski cut the cable of the torpedo-hoist himself. Then, taking advantage of the apparent breakdown, he came up on deck and berated the Estonian dockyard workers for being careless. But it was a Sunday and the civilian labourers were happy to have an excuse to stop work. The foreman apologized and, without making any attempt to investigate the cause of the hoist failure, accepted full responsibility. There was, he said, plenty of time. They would be back on Monday morning to splice a new wire and finish off the job. With a cheery wave, they clambered aboard the lorry and drove off.

Now only the armed sentries remained, but they presented no problem, for the Poles had taken care to cultivate friendly relations with their erstwhile captors. It was all part of Grudzinski's elaborate and carefully planned scenario to deceive the Estonians. Unfamiliar with naval routine, the watching soldiers had no reason to suspect that *Orzel*'s crew were busy preparing for departure. Even the Estonian officers fell victim to the bluff. At six o'clock that evening Piasecki switched on the submarine's gyro-compass and the soft hum of the machinery attracted the attention of an alert young Army lieutenant who was standing in the control room. *Orzel's* Executive Officer laughingly explained that it was only the sound of the night ventilation fans and the Estonian accepted the lie without further question.

Grudzinski's main worry was how he could prevent the authorities from draining the fuel bunkers, but for some reason such a step never occurred to the Estonians, though this would have ensured the complete immobilization of the submarine. Nevertheless the Lieutenant-Commander placed two brawny seamen armed with heavy steel bars by the vital fuel valves – just in case.

After a cooked supper, which the sailors shared with the guards, the crew climbed into their bunks and settled down for the night. Grudzinski's outward show of co-operation proved to be so convincing that, just after nine o'clock, the Estonian Commandant withdrew the guards on the quayside and left only two soldiers aboard the *Orzel* to keep an eye on things until the morning.

Zero hour had been set for midnight but the unexpected arrival of an Estonian officer exactly on the stroke of twelve led to a hasty postponement of the escape plan and two hours passed before Grudzinski considered it safe to proceed. The pre-arranged signal was given and the soldier standing guard on the bridge was swiftly overcome by two silent figures who emerged from the shadows and seized him before he could raise the alarm. Down below, in the brightly lit control-room, his companion was disposed of with similar rapidity – on finding himself facing a Petty Officer armed with a loaded revolver he had promptly fainted! While the two prisoners were being bound and gagged, one of *Orzel's* senior ratings ran down the deserted quayside with an axe and cut through the main elecricity cable, plunging the entire dockyard into darkness.

The sudden blackout led to confusion ashore and several minutes passed before anyone connected the power-failure with the Polish submarine. By the time they had woken up to the possibility of an attempt to escape the *Orzel* had already slipped her mooring cables and was reversing away from the quayside on her electric motors.*

There was a heart-stopping moment when *Orzel's* bows grounded on a submerged mudbank soon after she had cleared the gates of the dockyard basin, but, despite the danger, there was no panic and Grudzinski responded to the emergency with unruffled

---

* A submarine's diesel engines cannot run astern. Any manoeuvring which requires the vessel to proceed in reverse has to be powered by the electric motors.

calm. Having flooded the submarine's after-tanks to take the stern deeper, he blew the forward tanks to raise the bows.

'Grouper up – full astern both!'

The hum of the electric motors rose to a shrill whine. The submarine shuddered and then, lurching gently, slid into deep water. Grudzinski maintained full starboard helm and the vessel circled until her stem was pointing towards the open sea.

'Midships . . . steer Green zero-two-zero. Switches off – stop motors. In clutches. Full ahead both!'

Black smoke erupted from the exhausts as the diesel units rumbled to life and, almost simultaneously, the Estonian defences came into action. Gun flashes lit the night sky and towering geysers of water leapt skywards as the shells exploded in the sea on all sides of the submarine. Machine-gun and rifle bullets ripped through the darkness as the soldiers reached the seaward end of the quay and bullets rattled against the hull. But, without searchlights, it was impossible to aim accurately and with every passing minute *Orzel* was distancing herself further and further from the hornet's nest astern.

Grudzinski and the helmsman, the only two members of the crew to remain on the bridge, had to crouch behind the conning-tower coaming to shield themselves from the bullets and shell splinters as they steered the vessel across the outer harbour, but they ran the gauntlet safely and, within minutes, the submarine had broken past the harbour entrance and was plunging her bows into the ice-cold waters of the Baltic. Having disposed of one danger, however, they now faced another. The moment they ran clear of the dockyard the shore searchlights – unaffected by the failure of the dockyard power-supply – flickered into life and the massive 11-inch guns of the coastal defence batteries opened fire. But Grudzinski had reached deep water by this time and, returning the submarine to her true element, he took *Orzel* into the safety of the depths.

The first priority was to release the two Estonian prisoners and the submarine was put on a course for Sweden, although, without charts, Grudzinski was finding navigation something of a problem. Radio requests to the beleaguered naval base at Hel for assistance were jammed by the Germans; the fortress was destined to fall to the enemy within the next few days. The submarine *Rys* picked up *Orzel*'s signal and, replying in plain language, reported that she was badly damaged and making for internment in Sweden. She was, however, anxious to help and her captain offered to meet *Orzel* and hand over his own charts which were no longer needed. But Grudzinski was unwilling to give away his position and was forced to refuse.

116

Remaining submerged throughout the day and only surfacing at night, *Orzel* arrived off the coast of Gotland on 19 September. The submarine's collapsible boat was lowered into the water and the two prisoners were brought up on deck. They protested loudly, however, and seemed surprisingly opposed to leaving the vessel despite everything that had happened. An officer passed them a bundle of money together with several bottles of vodka and the Navigating Officer told them in which direction to row. The submarine was barely two miles from the Swedish shore, but it was a pitch-black night and, lacking confidence in the fragile rubber boat, they seemed unconvinced by his assurances. Finally Grudzinski handed them a letter which he told them to give to the Estonian authorities on their return to Tallin. The letter, which explained the circumstances of the escape, totally absolved the two guards of any complicity in the operation and would, he hoped, save them from punishment. Then, after a final wave, he closed the conning-tower hatch and *Orzel* slid beneath the surface, leaving the frightened soldiers to find their own salvation.

Grudzinski and his men patrolled the Baltic for a further sixteen days without sighting a single worthwhile target. The weather continued fine with good visibility and this forced *Orzel* to remain submerged for most of the day and much of the night. It was not a pleasant existence but there was little else they could do. Their time was, however, not wasted and, headed by the Torpedo Officer, the occupants of the wardroom took the opportunity to pool their knowledge and prepare hand-drawn maps from memory. The resulting charts which proved to be remarkably accurate when they were ultimately put to the test.

The war situation, as gleaned from news broadcasts picked up on the submarine's radio, was bad. Warsaw had fallen and, finally, after a gallant resistance, Hel surrendered. It was clear that organized resistance in Poland had virtually ceased and that a return to the homeland was out of the question. It was also unanimously agreed that they would not seek internment in Sweden. A BBC news bulletin picked up in mid-Baltic revealed that their flotilla-mate *Wilk* had successfully escaped to Britain and was now serving with the Free Polish Navy in exile. Inspired by the news, *Orzel*'s crew whole-heartedly supported their Captain's declared intention to do the same, despite the very different conditions that now prevailed.

Fuel was running short and water was already rationed – no one had been allowed to wash or shave for the past week. More important, *Wilk* had been able to rely on the accuracy of her charts, supplemented by the information on currents, landmarks

117

and other details in her Pilot's Guides, when she made her passage through The Sound. In addition her deck guns were in working order. But even with these advantages her captain and crew had, like Max Horton in 1914, encountered problems and dangers in abundance. Without charts or guns how could *Orzel* possibly succeed? Grudzinski did not know, but he was determined to try!

The submarine arrived off the entrance to The Sound on Thursday, 12 October but German patrols made it impossible to break through in daylight and *Orzel* was forced to submerge and wait the dusk. Fortunately it was a dark and moonless night – conditions which favoured the Poles – but The Sound proved to be alive with traffic and they narrowly avoided colliding with a merchant ship when they first rose to the surface to check their position. Grudzinski promptly submerged again but the freighter's captain was sufficiently unnerved to ignore the black-out regulations and, switching on his navigation lights, he hurriedly cleared the area for fear of an accident.

Grudzinski brought the submarine cautiously to the surface again and, with only a hand-drawn map to guide him, he decided to keep close to the Swedish side of the strait as a precaution against possible German minefields. Even so, he judged the risks to be so great that the entire crew, except for a few brave volunteers manning the engine-room, were assembled on deck wearing their life-jackets. Heavy rain made conditions unpleasant for the men sheltering in the lee of the conning-tower but the reduced visibility favoured the submarine and helped to shield its fleeting and shadowy shape from enemy attention.

German searchlights probed the surface ahead of *Orzel*'s bows but this time luck proved to be on their side for not one of the questing beams found the submarine as it rumbled northwards and then north-westwards. Despite his lack of charts, Grudzinski managed to keep in the deep-water channel, although, like Horton, he knew that he had insufficient depth to submerge completely if they were sighted by the enemy. But that was a chance that had to be taken. It was a nail-biting passage but good pilotage and excellent seamanship brought them through the most dangerous section without mishap and, shortly before dawn, *Orzel* submerged in 90 feet of water and remained on the bottom throughout the whole of Friday the 13th – a date that would have made Baron von Spiegel quake in his shoes!

At dusk Grudzinski brought the submarine back to the surface and within an hour or so *Orzel* thrust her bows into the Kattegat. Their ordeal was nearly over and, on passing clear of the Skagerrak, Grudzinski transmitted a radio signal *en clair* to the

10. *Korvettenkapitan* Otto Kretschmer, the top-scoring U-boat ace of World War II, returns smiling from a record-breaking combat patrol.

11. Commander Sam Dealey – the skipper who specialized in sinking destroyers.

12. *Kapitanleutnant* Otto Weddigen. His attack on the cruisers *Aboukir*, *Hogue* and *Cressey* in September, 1914, aroused the world to the dangers of submarine warfare.

13. *Chu-Sa* Mochitsura Hashimoto who took part in the attack on Pearl Harbor and was still on combat patrol when the war ended.

British Admiralty reporting his approximate position and asking for instructions. He knew he was taking a gamble for the enemy might be eavesdropping, but, without charts or code books, there was little else he could do. By good fortune his call for help was picked up by the Royal Navy and at 11 am on Saturday 14 September the destroyer *Valorous*, a singularly apt name in the circumstances, made contact with the waiting submarine and escorted her safely to the nearest British base.

It had been an epic voyage and one which it is impossible to parallel in the entire span of submarine history. In recognition of his inspired leadership during the *Orzel*'s heroic break-out from internment at Tallin and her subsequent dash for freedom through the heavily patrolled waters of The Sound without charts, navigational aids, or guns, Lt-Cdr Jan Grudzinski was awarded Poland's highest military honour – the *Virtuti Militari* – which was personally bestowed on him by the Polish Commander-in-Chief in exile, General Sikorski.

* * *

After repairs and refitting, *Orzel* joined the Royal Navy's 2nd Submarine Flotilla at Rosyth where she was to serve alongside such famous commanders and submarines as Lt-Cdr C. H. Hutchinson, *Truant*; Lt-Cdr E. F. Pizey, *Triton*; Lt-Cdr H. J. Caldwell, *Tarpon*; and Lt-Cdr W. F. Haselfoot, *Thistle*. She arrived in time to take part in the Norwegian campaign and, in fact, the Polish vessel was the first Allied submarine to make a kill when Hitler launched his attack on Scandinavia.

Operation *Weser*, the invasion and occupation of Norway and Denmark, began on the night of 6–7 April, 1940, when six groups of German warships and transports left Hamburg at carefully calculated intervals so that they would all arrive at their various objectives simultaneously at zero hour – 4.30 am on the 9th. It was an ambitious and superbly organized operation which stretched German naval resources to the limit. Surprise was essential if the plan was to meet with success. Should the Royal Navy have any cause to suspect what was about to happen the heavy ships of the Home Fleet could strike at the invasion forces while they were still at sea and destroy them before a landing could be made.

At 10.30 am on the morning of 8 April *Orzel* was patrolling submerged off the Norwegian coast in the vicinity of Kristiansand when a drab-painted passenger ship came into view. Grudzinski was called to the periscope by the Officer-of-the-Watch and, having examined the vessel at a distance, he decided to move closer. She was flying no identifying colours but he was able to read the name *Rio de Janeiro* on the bows. Although an attempt had been made to obliterate the port of registration with paint it had not been overly successful and Grudzinski, with the aid of his high-magnification periscope, was able to decipher it as *Hamburg*. An examination of the reference books in the control-room showed the ship to be a 9,800-ton German passenger liner built for the South American trade. It seemed a strange place for her to be, especially as she was steaming northwards along the coast in the direction of Bergen. Grudzinski had already noticed a significant increase in German air activity in the previous 24 hours, but he considered a Nazi invasion of Norway to be an unlikely possibility. Nevertheless the ship interested him and, in accordance with the rules of International Law, he brought *Orzel* to the surface and flashed a challenge: *Stop engines. The Master with ship's papers is to report on board immediately*.

The German ship did not stop to answer the order. White water frothed from her stern as she increased speed and she altered course to starboard in the direction of the Norwegian coast and the safety of territorial waters. Grudzinski ordered full speed ahead and set off in pursuit, while Andzej Piasecki, *Orzel*'s Second-in-Command, clipped a machine gun to the conning-tower mounting and fired a burst, the flying chips of paint testifying to the accuracy of his aim.

The *Rio de Janeiro* slowed and an acknowledging signal fluttered up her mast. But the Germans were only playing for time. Although a boat was lowered, it made little attempt to close the submarine and, a short while later, Piasecki spotted two Norwegian gunboats approaching to investigate the strange antics of the merchant ship. Despite this new complication Grudzinski was determined to obey the rules of war and another signal followed: *Abandon ship immediately. Intend to fire torpedo in five minutes time*.

Once again the enemy ship failed to respond. Not a soul was visible on deck and the lifeboat, lowered earlier, was still making no attempt to approach the *Orzel*. Grudzinski waited for the minutes to tick by. Number Two tube was flooded in readiness for the attack and, at the precise moment when the time limit expired, the Polish commander gave the order to fire. It was exactly 12.05 pm. The opening shot in Operation *Weser* had been fired sixteen hours earlier than Hitler and Raeder had planned. Did Grudzinski's attack mean that Germany had lost the essential element of surprise upon which the success of the invasion depended?

Orzel's torpedo struck the vessel amidships and, as a column of smoke and steam rose skywards, hundreds of soldiers in field-grey uniforms suddenly appeared on deck. The mysterious ship was obviously a transport. She began listing to starboard and the scenes of panic on her decks almost defied description as the soldiers ran wildly in all directions. Some threw pieces of wood and lifebelts over the side and leapt into the ice-cold water. Others clung to the rails, too terrified to jump. In the chaos and confusion of the attack no attempt was made to lower the lifeboats which were still hanging from their davits.

The approach of an aircraft from the direction of the Norwegian coast forced Grudzinski to dive, but the submarine was brought level at 30 feet and he continued to watch the scene through the periscope. But the *Rio de Janeiro* stubbornly refused to sink and when the Norwegian gunboats reached the crippled ship and began to rescue survivors, unaware that the soldiers were on their way to invade their homeland, he decided to finish her off. Circling slowly, he brought the submerged *Orzel* on to the other side of the transport and fired Number Three tube. One minute later the torpedo struck home and, with its back broken, the vessel quickly vanished beneath the waves. Despite the humanitarian efforts of the gunboats, hundreds of German soldiers drowned or died of exposure in the freezing sea and the surface was scattered with lifeless bodies. Sub-Lieutenant Eryk Sopocko recalled the horror of the scene: 'They keep together with folds of uniforms clutched tightly in a last spasmodic grasp. The one on the right is face downwards in the water . . . the faces of the two others, livid red and screwed up in a contortion of dread and fatigue, leaving a pitiful impression. Those two I shall never forget. They were both boys: capless, with yellow hair.'

By the time *Orzel* withdrew a Norwegian destroyer had arrived on the scene and the survivors were hurried ashore for interrogation. Some said that they were part of the 1st Sea Transport Division and many admitted that their intended destination was Bergen. Most claimed, however, that they were only being sent to save Norway from a British invasion – an apparently far-fetched story that actually had a substantial element of truth in it. Although not convinced that an invasion by either the Third Reich or the Allies was imminent the Norwegian authorities took the precaution of imposing a black-out that evening and put their coastal batteries on full alert.

It was a night of fear and confusion. Aware that the *Rio de Janeiro* had been sunk and that some of the troops on board were now in Norwegian hands, the German General Staff was terrified that the secret of their invasion plan would be exposed. When the Norwegian evening newspapers splashed the story in banner headlines it seemed that Germany's worst fears were justified. But this was the period of the so-called 'phoney war' and such reports from neutral sources were given little credence, similar scare stories appeared in European and American newspapers nearly every day. Unsure who was invading who, and already highly suspect of British motives, the Norwegian Government did not formally report the episode to London. But although the Admiralty received the news during the afternoon, presumably via the British Embassy in Oslo, it was not passed on to Admiral Forbes, at sea with the Home fleet, until late that evening. Thus a unique opportunity to crush the invasion force while it was at sea was lost because of a hiccup in communications. Germany was able to retain the advantage of surprise, despite *Orzel*'s intervention, and the following day the bulk of her troops disembarked without opposition at various Norwegian ports to begin their five-year occupation of that unhappy country.

There was, however, stiff resistance in some areas and the campaign was fiercely fought on land, in the air and at sea. Both navies sustained heavy casualties and the *Kriegsmarine* never really recovered from the disproportionate losses which it suffered. The Royal Navy's submarines, especially those of the 2nd Flotilla at Rosyth, bore the brunt of the underwater war and it is estimated that 75% of all British boats engaged in the Norwegian campaign were lost – due mainly to the short summer nights around the Arctic Circle which made surfacing to recharge batteries almost a suicidal undertaking.

Hitler's blitzkrieg attack on Holland, Belgium and France in May had the effect of moving the focus of world attention away from Norway. But, in point of fact, the battle for Scandinavia did not end until 8 June when the Allies finally withdrew from the Narvik area in two well-guarded convoys packed with British, French and Polish troops. The cruiser *Devonshire*, sailing independently, carried King Haakon and the Norwegian Government into exile, while another independent group, centred around the carrier *Glorious*, was already at sea and steaming for Scapa Flow.

That afternoon the *Glorious* and her two escorting destroyers were sighted and attacked by the *Scharnhorst* and *Gneisenau*. The carrier was inexplicably caught by surprise for she was not flying a combat air patrol and had no machines ranged on deck ready for take-off. In fact she did not even have a lookout on duty in the crow's nest. Pounded by 11-inch guns and fighting a battle for which she had never been designed, *Glorious* quickly succumbed. Her two attendant destroyers, *Ardent* and *Acasta*, sacrificed themselves in a brave but vain attempt to torpedo the enemy battlecruisers and save the carrier. Only one man survived from the *Acasta* and the loss of life from the three ships was horrendous – 1,519 officers and men killed and missing.

But the collapse of France and the drama of Dunkirk drove even this tragedy from the headlines and, not surprisingly, few noticed the brief communiqué issued by the Polish Admiralty-in-exile on 11 June: *Owing to lack of information and being long overdue, the submarine* Orzel *must be presumed lost*. Like so many submarines lost in wartime, the precise circumstances of *Orzel*'s end have never been established but it is thought that she struck a mine while on patrol in the Skagerrak.

Lieutenant-Commander Jan Grudzinski and the gallant men who served with him under the banner of Poland's White Eagle had paid the price of freedom. They were at least spared the agony of witnessing their nation's subsequent enslavement at the hands of the Communists.

TEN

Lieutenant-Commander Rupert Philip Lonsdale, RN

'Please, O Lord, deliver us.'

On Sunday 5 May, only a month before the *Orzel* vanished in the Skagerrak, His Majesty's submarine *Seal* ended her career some 100 miles further east, following a successful minelaying mission deep inside the Kattegat – an area of notorious memory for both the Polish boat, during her escape from the Baltic in September, 1939, and for Max Horton's *E.9* twenty-five years earlier in 1914. But, unlike *Orzel*, there was no mystery about the British vessel's untimely end. For *Seal*, crippled by the explosion of a mine, damaged by bombs and cannon shells, without engine-power, and unable either to steer or dive, was forced to surrender to the enemy. As a final humiliation, her captain, Lt-Cdr Rupert Lonsdale, was ordered to swim from the sinking submarine to a waiting German seaplane to complete the formalities.

Lonsdale had displayed courage of the highest order throughout *Seal*'s twenty-two hour ordeal. Leading by example, there is little doubt that his calm determination and faith saved the crew from certain death when the submarine sank to the bottom of the Kattegat after an enemy mine had blown a hole in the pressure hull. His physical bravery, too, was beyond dispute. When *Seal* was finally persuaded to the surface he personally fought one of the submarine's two Lewis machine-guns and, despite being under heavy fire, held two German aircraft at bay until both weapons jammed irrevocably.

Many other submarine commanders have demonstrated similar heroism in the face of the enemy, and many have inspired their men in the terrifying atmosphere of a flooded and sinking boat, but few have matched Lonsdale's moral courage. Realizing that nothing more could be done to save the *Seal*, he took the unprecedented step of displaying the white flag of surrender in order to preserve the lives of the gallant men who served with him. It was a decision which ultimately, and inevitably, led to court-martial charges against him after his return from prison-camp at the end of the war.

The minelaying submarine *Seal*, launched in September, 1938, and commissioned into the Royal Navy in May of the following year, was developed from the experimental *M.3* – herself an off-shoot of the infamous steam-driven K-class boats of World War One of which no fewer than eight* were lost by accident. A member of the *Porpoise*-class, she had a deep-load displacement of 1,810 tons in surface trim with a full complement of mines aboard, and a hefty 2,155 tons submerged. Measuring 293 feet from stem to stern and with a beam of 25½ feet, her twin Admiralty-pattern diesel engines could drive her at 16 knots on the surface while her 1,630 SHP electric motors gave a maximum underwater speed of 8¾ knots.

The *Seal* was fitted with a set of rails on top of the pressure hull on which she could carry fifty Mk XVI mines, the canisters being dropped over the stern by a system of powered conveyor chains similar to those employed in the Royal Navy's surface minelayers. The entire mine compartment was housed inside a slab-sided free-flooding external casing which stretched from the conning-tower to the stern – a feature that gave the class a distinctive flush-decked appearance. But the *Seal*, like her sisters *Cachalot, Grampus, Narwhal, Porpoise* and *Rorqual*, of which only the latter was to survive the war, were equally useful for normal anti-shipping patrol duties and a single 4-inch deck gun, two .303-inch Lewis machine-guns, plus six 21-inch torpedo tubes, ensured that they could give a good account of themselves in any encounter with the enemy.

On 4 August, 1939, *Seal* left Portsmouth's Fort Blockhouse en route for the Far East and the China Station. Service in Hong Kong was always popular in the Royal Navy and *Seal* was a particularly happy ship as she steamed eastwards through the Mediterranean towards Malta and the Suez Canal. The crew had settled down well since commissioning and both officers and men approved and

* *K.1, K.4, K.5, K.13, K.15, K.17, M.1* and *M.2* – the *M*-class boats being diesel-engined versions of the original design.

respected their skipper. Softly spoken and fair-minded, Lt-Cdr Lonsdale was a professional to his fingertips and no one had ever heard him raise his voice or seen him lose his temper. He was, as one member of the crew recalled, 'a quiet and good-living man'. Another, misreading the outward signs, concluded that he was 'too much of a gentleman to be a good submarine captain'. Subsequent events were to demonstrate the inaccuracy of this somewhat superficial assessment. Lonsdale was certainly a gentleman in the best sense of the word, but, as he came to prove, he was also a damned good submarine commander.

Seal had already reached Aden when the Admiralty's War Signal was received and the crew rather unexpectedly found themselves on combat patrol in the Straits of Bab el Mandeb in search of German merchant ships seeking safety in the neutral harbours of Italian Eritrea. There was momentary excitement when an alert British tanker, mistaking her for a U-boat, attempted to ram the submarine, but Lonsdale's prompt reaction averted disaster and *Seal* escaped undamaged. A similar patrol followed and, on its completion, the boat was ordered to Alexandria for stores and extra torpedoes. But, instead of returning home as expected, Lonsdale was sent back to the Red Sea again. Fortunately his sailing orders were rescinded before *Seal* reached Aden and by mid-October the submarine was safely back in her berth at Fort Blockhouse.

Seal's first patrol in home waters took her to the vicinity of the Dogger Bank where, after the turgid heat of the Red Sea, the crew had a taste of the heavy seas and bitingly cold gales of the North Sea. They also enjoyed their first contact with the enemy when a German aircraft appeared overhead while they were running down-Channel on their way home. Lonsdale took *Seal* down in an emergency dive in double-quick time and the submarine was safely beneath the waves by the time the bombs exploded.

Although the Royal Navy possessed only six minelaying submarines, the Admiralty planners chose to put *Seal* on convoy escort duties at a time when her special services could have no doubt been more meaningfully utilised and on 11 November, 1939, she left Fort Blockhouse to join the escort of a convoy bound for Halifax, Nova Scotia. Most submarine crews hated escort work and *Seal*'s men were no exception. The misery of the North Atlantic weather did little to improve their feelings. But, as always, Lonsdale was able to maintain morale and spirits lifted appreciably when *Seal* returned with an east-bound convoy in time for Christmas and a spot of well-earned leave.

A transfer to the 6th Submarine Flotilla at Rosyth followed in the New Year but, to their disgust, *Seal*'s crew once again found themselves on convoy escort duty, sailing to Norway with thirty-two assorted merchant ships under her wing and returning a few days later with a homeward-bound convoy. After another brief rest period, however, *Seal* and her crew finally set out on a fourteen-day war patrol off the Norwegian coast, a routine that was to continue without respite for several months during one of the worst winters on record. Their target was Germany's vital iron-ore trade. But, as the enemy bulk carriers kept well inside Norwegian territorial waters, it was impossible to get at them and these patrols were singularly frustrating for Lonsdale and the other captains involved.

The Nazi invasion of Norway offered a new opportunity to strike at the enemy and it was one which the Royal Navy's submarines were quick to exploit, although, sadly, the flotillas suffered grievous losses in the process. On one celebrated occasion *Seal* penetrated deep inside Stavanger fjord in search of shipping – a daring errand that demanded split-second reactions from both captain and crew. The operation began in dramatic style when the submarine encountered an Estonian merchant vessel in dense fog. Lonsdale's prompt use of the helm averted a major disaster but a collision was unavoidable and the neutral ship, striking *Seal*'s stern, ripped away her after hydroplane guard and started several leaks in the pressure hull.

Although the damage was not dangerous it was sufficiently severe to make deep diving unsafe and, on the basis of the Admiralty's operational guidelines, Lonsdale would have been fully entitled to have aborted the patrol and returned home. But, shrugging off the risks and relying on temporary repairs, he maintained course for Stavanger. The task of penetrating the fjord had been originally assigned to one of the smaller *S*-class boats but when the submarine in question failed to return from patrol the mission was given to *Seal* – a much larger and more ungainly vessel fundamentally unsuited for this type of operation in restricted waters. However, thanks to *Seal*'s new-fangled Asdic apparatus and the skill of her navigation officer, Trevor Beet, plus Lonsdale's own iron nerve and determination, the submarine successfully reached the land-locked harbour of Stavanger after a hazardous four-hour submerged passage through the cold black waters of the fjord during which she only rose to periscope depth on two brief occasions.

But their brave efforts proved to be in vain. Lonsdale found four merchant ships in harbour, all flying neutral flags. He had little doubt that they were, in fact, German transports or supply ships waiting to unload. But Lonsdale was not prepared to compromise his principles and break International Law on the basis of a supposition. There was a groan of disappointment when he announced his decision. But in their hearts the men knew that their Captain was right and they admired his moral courage in refusing to yield to the temptation of some easy prizes.

Returning through the fjord, the *Seal* sighted an enemy torpedo-boat, but a check of the reference books in the control-room showed that the draught of the German vessel was too shallow for a successful torpedo attack and Lonsdale could do nothing to prevent its escape. *Seal* herself enjoyed a similar reprieve while on her way back to Rosyth. Running on the surface off the Scottish coast a lookout spotted the tracks of no fewer than *three* torpedoes coming towards the submarine. It was impossible to alter course in time but, miraculously, all three torpedoes passed safely ahead of the bows. Lonsdale took the boat down immediately and remained submerged for the next three hours but fortunately there were no further excitements.

Just how lucky the submarine's crew had been was not apparent until they berthed at Rosyth and learned that their flotilla-mate *Thistle* had been sunk by a German U-boat in virtually the same position in which *Seal* had been attacked. In the circumstances it was hardly suprising that Lonsdale should be regarded by his crew as 'a ruddy marvel' for there was little doubt that Providence was affording the submarine some very special protection.

It had been intended to send the *Seal* south to Chatham for dry-docking and repairs following her collision off Norway. But, at the very last moment, priority had to be given to her more heavily damaged sister-submarine *Cachalot* and Lonsdale was ordered, instead, to Blyth. The stern plates were repaired and other equipment was checked and replaced as necessary but the work fell far short of a full dockyard refit and, as a matter of operational necessity, the *Seal* was back in service within a week.

Operation FD-7, an ambitious scheme to lay a minefield in the Kattegat, had been under consideration for several weeks and, with *Cachalot* in drydock and out of commission, a substitute was urgently needed to take her place. *Seal* was the obvious choice and Lonsdale was not surprised when he was ordered south to Immingham to take on a cargo of mines. It was not a mission for the faint-hearted. *Seal* would have to pass through the Skagerrak, the graveyard of many gallant British submarines, round The Skaw, and then proceed into the Kattegat – the stretch of shallow water that separates Denmark from Sweden. Deep inside enemy-controlled territory, it was one of the most dangerous areas in the world for submarine operations and Lonsdale knew that if they were discovered by the Germans their chances of survival were minimal.

Having embarked a full complement of fifty Mk XVI mines, *Seal* left the Humber estuary during the evening of 29 April and steered north-west until she was safely clear of Britain's East Coast minefields. Her sister-ship, *Narwhal*, was already engaged on the first stage of Operation FD-7 and, as Lonsdale was under orders not to enter the Kattegat until *Narwhal* had cleared The Skaw at the conclusion of her mission, there was no pressing urgency.

Seal made no attempt to submerge when she reached the Skagerrak, for Lonsdale was anxious to conserve his batteries. The hours of darkness in northern lattitudes at this time of the year were insufficient for a submarine to complete a full charge and, in his considered opinion, it was safer to run on the surface in daylight with the benefit of good visibility than risk being surprised at night. Not every captain would have agreed with his theory, but Lonsdale neither sought nor needed the approval of other men.

They reached the vicinity of The Skaw on the evening of 3 May and reduced speed while they waited for *Narwhal*'s clearance signal. When nothing had been received by midnight, however, Lonsdale decided they would have to push on if they were to be inside the Kattegat by dawn. Moving slowly ahead on the main engines, *Seal* passed The Skaw at 1.30 am and altered course south. A short while later *Narwhal* appeared out of the mists like a phantom. She was steaming north on a reciprocal course and the two submarines passed close to each other in the darkness. There was no exchange of signals for the flashing Aldis lamps might have been seen from the shore and within minutes the homeward-bound submarine was astern and fading quietly into the night. *Narwhal*'s work was done. She had laid her minefield and, by way of a bonus, had fired six torpedoes at enemy targets. Would *Seal* be equally lucky?

Dawn was due at 2.30 am and the crew had been warned to prepare for diving during the final minutes of darkness before the sun peeped over the eastern horizon. Lonsdale himself was on the bridge together with the Officer-of-the-Watch and two lookouts. Suddenly the urgent throb of an aero-engine could be discerned above the rumble of the diesel exhausts. Nothing was visible in the night sky but the sound itself was a sufficient warning.

'Dive – dive – dive!'

There was a disciplined scramble to squeeze through the upper hatch and slide down the ladder into the control room for, with the submarine trimmed down and running awash; her conning-tower would dip beneath the surface more quickly than usual. But practice and training ensured there were no mishaps. The bridge was cleared in double-quick time and, as Lonsdale reached up to pull the hatch shut, he caught his first and only glimpse of the enemy aircraft almost directly overhead.

'Grouper up! Ninety feet!'

The diesels had been shut off at the first squawk of the diving klaxon and *Seal* was already running on her electric motors.

'Ninety feet, sir,' Butler acknowledged. 'Blow Q'.*

Seal slipped obediently beneath the waves and was safely on her way to the depths when the bomb detonated on the surface. Nevertheless the awesome crack of the explosion and the submarine's jolting response to the underwater blast wave was sufficient to be unpleasant, even though the main force was directed upwards. A quick inspection revealed two leaks in the pressure hull, plus an electrical fault to the servo-motors controlling the bow hydroplanes, and temporary repairs were put in hand immediately. The leaks were soon caulked, but it took more than five hours to sort out the problem with the hydroplane machinery and by the time the work had been completed *Seal* was already close to Lesso, the island directly opposite the Swedish harbour of Gothenburg.

The time was fast approaching when Lonsdale would have to decide in which of three pre-selected areas he was to lay his cargo of mines. But, for the immediate moment, his attention was concentrated on a number of anti-submarine trawlers which were sweeping directly ahead of *Seal*. He was not surprised by this sudden surge of activity. *Narwhal*'s recent presence in the Kattegat was obviously known to the Germans and *Seal*'s own clash with the patrol aircraft must have alerted the enemy to the fact that another British submarine was also now deep inside their home waters. But the trawlers were unfortunately astride the course he needed to steer if he was to reach the primary target area set down in FD-7 and that meant he would have to select one of the alternative sites. In the event he chose the nearest to hand, even though this would mean laying his lethal clutch of eggs directly under the noses of the searching trawlers.

Having announced his decision, Lonsdale passed the necessary orders to the mining compartment and at 8.59 am precisely the first canister tumbled over the stern, its sinker descending to the bottom of the Kattegat to anchor it securely in position at the

* The quick-diving tank, 'Q', had to be blown clear of ballast as soon as the submarine submerged in order to restore neutral, as opposed to negative, buoyancy.

required depth. As each mine fell away the Mining ERA had to compensate for the loss of weight by admitting an equal equivalent of water into the after ballast tanks. It was a delicate task requiring concentration and skill, for a minor error in either the timing or the quantity could lead to the submarine rising to the surface. With the enemy so close, even the slightest variation in the submarine's depth could be fatal. But Ernie Truman knew what he was doing and never once during the forty-five minute laying operation did he fail to operate his flooding valves to perfection.

With the minefield successfully laid it was time to withdraw and at 9.45 am Lonsdale reversed course through 180° and began the cat-and-mouse game that was destined to continue for the next nine hours. The odds, in fact, slightly favoured the submarine, for, in order to detect the faint hum of *Seal*'s motors with their hydrophones, the trawlers of the 12th Anti-Submarine Flotilla had to shut down their own engines and lie stopped in the water while their operators listened for tell-tale sounds through their head-phones. The submarine, however, was equipped with Asdic – an early form of sonar sound ranging – and thanks to this still top-secret gadgetry Lonsdale knew when the hunters had stopped to eavesdrop. It was thus an easy matter to switch off *Seal*'s motors at exactly the right moment and deprive the enemy of the sound-source he needed if he was to locate the submarine.

The tension at times was almost unbearable. No one could be sure what was happening up top and every man in *Seal* was uncomfortably aware that there was insufficient depth of water under the keel to dive deep and avoid danger in the event of a depth-charge attack, the maximum depth of water in this part of the Kattegat being a bare 90 feet. And it was painfully apparent to the Asdic operator and to Lonsdale, during his periodic and very brief periscope observations, that *the enemy was closing the gap*.

At 3 pm, however, the odds swung further against the submarine when Lonsdale sighted another group of modern anti-submarine motor launches – nine vessels in all – approaching from the north-east. But, refusing to be forced into decisions that he might later regret, Lonsdale persevered with his tactics and, after altering course towards the Danish coast for a short period, he continued to move slowly north at minimum speed. He was now in the unenviable position of buying time, for he was acutely conscious that they had no possibility of escape before nightfall. And that meant doing virtually nothing, not the easiest course of action with death and danger threatening from all sides. For one thing was utterly certain. If the enemy chose to launch a depth-charge attack *Seal* stood no chance whatsoever of surviving.

At around six o'clock Lonsdale decided to go to the bottom and lie doggo until darkness descended over the Kattegat. Diving orders were passed to the planesmen and the submarine's bows tilted obediently. But a layer of salt water at a depth of sixty feet prevented the boat from descending any further without the added thrust of her motors and Lonsdale was content to let the submarine 'sit' on this natural cushion of buoyancy with her machinery stopped. It seemed a perfect solution to their dilemma, but, minutes later, *Seal* suddenly shuddered and lost trim for a few frightening seconds. According to the depth-gauges her stern had risen several feet and a message from the motor-room warned that the sound of a wire scraping against the hull had been heard on the starboard side. Almost simultaneously Higgins reported that the aft hydroplanes were jammed.

Lonsdale wondered whether the submarine had snagged the mooring cable of a German mine in a newly-laid field not yet marked on their charts – or whether, as seemed more likely, the trawlers were using sweep wires to locate their prey. But moments later *Seal* regained her trim unaided and the emergency, whatever may have been its cause, seemed to be over. At 6.30 pm the men were stood down from Diving Stations and instructions were passed to the cooks to prepare an evening meal. It seems almost incredible that *Seal*'s crew should feel like eating while they were trapped on the bottom in relatively shallow water with nearly twenty enemy anti-submarine patrol boats intent on their destruction milling around overhead, but the British sailor enjoys a healthy appetite no matter what dangers may lie ahead.

However, they were destined never to enjoy their meal. A few minutes before seven o'clock a tremendous explosion rocked the submarine and a sudden increase in air pressure warned that one or more compartments were flooding. *Seal*'s stern began to sink and, as the watertight doors were slammed shut, the men in the aft section hurried forward with the sea lapping their ankles. As the disciplined confusion came under control Lonsdale had time to take stock of the situation. There had been no further explosions, and there had been no hydrophone reports of propeller noises. These two facts seemed to rule out a depth-charge attack and left only one plausible explanation – the *Seal* had fallen victim to a German mine. And the loss of trim that had occurred half an hour earlier had probably been caused by the mine's mooring cable fouling the after hydroplanes.

The long-awaited evening meal now lay scattered on the deck – a soggy mixture of meat, gravy, vegetables and broken china, but the mere fact of still being alive was more than adequate recompense for a lost dinner, and the pangs of hunger quickly vanished as the submarine was inspected for damage. The test-cock on the watertight door leading into the motor-room from the engine compartment remained dry when tested and a visual check through the circular glass port revealed no sign of flooding. Suddenly they heard fists thumping against the heavy rubber-sealed door and, when it was opened, two wet and exhausted men tumbled through the hatchway and collapsed on the deck.

Leading Stoker Tom Vidler and Able Seaman Mickey Reynolds had been trapped in the stern when the watertight doors closed. But, with the sea rising steadily up their legs and groggy from the concussive effects of the blast, they had managed to reach the motor-room where, with the self-sacrifice of the true submariner, they had stuggled to close the rear watertight door before seeking their own safety. Thanks to their efforts, the vital compartment was saved from flooding and, despite their exhausted condition, they were sufficiently coherent to tell Lonsdale what had happened in the stern.

Their account was scarcely reassuring. The explosion had torn a hole in the pressure hull and the sea was flooding in through the after escape chamber. But the situation had stabilized. For, with the submarine's stern firmly stuck in the silty bottom of the Kattegat, the opening had been sealed by mud and no further water was entering the vessel. Lonsdale called his officers together in the wardroom and, conscious that, 'with God all things are possible', he decided to send a party into the motor-room to close the escape chamber doors so that the flooded compartments could be pumped clear. Clark, the Engineer Officer, and four volunteers – one of whom included the indefatigable Tom Vidler – entered the motor-room and closed the watertight door behind them. Then, locked inside their steel prison, they moved aft and carefully opened the hatch into the stoker's mess space. The compartment was flooded chest-high and the only way to reach the after door of the escape chamber was to take a deep breath and plunge head-first into the ice-cold water. Several attempts were made but, not surprisingly, the conditions defeated them. After a brief rest they next tried to close the for'ard door of the escape chamber. This time they were more successful and managed to pull it back onto its rubber seating where the weight of water held it in place. But for some inexplicable reason they were unable to secure the dog catches and lock it properly.

Finally, having closed every valve they could find, the little group made their way back to the warmth and security of the engine room and thankfully clipped the watertight door shut behind them. Rough calculations showed that the *Seal* had shipped some 130 tons of sea water. As her total ballast capacity was 380 tons there would be no difficulty in restoring positive buoyancy once all the tanks had been blown. But, despite the claustrophobic tension inside the boat and an instinctive desire to lift the partially flooded submarine to the surface as quickly as possible, Lonsdale advised caution and decided to delay the attempt until ten o'clock and darkness.

The men passed the time playing cards and Lonsdale, aware that the excitement of cash stakes would draw their minds away from *Seal*'s terrifying predicament, thoughtfully gave permission for them to ignore King's Regulations and gamble for money. While he and the First Lieutenant prepared a coded situation report for transmission to the Admiralty when they broke surface the other officers began preparing the confidential books and documents for destruction. The rum ration was served and Lonsdale took the opportunity to move up and down the boat so that the men would be reassured by his presence. A little later sandwiches were passed around but it was clear that time was running out. The air was noticeably staler and many of the men were already having difficulty breathing.

Diving Stations were piped just before 10.30 pm and a few minutes later Lonsdale gave the order to surface. The high-pressure air valves were opened and, as the tanks emptied, *Seal* lurched upwards. But, despite maximum power from the motors, her bows stubbornly refused to lift beyond 75 feet while the weight of water in the flooded rear compartments kept the stern firmly stuck in the muddy bottom of the Kattegat. Lonsdale kept the power on for nearly two minutes, but *Seal* failed to respond and he was finally forced to shut down the motors and delay blowing in order to conserve his batteries and compressed air reserves. The submarine hung in the limbo of the depths for a few seconds and then slowly settled back to the seabed – her keel nestling softly into a womb of mud. Until this moment there had been hope. Now, suddenly, there was despair. They had already been submerged for eighteen hours and, with the air inside the boat compressed by the flooding, the carbon dioxide content was beginning to reach a dangerously high level. Several men had already collapsed; others were having considerable difficulty in breathing. But Lonsdale, as usual, remained a tower of strength and every man trapped inside the crippled submarine drew comfort and inspiration from his determination.

They next tried releasing *Seal*'s eleven-ton 'drop keel' in a desperate last-ditch attempt to regain positive buoyancy but this also failed and the submarine emerged in a worse position than before with her stern still firmly grounded in the mud and her bows inclined at an angle of 45°. A few minutes later Lonsdale tried again. Again the vessel refused to budge. One of the senior ratings suggested using the boat's DSEA* kits but the idea was promptly vetoed by the Engineer Officer on the grounds that the men were too exhausted and befuddled by carbon dioxide poisoning to follow the escape chamber routine correctly. As he pointed out, a single mistake in operating the valves could flood the entire boat.

There was only one hope left to them. Conscious of his own faith, Lonsdale invited everyone who so wished to assemble in the control room and join him in prayers. Several could not even find the energy to accept the invitation while others, sceptical of religion, were content to remain on their bunks quietly awaiting death. But a surprising number of men made their way to the cramped and crowded control room to join their skipper.

Lonsdale quietly explained that their survival now rested in God's hands and, before leading them in the Lord's Prayer, he delivered his own brief but poignant plea to the Almighty:

'Dear God, we have tried everything in our power to save ourselves and we have failed. Yet we believe that You can do things which are impossible to men. Please, O Lord, deliver us.'

There was a muttered Amen and then, led by their Captain, the assembled sailors began to recite the Lord's Prayer, following which there was a brief period of silence while the men offered up their own individual prayers. Taking advantage of the renewed hope created by this spiritual interlude, Lonsdale began preparations for a final attempt to reach the surface. The Engineer Officer, Lieutenant Clark, assisted by members of his staff, entered the flooded stern compartments for the third time to open the valve to the salvage-blow – an act of exceptional heroism in his exhausted condition. All crewmen with no specific duties to perform were sent forward to add their weight as ballast in the fore-ends. The conditions inside the submarine, however, were so bad that even this small physical effort proved too much for some of the exhausted sailors.

The electric motors vibrated as Lonsdale called for maximum power and the port unit caught fire. But there was so little oxygen in the atmosphere that, lacking the materials of combustion, the

* Davis Submerged Escape Appartus – a self-contained breathing kit used for escaping from a sunken submarine.

135

flames died at birth. Acrid blue smoke was also beginning to seep from the starboard motor as *Seal* struggled to escape from the cloying embrace of the mud but then, suddenly, Lonsdale's final gamble reaped its reward. The submarine lurched violently and, tearing itself free, steadied up on to an even keel. With every possible blowing valve open the hiss of the pressurised air echoed through the boat and, as *Seal* rose upwards, the red pointer needles of the depth gauges swung around the dials . . . 70 . . . 60 . . . 50 . . .

The submarine broke surface in the inhospitable emptiness of the Kattegat at 1.30 am and, having first taken precautions to vent the pent-up force of compressed air inside the vessel through a valve in the conning-tower, Lonsdale unclipped the upper hatch and climbed onto the bridge. They were not out of the woods yet, but they were at least breathing God's clean fresh air again. And that was a miracle for which none would have dared hope an hour earlier.

Although most of the men recovered quickly, many were violently sick. They were surprised by the absence of enemy ships, for everyone had supposed that the German Navy would be waiting in force to greet them. But Lonsdale could not afford the luxury of self-congratulation and he was soon involved in the next stage of their escape. The signal which he had composed earlier, informing the Admiralty of the damage which *Seal* had sustained and advising that he intended to make for Sweden, was duly transmitted. And, at the same time, the submarine's top-secret Asdic equipment was dismantled, smashed into pieces with hammers, and then thrown over the side in buckets. In the wireless room Futer waited until his signal had been acknowledged. Then, closing down his transmitter, he began to destroy *Seal*'s radio apparatus.

The starboard diesel was restarted but its companion proved more obstinate and the engineering staff spent some time coaxing it to life. Meanwhile it was found that the submarine's rudder had been smashed by the explosion and Lonsdale was forced to achieve a 'straight' course by using the port and starboard engines alternately. But even this makeshift solution did not survive for long. Damage to the lubrication system eventually led to a loss of oil pressure and when they tried to connect the starboard engine clutch to the starboard electric motor sea-water in the motor-room caused a short circuit and the resulting fumes were so severe that the compartment had to be temporarily evacuated. It was clear that, at this rate, their chances of reaching Sweden were diminishing with every minute, for *Seal* was now reduced to circling slowly and painfully on one engine. Unable to dive, she was at the mercy of any enemy ship that might find her.

In the event it was an Arado AR 196 seaplane from No 706 Coastal Defence Wing that discovered the submarine wallowing helplessly in the water soon after dawn. The aircraft's commander, Lieutenant Mehrens, ordered the pilot to circle the mysterious vessel while he flashed a challenge. But the reply was unintelligible and on the next low-level sweep he identified the conning-tower markings as British. Opening the throttle, the pilot of the Arado climbed for altitude, banked sharply, and hurtled down on its first bombing run with machine-guns blazing. Swerving away, it returned for a second attack and this time its wing-mounted cannons pumped armour-piercing shells into the submarine's exposed ballast tanks.

Two men, one of whom was *Seal*'s First Lieutenant, Butler, were wounded in the first sweep and Lonsdale hurriedly cleared the bridge to avoid further casualties. Only Leading Seaman Mayes remained up top alongside his captain and the two men manned the submarine's Lewis-guns in total disregard for their personal safety in an attempt to fight off the seaplane. After expending several drums of ammunition, Mayes' weapon jammed and, while he dropped down through the hatchway to fetch replacement parts, Lonsdale remained alone on the exposed bridge as he fought his lone battle with the enemy.

But the end could not be long delayed. *Seal* was down by the stern and water was pouring into her shell damaged ballast tanks. The batteries were too exhausted to operate the pumps, the main blower failed and, the last straw, the submarine's sole remaining power unit, the starboard diesel engine, seized solid, leaving *Seal* drifting helplessly before the wind, unable to dive and sinking by the stern.

Suddenly the breech mechanism of Lonsdale's machine-gun jammed and he could fight no longer. What should he do next? It was a fearful decision for a Royal Navy officer to make. But not even the tradition of centuries could persuade him to prolong the struggle and put at risk the lives of the sixty men entrusted to his care. When a second seaplane joined the fray and raked the conning-tower with bullets, Lonsdale weighed the conflicting demands of duty and compassion. Suddenly an anonymous voice shouted up to him from the control-room:

'We'll have to surrender, sir. Nothing for you to worry about, sir. God knows, you've done all you could.'

At that moment Lonsdale knew what he had to do. Thrusting his head into the hatchway, he told someone to fetch the tablecloth from the wardroom. Moments later it was passed up to him and, walking across to the engaged side of the bridge, he streamed the square of white linen in the wind.

While its companion continued to circle warily, the second seaplane landed in the water and taxied close to the submarine. *Leutnant* Karl Schmidt pulled back the cockpit canopy and shouted for the Captain. Lonsdale raised his arm.

'Jump into the water, *Herr Kapitan*. Swim across to me and come aboard.'

Lonsdale nodded and, slipping off his shoes, he climbed down the bullet-gashed ballast tank and jumped into the ice-cold water.

* * *

Both Lonsdale and the officers he had left behind on the submarine were convinced that *Seal* was too badly damaged to remain afloat for more than a few hours. But, having taken off the crew, German salvage experts took the crippled vessel in tow and, against all the odds, succeeded in getting her back to Kiel. She was subsequently refitted and commissioned into the *Kriegsmarine* as *UB-1* but never achieved operational status. After exploiting the propaganda value of their unexpected prize, the German Navy abandoned her in a dockyard basin at Kiel and left her to rust. She was subsequently sunk during an air raid and was finally raised and scrapped in 1945.

Lonsdale and his men spent the rest of the war in prison camps. One member of the crew had fallen overboard and drowned while the survivors were being transferred to a German rescue ship at the time of the surrender and Petty Officer Barnes, who escaped with an army colleague from Stalag XXA in Poland, was shot dead by Russian soldiers when he tried to cross the Soviet border. Two others, however, engineered a more successful dash for freedom from Colditz and managed to reach England via neutral Switzerland. Prison life for the remainder was hard and, in the latter days of the war, precarious, but happily all survived and returned home safely.

As the Commanding Officer of *Seal*, Lonsdale's court-martial was an inevitable consequence of the submarine's surrender – a burden he shared with Lieutenant Trevor Beet who, taking over from the wounded Butler, had been in *de facto* command when the actual act of capitulation had taken place. Beet was the first to be tried and, as anticipated, was 'honourably acquitted' after a four-hour hearing on 10 April, 1946. A brief adjournment followed and then Lt-Cdr Rupert Lonsdale was brought into the courtroom to face charges of, firstly, failing to take immediate action to engage enemy aircraft when they attacked and, secondly, failing to take steps to ensure the sinking of *Seal* when it seemed possible she could fall into enemy hands. Lonsdale entered a plea of Not Guilty on both counts.

The hearing lasted two days but, although very little information came out in evidence, it was revealed that, on learning of Lonsdale's intention to make for Sweden, the Flag Officer (Submarines) – the great Max Horton himself – had sent *Seal*'s captain a personal signal: *Safety of personnel should be your first consideration after destruction of Asdic.* Unfortunately the *Seal*'s radio equipment had been destroyed by the time Horton's signal was transmitted and it was never received. But the wording leaves little doubt that Sir Max supported Lonsdale's courageous decision. It was also revealed that British submarines were not supplied with scuttling charges at that period of the war.

Several of *Seal*'s officers were called as witnesses and both Prosecution and Defence made much of the stultifying effects of carbon dioxide poisoning on the human brain. But Lonsdale offered no excuses and made it clear that he accepted full responsibility for his decision and its consequences. The court-martial board retired for 45 minutes, and when Lonsdale returned to the courtroom to hear the verdict he saw the hilt of his sword pointing towards him in the time-hallowed tradition – he had been honourably acquitted on both charges.

Rupert Lonsdale's experiences both in *Seal* and, later, as a prisoner-of-war, had a profound spiritual influence on him. He had always been conscious of his faith but, as the months and years passed, he knew beyond question that his life had been spared by the direct intervention of God.

He resigned his commission in the Royal Navy in June, 1946, and, shortly afterwards, began training at a theological college. Two years later he was ordained into the Anglican Church.

—ELEVEN—

Korvettenkapitan Otto Kretschmer

'My sincere congratulations on your success.'

It is a matter of historical fact that the German Navy lost a total of forty-one submarines during the month of May, 1943, and most experts agree that this particular period marked the turning point in the Allies' long-fought struggle against Hitler's U-boats. But to many veterans of the *Unterseeboots Flotille* the carnage of May, 1943, had less impact on the Battle of the Atlantic than the events of March, 1941, when, in the space of ten days, Admiral Doenitz lost his three top aces – Gunther Prien, Joachim Schepke and Otto Kretschmer.

It was a devastating blow for the *Kriegsmarine* and one from which it never fully recovered. With the war now into its second year, the U-boat arm was expanding rapidly. New vessels were coming off the slipways in ever-increasing numbers and additional officers and crews were being turned out by the training schools along the Baltic coast of northern Germany where the harsh realism of the exercises often led to the loss of both U-boats and men.* But to achieve victory Doenitz needed the support and expertise of his experienced captains, men who could lead and inspire these new officers and crews – battle-tested veterans whose intimate knowledge of combat conditions in the Atlantic were vital for the survival of the newly trained recruits and their submarines.

* At least twenty-six U-boats were lost during training or while engaged on exercises.)

140

And of all the aces Prien, Schepke and Kretschmer were the *crème de la crème*. Even Churchill, writing after the war, was moved to observe: 'Few U-boat commanders were their equals in ruthless ability and daring'. High praise indeed from such a doughty and implacable foe.

Korvettenkapitan Gunther Prien, who had gained world-wide fame in the early days of the war by penetrating the defences of the British fleet base at Scapa Flow in *U-47* and sinking the battleship *Royal Oak*, was the first to go. Yet such were the uncertainties of the U-boat war that, although he was killed on 8 March, several weeks passed before BdU* was able to confirm his fate. Even when the facts of his death were finally established, the news was held back from the German public until 23 May – six weeks after he met his end at the hands of a British destroyer.

The bait that lured Prien to disaster was Convoy OB-293 and it was his own boat, *U-47*, that first located the target south of Iceland. Curbing his aggressive instincts, Prien kept his prey under close surveillance while his radio-operator transmitted details of the convoy's position and course to all U-boats in the vicinity. Then he waited for the other submarines in the area to concentrate for a wolf-pack attack. Joachim Matz and *U-70* joined up with Prien during the early hours of 7 March and Otto Kretschmer with *U-99* arrived some time later. With dawn breaking, and hopeful that other U-boats would join the pack during the day, the three submarines fell back and shadowed the convoy from a discreet distance while they waited for darkness to descend again.

Many normally reliable reference books show *U-47* as being sunk by the British corvettes *Arbutus* and *Camellia* on the afternoon of the 7th with Matz's *U-70* being destroyed by *Wolverine* the following day. These details, however, are erroneous. Admiralty records confirm that the U-boat which fell victim to the corvettes on the 7th was *U-70* and that Prien's boat, *U-47*, was sunk the next day by the destroyer *Wolverine*. As Matz and twenty-five members of his crew were picked up following the sinking of the *U-70* on the 7th, it is difficult to understand the reason for the error. But confusion is a not unusual corollary of the war beneath the sea.

It has often been claimed that Prien and his crew were not aboard the *U-47* when it was sunk, and the favourite story is that they died in a punishment battalion on the Russian Front following a court-martial for mutiny. Post-war research has failed to find any

* Befehlshaber der Untersee-boot = Commander U-boats.

factual basis for this and similar tales and most historians now agree that Prien went down with his boat on 8 March, 1941.

In his Official Report of Proceedings, Lt-Cdr J. M. Rowland, the skipper of the *Wolverine*, stated that the action started when diesel exhaust smoke was observed at 0023 on 8 March. Having made a signal to *Verity* that he could see something ahead Rowland increased speed to 22 knots and, at 0029, a U-boat was sighted on the surface.

Prien zig-zagged wildly in his efforts to escape but he made no attempt to submerge and seemed content to make a run for it. German submarine commanders were well aware that British destroyers had to slow to 10 knots in order to use their Asdic and hydrophone apparatus whenever they lost visual contact with their target. Exploiting this weakness, they soon discovered that, with a modicum of luck, they could outrun their pursuers provided they did not dive and thus expose themselves to Asdic detection. It needed strong nerves to face out a well-armed destroyer on the surface. But those who did lived to fight another day whereas those who dived frequently succumbed to depth-charge attacks.

Despite his reluctance to submerge, Prien was finally forced to dive when a starshell, fired by *Verity* at 0030, pinpointed the submarine on the surface. *U-47* dived before the enemy's guns could open fire and the two destroyers quartered the area in a frantic search for their prey. A tense quarter of an hour passed before *Wolverine* obtained a firm Asdic contact 5° off her port bow. Three minutes later a pattern of ten depth-charges tumbled from the racks. But no results were observed and, with *Verity* in support, Rowland pursued his quarry in a hunt that was to last for five hours.

Depth-charges were dropped each time the Asdic equipment made contact and a strong smell of diesel fuel in the air plus a long slick of oil on the surface suggested that the U-boat had been damaged. But with the sounds of its propellers still audible on the hydrophones, it was clear that *U-47* was far from crippled.

At around 4 o'clock Prien fired a torpedo in the apparent hope that the noise of its thermal engine would lure the destroyer away on a false scent. But Rowland, an ex-submariner himself, was not so easily bluffed and he made sure that his Asdic operator did not confuse the decoy with the real prey. This cat-and-mouse game continued for another hour with Prien using every trick in the book, plus a few others, to escape from his hunters. Bursts of speed were accompanied by violent alterations of course. These manoeuvres were interspersed with periods of total silence with the U-boat lying doggo on the bottom with her motors shut off.

But, despite losing Asdic contact with monotonous regularity, Lt-Cdr Rowland refused to give up and he clung to his slippery adversary like a jealous bulldog.

Realizing that he was at the mercy of the enemy's underwater detectors, Prien decided to return to the surface and rely on speed and the low silhouette of the submarine to make his escape. It was a tactic originally devised by his former team-mate Otto Kretschmer and at this stage of the war it inevitably caught the British unawares, for it was the complete antithesis of all submarine theory which held that submergence was the best and only means of defence. However, having studied the problem, Kretschmer had realized that the chances of finding a U-boat were greatly reduced if the submarine was *surfaced*, for this rendered the Royal Navy's underwater detection devices useless. In addition depth-charges were of little utility against a surface U-boat and the only alternative, gunfire, was notoriously inaccurate against such a small and fleeting target, especially as most convoy attacks were made at night. Later in the war, of course, guns were laid by radar and many of these disadvantages lost their validity. But in 1941, with shipborne radar still in its infancy, there is little doubt that Kretschmer was right. Remaining on the surface at night was the U-boat's best form of defence.

Rowland, alerted by loud noises over the hydrophones, gambled on his personal judgement and, increasing speed to 20 knots, altered course towards the HE*. At 5.18 am the wake of a U-boat was detected on the starboard bow and a minute later the submarine itself came into view, trimmed low in the water and steaming at high speed. *Wolverine*'s stern tucked down as her engines roared to maximum revolutions. Her captain moved to the bridge voice-pipes.

'Stand by to ram!'

Sensing danger, Prien tried to crash-dive to safety and *U-47* was already sliding swiftly beneath the surface by the time the *Wolverine* reached the diving position. 'I don't think I missed the conning-tower by more than a few feet – perhaps a few inches,' Rowland recalled later. 'The ten depth-charges we fired fell exactly on the spot where the submarine dived.'

Despite the pin-point accuracy of the attack, however, no wreckage appeared on the surface and a disappointed Rowland could only report a 'probable' kill when *Wolverine* rejoined Convoy OB-293. But the Admiralty had few doubts. Information given by U-boat survivors together with other intelligence sources

* Hydrophone Effect.

all suggested that Rowland had sunk his victim. And, as further details were assembled, it became clear that he had destroyed one of Germany's most famous commanders – Gunther Prien. A few weeks later Lt-Cdr Rowland was awarded a DSC for his success.

With the loss of *U-70* the previous day, and now *U-47*, the attack on Convoy OB-293 petered out, although the wolf-pack claimed several victims before withdrawing. Kretschmer himself inflicted mortal damage on the 20,000-ton factory ship *Ter je Viken* and sank the tanker *Athelbeach* during the early stages of the assault. But, having witnessed the destruction of Matz's *U-70* at close quarters – the concussion of the exploding depth-charges had badly shaken his own boat – he broke off the action and steered away from the convoy.

The next day he set of in search of fresh targets. But the ocean proved to be disappointingly empty, although he glimpsed an escort ship during the afternoon of 15 March. A few hours later *Kapitanleutnant* Lemp and *U-110* sighted Convoy HX-112 south-east of Iceland and, taking up a shadowing position astern of the target, he transmitted an urgent wolf-pack call to all submarines in the area. Kretschmer responded eagerly but, on reaching the reported position, no ships were visible and, as a precaution against air patrols, he submerged. But his hydrophones soon picked up faint HE to the south and, returning to the surface, he set off in pursuit. Joachim Schepke also picked up Lemp's rallying signal and *U-100*, too, was now speeding to join *U-99* and *U-110* in their rendezvous with disaster. For, unbeknown to the three U-boat aces, the destroyer escort of Convoy HX-112 was under the command of Commander (later Captain) Donald Macintyre, an anti-submarine expert who was destined to end the war with seven U-boats to his credit. A battle of the giants was about to begin.

* * *

Otto Kretschmer, the son of a schoolteacher from Lower Silesia, was just 24 years old when he transferred from the big ship Navy to join the newly-formed but still secret U-boat service in 1934. Both Gunther Prien and Joachim Schepke were members of the same intake term at the euphemistically-titled anti-submarine school at Kiel and the three remained constant companions whenever shore leave gave them an opportunity of meeting, although, as Kretschmer's biographer observed, they were bound together more by bonds of professional rivalry than personal affection.

Kretschmer's first appointment after graduating from the Periscope School was as Second Officer of *U-35*. But by the time of the Munich crisis, which rose to boiling point in September, 1938, he was already in command of his own boat, *U-23*, a Type IIB coastal defence submarine of 279 tons surface displacement armed with a single 20-mm AA gun and three torpedo tubes. However, when *U-23* left Kiel under sealed orders she sailed without torpedoes and carried, instead, eight of Hitler's much vaunted secret weapon – the magnetic mine. As Kretschmer was widely regarded as the *Kriesmarine*'s finest torpedo marksman it seems odd that his first patrol under combat conditions should find him engaged in a mundane mining operation.

With the crisis deepening by the hour and diplomats scurrying across Europe in search of a peace formula, *U-23* reached Britain's east coast and took up its assigned position 15 miles off the Humber estuary. Although his secret War Orders were still sealed inside their envelope, there was little doubt in Kretschmer's mind that, when opened, he would be directed to sow his deadly cargo in the busy shipping lanes that led into the port of Hull. But Prime Minister Chamberlain's famous 'scrap of paper' resolved the crisis and after spending three days on his war station Kretschmer, with the other twenty-four U-boat captains patrolling off the British Isles, was recalled to Germany.

On their return to Kiel, and in the course of de-briefing discussions, the secret War Orders were opened and Doenitz, having listened to the complaints and objections of Kretschmer and his fellow U-boat captains, agreed that the orders would be modified if a similar emergency occurred in the future. 'I have no intention of throwing away either you or your boats,' he reassured them. 'You cost too much to be lost easily.'

But when the threat of war loomed again in September, 1939, and Hitler invaded Poland the Admiral's promise was quickly forgotten. For the second time within a year Kretschmer found himself patrolling off the Humber with a cargo of magnetic mines and no torpedoes – hardly the prospect of glory he had anticipated when he first volunteered for U-boat service. However, in a repeat of the 1938 operation, Kretschmer and *U-23* were recalled to Germany after three days and no mines were laid. His arrival in Wilhelmshaven coincided with an RAF bombing attack on the cruiser *Emden*. But, concentrating on the big ship, the British pilots ignored the insignificant submarine in the centre of the basin and Kretschmer enjoyed the luxury of observing the attack as a bystander, although *U-23*'s 20mm AA gun joined in the flak barrage and made her own tiny contribution to beating off the raiders.

Kretschmer's hopes of being sent on an offensive patrol were quickly dashed when he was once again ordered to lay magnetic mines, this time off the Scottish coast in the area of the Firth of Forth. But he was at least afforded the compensation of carrying a reduced complement of torpedoes which he was authorized to use, if the occasion arose, after the mines had been laid. It was an opportunity not to be missed.

Having completed the mining operation, Kretschmer brought *U-23* to the surface and set off in search of targets. He did not have long to wait. Later that night he sighted a darkened merchant ship and fired all three of his precious torpedoes at it. But, to his consternation, not a single weapon struck or exploded and, unable to believe his bad luck, he returned to Wilhelmshaven feeling more than a little downcast.

He was not, however, alone. U-boat HQ was quickly filled with irate captains complaining about missed targets and faulty torpedoes. The *Kriegsmarine*'s technical experts soon discovered that the new magnetic pistols of the standard thermal-engined *G-7a* torpedoes were defective and, while scientists searched for a solution, existing weapons were modified to include conventional impact triggers – an improvement which Kretschmer swiftly celebrated by sinking his first victim, the 500-ton coaster *Glen Farg*, which he despatched with a single torpedo after ensuring that the crew were safely in the lifeboats.

Although by the end of 1939 Kretschmer had increased his total tally to three ships – having sunk the *Deptford* (4,101 tons) and *Magnus* (1,339 tons) just before Christmas – he was aware that other captains were being far more successful. Prien, with the battleship *Royal Oak* to his credit, was clearly the Navy's top submarine commander but several others had also done well, notably *Oberleutnant* Schuhart who had sunk the carrier *Courageous* in the Channel. Nevertheless Doenitz and the *Kriegsmarine* top-brass were more than satisfied with the young commander of *U-23* and he was given the Iron Cross (2nd class) for his torpedo attacks on merchant shipping plus an Iron Cross (1st class) for minelaying operations. It was a satisfactory start to Kretschmer's war.

As he gained experience his score gradually increased and during the first few months of 1940 he sank the motor tanker *Denmark* (10,517 tons), the freighter *Polzella* and another coaster, *Baltanglia*. Finally, on 18 February, he gained the prize for which all submarine commanders yearn – a destroyer. In so doing Kretschmer set a new fashion in submarine tactics. *U-23* was surfaced off Duncansby Head when the convoy came into view and, to his consternation, he found himself lying between two destroyers patrolling the outer wing of the convoy. With one of the warships to port and the other to starboard *U-23* seemed trapped like a fly in a spider's web. Having studied and analysed British anti-submarine tactics, Kretschmer knew that if he dived – the natural and normal reaction of any U-boat captain at that period of the war – he would be quickly detected by the enemy's Asdic and then blasted to eternity with depth-charges. By remaining on the surface, however, the chances of the enemy spotting the U-boat were only as good as their lookout's eyes. And, lying low in the water with only her conning-tower visible, *U-23* had a distinct advantage over her more powerful but easily visible adversaries.

Unfortunately the practical situation was not quite so clear-cut as the theoretical. For although Kretschmer intended to remain surfaced and rely on his speed to get away, his only avenue of escape was blocked by one of the two destroyers. Without a moment's hesitation he swung *U-23*'s bows towards the starboard warship and fired two torpedoes in quick succession before turning away and steaming seawards. Less than two minutes later the torpedoes slammed into the destroyer *Daring* and, with flames blazing amidships and steam shrieking from her ruptured boilers, she rolled over onto her beam-ends and slid beneath the water.

Once clear of the convoy, Kretschmer came up with a straggler, the 5,225-ton freighter *Tiberton*, and sent her to the bottom with two torpedoes. Three nights later he despatched the *Loch Maddy* (4,996 tons) east of the Orkneys. With nine ships to his credit and a total bag of more than 30,000 tons, Kretschmer's reputation was rapidly growing and his skill was acknowledged by *BdU* when, on 1 May, 1940, he was appointed to command the brand-new Type VIIB submarine *U-99*. Displacing 753 tons in surface trim and with a maximum speed of 17¼ knots, she was the ideal vessel for Kretschmer's revolutionary new tactics. Measuring 218 feet in length, she carried a 3.5-inch deck gun plus a 20mm AA gun and five torpedo tubes – four forward and one in the stern – with an outfit of twelve torpedoes.

U-99's career got off to a shaky start, however, when the pilot of one of the *Scharnhorst*'s Arado float-planes mistook the U-boat for a British submarine and carried out a bombing attack which resulted in a near miss and serious damage to *U-99*'s periscopes. But the U-boat's first patrol quickly demonstrated that no permanent harm had been done and by the time Kretschmer returned to his new base at Lorient in Occupied France he had added a further six vessels to his tally.

More significantly, *U-99* had successfully endured a massive depth-charge attack during which Kretschmer was forced to take his boat down to 700 feet – 150 feet below the submarine's safe diving depth.* *U-99*'s War Diary recorded no fewer than 127 depth-charge explosions in the course of this one single attack and, for Kretschmer, it was a taste of the other side of the coin. But his success in extricating his boat and his men from near-certain destruction raised morale to an unprecedented height and was an inspiration to the entire flotilla.

U-99 left for her next patrol on 24 July and, by the time Kretschmer returned to Lorient on 8 August, he had set a new record for the number of ships sunk by a World War Two U-boat commander in the course of a single patrol. His prowess was rewarded with the Knight's Cross to the Iron Cross. In the early part of the cruise he sank the Blue Star liner *Auckland Star* and followed this with the *Clan Menzies, Jamaica Progress* and *Jersey City*. But there were other excitements. He was attacked by an unidentified submarine which, fortunately, missed and was the target of various Coastal Command aircraft including a Sunderland flying-boat. There were also several brushes with enemy escort ships.

His greatest triumph came, however, during a night convoy attack when, for the first time, Kretschmer put theory into practice and got into the centre of the formation by dashing through the escort screen at full speed *on the surface*! *U-99* had only four torpedoes left but in half an hour of mayhem Kretschmer sank three tankers and caused two other vessels to collide. It was an impressive achievement and demonstrated the soundness of his tactics of attacking only at night, on the surface, and from *inside* the convoy where the cluttered mass of shipping rendered the escorts' radar and sonar detection devices virtually useless.

A detailed account of Kretschmer's subsequent successes would quickly degenerate into an ever-increasing list of ships' names and tonnages. But certain highlights in his later career merit special attention. And, of course, it must be acknowledged that his new method of attack, which was taken up and developed by Doenitz in conjunction with the wolf-pack concept, caused such tremendous losses to Allied shipping in the Atlantic that it kept the fate of the war very much in the balance for two more years.†

The attack on Convoy SC-7 in October, 1940, demonstrated the effectiveness of getting a surfaced U-boat inside a convoy. On this occasion SC-7 had been sighted and shadowed by *U-93* and, by the

* Von Tiesenhausen's U-331 reached a depth of 860 feet after torpedoing the battleship *Barham* on 25 November, 1941, a figure not exceeded by any other U-boat in the Second World War.
† Neither must it be forgotten that Kretschmer's tactics were also copied by US Navy submarine commanders with great success in the Pacific.

time the assault began, no fewer than eight submarines had homed-in on the unsuspecting merchant ships. But, while seven U-boats of the wolf-pack launched submerged attacks from outside the port wing escort screen of the convoy, Kretschmer took *U-99* to the starboard side of the group, steered the submarine through the escort screen at high speed and placed himself in the middle of the lumbering lines of slow-moving merchantmen.

His first torpedo missed but the second slammed home and sent its victim to the bottom in twenty seconds flat. Steaming down the line of ships, he let fly a third torpedo which again missed and was rewarded for his temerity by a burst of gunfire from a 4-inch quick-firer on the poop of one of the freighters. To add insult to injury the freighter's Master ported his helm in an attempt to ram the U-boat, but Kretschmer adroitly evaded the attack and fired a torpedo which missed its intended target and struck the *Empire Brigade* in the next column. His fifth shot scored another hit but the sixth failed to find a target. Undismayed, he loosed two more torpedoes and two more merchantmen went down. His task was simplified by the fact that the escort commander thought the ships were being sunk by torpedoes fired from U-boats *outside* the convoy.

While the crew sweated to reload the tubes, Kretschmer prepared to renew the attack. Still steaming hard, and surrounded by sinking and burning ships, *U-99* tore through the heart of the convoy once again and sank three more vessels – *Thalia, Shetaticka* and *Sedgepool*. Then, pulling clear of the massed merchantmen and taking care to keep well away from the escorts, he picked off a lone straggler with his last torpedo. By the time the battle was over SC-7 had lost seventeen ships to the eight U-boats making up the wolf-pack. *And nine of those seventeen victims had fallen to U-99's torpedoes*! Faced by such overwhelming proof, most U-boat captains were grudgingly prepared to accept that Kretschmer's new tactics held the key to victory at sea. But when it came to the crunch few had the courage to follow in his footsteps.

Further successes included the sinking of the armed merchant cruisers *Laurentic* (18,724 tons) and *Patroclus* (11,314 tons) on the same day. On 4 November, 1940, it was announced that Kretschmer had been given one of Germany's highest decorations, the Oak Leaves to the Iron Cross, an award that led to a meeting with Adolf Hitler in the course of which the *Fuehrer* personally bestowed *U-99*'s captain with the honour. He was subsequently invited to lunch with Hitler and his personal staff. Kretschmer's only memory of the occasion was the complete absence of meat from the menu.

A spell of leave followed and, as it came to an end, Kretschmer met up with his old comrades Prien and Schepke for a celebratory dinner. All three captains were now officially credited with sinking more than 200,000 tons of shipping, although in Schepke's case, there was a certain element of doubt about the reliability of his claims.*

A few days later *U-99* was back at sea again and on 1 December, in the teeth of a wild Atlantic storm, Kretschmer sank the Armed Merchant Cruiser *Forfar*, although it took a total of five torpedoes to put her down. But worsening weather plus engine troubles forced him to cut short his patrol, although he succeeded in winning three more scalps, *Samanager, Conch* and *Farmsum*, before returning to Lorient. But it had not been a happy trip. Weather conditions had been diabolical and, during the final days of the cruise, *U-99* had been heavily depth-charged by British destroyers.

Krestschmer's official tally now topped 250,000 tons – making him the first U-boat commander to exceed a quarter of a million in World War II. Doenitz invited him to accept an appointment on his personal staff or, if a desk job was not to his liking, to take over as Chief Instructor at the U-boat School. But Kretschmer politely refused both offers and told the Admiral that he would prefer to remain at sea.

And so, in accordance with his request, Kretschmer and *U-99* sailed from Lorient on 22 February, 1941, for another combat patrol – this time leaving harbour to the strains of a military band playing a stirring march especially composed in his honour. Prien and Schepke had left two days earlier and were already far out into the Atlantic searching for targets, but this time not one of the famous trio was destined to return home again. Gunther Prien, Joachim Schepke and Otto Kretschmer had all left Lorient for the last time.

* * *

As Kretschmer closed on Convoy HX-112, he was unaware that Prien was dead and he assumed that *U-47*'s failure to acknowledge *BdU*'s continuous requests for a report was due to a fault in the U-boat's radio equipment. Having withdrawn from the assault on Convoy OB-293 in its early stages, he had not witnessed the depth-charge attack during the small hours of 8 March and he had no suspicion that anything was wrong. In fact he was half-expecting to see Prien's boat, with its famous Roaring Bull mascot painted on

* See postscript at the end of chapter.

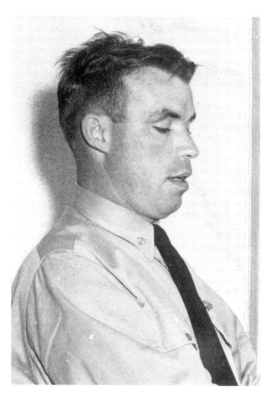

14. Commander Dudley Morton. After a legendary career in the *Wahoo* 'Mush' and his submarine paid the supreme penalty in October, 1943.

15. Admiral Andrew Cunningham – the man who ordered de la Penne to be held prisoner in the bowels of the *Valiant* after the human-torpedo attack on Alexandria.

16. *Kapitanleutnant* Freiherr von Spiegel von und zu Peckelsheim, the aristocrat who crossed swords with the Royal Navy's Head of Intelligence, Reginald Hall, and lost.

17. *Kapitan* Jan Grudzinski. The Polish skipper of the *Orzel* who ran the German gauntlet to reach England in 1939.

its conning-tower, in the wolf-pack which Lemp was assembling in the path of HX-112.

Joachim Schepke in *U-100* was the first member of the pack to go into action and, shortly before midnight on 15 March, he fired a salvo of four torpedoes into a large tanker which promptly erupted in flames. Macintyre's *Walker* and the other destroyers turned towards the presumed firing position but Schepke skilfully evaded them and avoided immediate retribution. Kretschmer arrived to join the pack the following day but, spotted by an alert destroyer, he was forced to submerge and cautiously took up a watching station astern of the slow-moving huddle of merchant ships, an area least likely to be searched by the escorts. But when night fell *U-99* returned to the surface, caught up with the convoy and, in accordance with Kretschmer's usual tactics, penetrated unseen into the middle of the dense mass of shipping. By the time he withdrew, *U-99* had used up all her remaining stock of torpedoes and he had sunk six vessels: the tankers *Fern, Bedouin, Franche Comte* and *Korsham*, plus two freighters, *Venitia* and *J. B. White*. It had been a good night's work even by Kretschmer's exacting standards.

Schepke, meanwhile, beset by mechanical trouble and damage to *U-100*'s propellers, had been forced to surface. He emerged into the cold North Atlantic air some two miles off the starboard side of the convoy, a relatively safe distance in normal conditions of night visibility. But on this occasion the enemy could see in the dark. The destroyer *Vanoc* was equipped with the newly issued Type-286 radar apparatus and *U-100* showed up on the cathode tube as soon as she broke surface. A W/T signal informed Macintyre of the radar plot and he responded without hesitation. The two destroyers, already moving at high speed, turned sharply under full helm and headed along the bearing given by *Vanoc*'s radar operator.

Travelling faster than her companion, the *Vanoc* caught the surfaced U-boat by surprise and her sharp steel bows sliced deeply into the submarine's side. Schepke, jammed against the periscope standards by the destroyer's stem, lost both his legs in the impact but was still alive as he was hurled into the sea by the force of the collision. *U-100*'s nose rose high into the air and hung motionless for a moment before sliding back beneath the waves for the last time. Only five men escaped from the sinking U-boat and *Vanoc*'s searchlight flashed out of the darkness as she slowed to pick them up.

U-99's Second Officer, Petersen, was on the submarine's bridge when *Vanoc* and *Walker* were sighted bearing down on the crippled *U-100*. Although the two destroyers were at least a quarter of a mile away, Petersen, unwisely in Kretschmer's opinion, hurriedly dived the U-boat to avoid being seen. The *Korvettenkapitan* had always argued that, once a U-boat had submerged, she became a perfect target for the Royal Navy's Asdic detectors, and in this instance his worst fears proved to be justified for, while *Walker* was cautiously circling *Vanoc* as the latter dragged *U-100*'s survivors from the water, her Asdic operator reported a positive contact. Macintyre found it difficult to believe that a second U-boat was so close at hand but, taking no chances, he increased speed and prepared to launch a depth-charge attack.

Caught like a rat in a trap, there was nothing Kretschmer could do to save his boat. A salvo of charges detonated all around the helpless *U-99* and the concussion of the explosion hurt his ears. The main lights went out, the glass of the dials and gauges splintered and, as cork insulation sprinkled down from the deckhead, water began leaking into the hull. A ruptured oil tank added evil-smelling diesel fuel to the general mess of broken glass, clothing, loose equipment and sea-water swirling around the deck of the submarine and this served to compound the chaos and confusion of the counter attack. Although the depth gauges were broken, Kretschmer estimated that *U-99* was already down to at least 700 feet, well below her diving limit, and he ordered the tanks to be blown. There was a heart-stopping moment when the main control-room valve jammed but it was finally hammered free with a wrench and there was a comforting scream of high pressure air as it opened.

U-99 broke surface astern of *Vanoc* but, because of her damaged propellers, Kretschmer could not use the engines to escape. Macintyre, hoping to capture the U-boat intact, opened fire on the listing vessel and, having ordered his men to shelter behind the protective lee of the conning-tower, Kretschmer went below to destroy the U-boat's confidential papers and code books while scuttling charges were prepared and laid. He had just returned to the deck when the sinking submarine lurched violently, throwing a number of the crew into the sea. In an effort to save life he ordered Petersen to flash a signal to the British destroyers.

From Captain to Captain . . . Please pick up my men drifting towards you in the water. Stop. I am sinking.

Macintyre ordered *Walker*'s guns to cease fire and a scrambling net was dropped over the side so that they could climb to safety. But when a boat was lowered to help with the rescue, Kretschmer mistakenly thought that the British intended to board the U-boat and *U-99*'s Chief Engineer, Schroeder, hurried below to check that the vents were open. Moments later Kretschmer and the remaining men found themselves in the water as *U-99* sank beneath their feet. The *Walker* turned towards them and within minutes the bedraggled survivors had been hauled to safety.

As befitted his rank, Kretschmer was taken to Macintyre's day cabin where he was given dry clothing and a generous tot of rum. Some hours later the destroyer's skipper went down to visit his prisoner. Kretschmer thanked him for rescuing his men and added quietly: 'I should like to say, however, how much I regret not having any torpedoes with which to attack you'. Then holding his hand out to Macintyre he smiled and continued: 'As it is, my sincere congratulations on your success.'

It was a gallant gesture by a gallant foe.

POSTSCRIPT

Wartime claims by submarine commanders, like those of fighter pilots, are often unintentionally exaggerated. The following details are based upon a post-war examination of German and Allied records:

Korvettenkapitan Kretschmer	43 ships.	263,682 BRT
Korvettenkapitan Lüth	46 ships.	228,429 BRT
Fregattenkapitan Schütze	33 ships.	212,036 BRT
Korvettenkapitan Topp	33 ships.	184,244 BRT
Kapitanleutnant Schultze	28 ships.	183,432 BRT
Kapitanleutnant Lehmann-Willenbrock	24 ships.	174,326 BRT
Korvettenkapitan Prien	30 ships.	160,006 BRT

Joachim Schepke's claim to have sunk over 200,000 BRT is now completely discredited. (Source: *U-boats in Action* by B. Herzog. [Podzun-Verlag 1970])

TWELVE

Commander Howard W. Gilmore, USN

'Take 'er down!'

Despite being a relatively small force – in terms of personnel it represented only 1.6% of the Navy's total strength – America's submarine service suffered a heavier proportion of casualties than any other combat branch of the US Navy in the Second World War. And, of the 374 officers and 3,131 enlisted men who gave their lives in the Pacific, none died more bravely than the skipper of the *USS Growler* – Commander Howard W. Gilmore.

Gilmore's combat career was sadly brief – it spanned less than eight months – but in that time he saw more action than most men experience in a lifetime. Unlike the majority of American submarine commanders, he received his baptism of fire not in the warm and sunny waters of South Pacific but in the fog-shrouded seas that surround the Aleutian Islands to the west of Alaska.

In accordance with a long-standing custom common to both the American and British navies, *Growler* was still under construction when Gilmore was appointed as her captain in 1941 and he kept a fatherly eye on the progress of his new baby as she slowly took shape on the building slip at the Electric Boat Company's yard at Groton, Connecticut. He was conscious, too, of a sense of history for the Company's connection with submarines dated back as far as 1898 – the year in which its founder, Isaac Rice, had engineered a merger with Holland's Submarine Torpedo Boat Company after the latter had proved unable to pay its debts. And the Irish-born owner of the insolvent business had designed and built the first operational submarine to join the US Navy, the *USS Holland* or *SS-1*.

The contrast between the two vessels was a measure of the progress that had been achieved during the ensuing forty years. The *Holland* had displaced only 64 tons in surface trim and 74 tons with all her ballast aboard. *Growler*'s equivalent vital statistics were 1,526 tons and 2,424 tons respectively. A single-shaft Otto gasoline engine pushed the little *Holland* along at 8 knots when surfaced while her batteries gave a submerged speed of 5 knots. *Growler*'s four massive twin-shaft 16-cylinder General Motors Type-278A diesel engines produced a useful 20¼ knots on the surface while her General Electric motors, fed by a 252-cell Exide battery, provided a comfortable underwater maximum of 8¾ knots – faster, in fact, than her pioneer predecessor could travel on the surface.

Growler was almost six times as long as John P. Holland's vessel, measuring 311¾ feet overall against *SS-1*'s 53¾ feet. But it was in terms of hitting power that the contrast was most marked. The *Holland* design included a single 18-inch torpedo tube in the bows, with storage capacity for two reload weapons, plus two pneumatic dynamite guns of 8-inch calibre. *Growler*, however, was equipped with six 21-inch tubes in the bows and four more in the stern – ten in all – and, with reloads, she carried a complete outfit of twenty-four torpedoes. In terms of sheer destructive ability *Growler* was a mega-killer. The weight of explosives in her torpedo warheads totalled 14,400 pounds. The *Holland*'s tipped the scales at just 600 pounds! In addition, and for surface action, the newer boat was armed with a fast-shooting 5-inch deck gun plus two .5-inch and two .300-inch surface/air machine guns.

Growler was launched with all the traditional ceremony on 2 November, 1941, just five weeks before the Japanese attack on Pearl Harbor. The cutting-edge of war brought a sharp realism to the training routines once the submarine was ready for sea. Her acceptance trials revealed no serious problems and Gilmore was already more than satisfied with the way his new team was shaping up. Long and hectic hours of drill and exercises soon brought both officers and enlisted men to a peak of enthusiasm and efficiency, and within a few weeks Gilmore had produced a superbly disciplined underwater fighting machine that was eager and anxious for battle.

Excitement ran high as *Growler* nosed her way into the Pacific and set course for Pearl Harbor, but the crew was given little time to savour the fleshpots of Honolulu. US Naval Intelligence had broken Japan's top-secret naval code and was building up details of

Admiral Yamamoto's grandiose *Operation MI*, an over-ambitious scheme to seize the strategically important island of Midway and to force the US Pacific Fleet into battle on terms favourable to Japan and which, it was hoped, would result in the total annihilation of American sea power. Admiral Chester Nimitz, himself an old submarine hand who had commanded the *Narwhal* in 1911 and the *Skipjack* in 1912, had no intention of allowing Yamamoto to succeed. With the priceless advantage of knowing in advance what his enemy intended to do, he laid his plans accordingly.

One very minor off-shoot of Nimitz's grand strategy was to place a defensive line of submarines in a wide arc 300 miles to the north of Oahu so that they could attack the Japanese fleet if it attempted to approach Hawaii. *Finback, Pike* and *Tarpon* were ordered to take station on the line and *Growler* was ordered to join her three sisters. It proved to be a dull and routine patrol, for the American victory at Midway – a battle that lasted from 4 to 6 June and which marked the turning point of the Pacific war – effectively prevented the main enemy force from getting to within a thousand miles of the Hawaiian Islands. But the northern section of Yamamoto's Combined Fleet struck at the Aleutians and occupied Kiska, Attu and other islands in the chain. And to counter this thrust Nimitz sent *Growler* and seven other fleet submarines to Dutch Harbour on Unalaska to support the six veteran S-boats already on station.

According to the calendar it was midsummer but someone had apparently forgotten to tell the weather-men. Thick fogs hung over the near-Arctic seas and the damp chill of the air froze the bones of the men on Watch on the exposed bridges of the submarines. It was a far cry from the tropical heat of Hawaii, but they stuck to their task and were soon rewarded for their perseverance. *Triton* claimed the first success when her skipper sighted the destroyer *Nenchi* on 3 July and, having shadowed it through the night, sent it to the bottom the following afternoon, an appropriate way to celebrate Independence Day. *Growler*'s turn came the next morning when three destroyers emerged from Kiska harbour while the submarine was patrolling off the entrance at periscope depth. In the early months of the war enemy destroyers were not regarded as suitable targets for submarine attack because of the risks involved. Most certainly any attempts to tangle with three simultaneously was tantamount to suicide, especially as the enemy was very much on the alert following the sinking of the *Nenchi* the previous day.

But Gilmore trusted his boat, his crew and his own judgement. Having brought *Growler* into a suitable position, he told the bow tubes to stand by and began passing the attack details to the officer working the Torpedo Data Computer.* The calm catechism of bearings, ranges and speeds continued until the TDC operator brought it to an abrupt conclusion.

'Solution, Captain.'

'Fire!'

Gilmore aimed one torpedo each at the two leading destroyers and he completed the four-shot salvo with two more at the third and last vessel. The first weapon unfortunately missed its intended target but the enemy was so alert that, within seconds of seeing the bubbling wake pass in front of its bows, the reprieved vessel had aimed and fired two torpedoes in the general direction of *Growler*'s periscope. Gilmore did not hang around to see any more.

'Full left rudder! All ahead full! Take her to two hundred, Mister Schade!'

As the submarine angled towards the bottom the Sound Operator sitting at the listening gear heard the swirl of the torpedo swish overhead and gave Gilmore a quick thumb's-up sign. But the grin was quickly wiped from his face.

'Propellers approaching zero-five-zero, Captain!'

'Rig for depth-charges!'

The heavy thud of the watertight doors slamming shut echoed through the length of the submarine and *Growler*'s crew braced themselves for attack. They did not have long to wait and, within minutes, the submarine was kicking and bucking like a frightened colt as the depth-charges exploded all around her. A seaplane joined the hunt and added its bombs to the general turmoil, but, fortunately for *Growler*, Japanese sonar was by no means perfect and, unable to obtain a firm contact on the submerged submarine, most of the depth-charges fell wide and caused no serious damage. Running at low speed and continually altering course, Gilmore skilfully evaded the predators on the surface and when the attack finally petered out he returned to periscope depth.

An enormous column of smoke testified to the accuracy of the three remaining torpedoes and numerous small boats were circling the area searching for survivors. Post-war records confirmed that Gilmore had sent the *Arare* to the bottom – a modern 1,961-ton destroyer which had only come into service in April, 1939 – and had also damaged a second which was subsequently towed back to Japan for repairs. In a secret report to his superiors in Tokyo the local Admiral observed: 'This was a daring and skilful attack . . .

---

*A similar type of attack calculator used in the Royal Navy was known less formally as the Fruit Machine or the Is-Was.

157

(and) was admirably executed'. It was not often that the Japanese handed such handsome bouquets to their enemy.

Growler's crew shed no tears of regret when the submarine left the fog-bound islands astern and headed south for the lush warmth of Pearl Harbor and Hawaii. But, once again, she was soon off – this time westwards for Formosa. During the thirteen days which the submarine spent on patrol off the Japanese-occupied island she sent four enemy supply ships to the bottom. Gilmore, of course, was delighted with both his crew and his submarine and everyone was in high spirits as they headed home. With only two patrols under her belt *Growler*'s score-card was already impressive: one destroyer and four freighters sunk and another destroyer seriously damaged. It was success beyond Gilmore's wildest dreams.

By the end of 1942 *Growler* was based in Australia and on New Year's Day, 1943, the submarine steamed out of Brisbane harbour for the start of her fourth mission. Gilmore's designated patrol area ranged between the Gilbert Islands in the east and Palau in the west, but he had been ordered to concentrate his attention on the Steffen Strait and the Japanese convoy route from Truk southwards to Rabaul. It was one of the toughest areas in the entire South Pacific war zone and, even as recently as 30 November, just a month before *Growler* set out on her patrol, the US Navy had suffered heavy losses in a savage night action off Tassafaronga.

Although the battle for Guadalcanal was still raging, the Japanese High Command, unbeknown to the Americans, had issued secret instructions on 4 January that the 13,000-strong garrison was to be evacuated. During the same month the enemy made three runs down The Slot with the famous 'Tokyo Express' – operations that convinced the Americans that the Japanese were reinforcing their troops on the island. But these high-speed missions were merely preparatory to the main evacuation operation which began on the night of 1 February when a force of twenty destroyers hurtled through the darkness and, closing the shore, lifted off a substantial number of soldiers.

A cruiser and twenty-two destroyers repeated the run four nights later with equal success and finally, during the dark hours of 7 February, another force of destroyers embarked the remaining survivors from the garrison, the three missions rescuing a total of 12,198 soldiers plus 832 Navy personnel. Carried out in complete secrecy under the very noses of the enemy, the operation was a remarkable achievement and must rank with the equally successful British evacuation of the Gallipoli peninsula in 1915. But while 7 February, 1943, marked the date on which the United States finally won victory in the Guadalcanal campaign it was destined to have a very different and tragic significance for the captain and crew of the *USS Growler*.

The fourth patrol, however, opened well. On the night of 16 January Gilmore intercepted a Japanese convoy and sent a transport to the bottom. He followed up this success by torpedoing another vessel three nights later. There was certainly no dearth of targets, for the battle for Guadalcanal was reaching its bloody climax and the convoys criss-crossing the waters to the north of the Solomon Islands were heavily defended by anti-submarine escorts of every size, shape and description. The US Navy was indeed fortunate to lose only one submarine by enemy action – the *Argonaut*, south-west of New Britain on 10 January – in the course of this bitterly contested campaign.

Growler continued to prowl her patrol area with the persistence and cunning of a fox stalking a chicken. But suddenly, thanks to a batch of faulty torpedoes, the submarine's run of luck came to an abrupt halt. Seven more convoys were attacked, but, due to the erratic performance of her normally reliable underwater weapons, not a single ship was destroyed. It was a numbing disappointment for a crew that had grown accustomed to success and many captains would have returned home in disgust. But Gilmore gritted his teeth and held on.

There were murmured whispers from the mess-decks that *Growler* was jinxed, but Gilmore wisely ignored such foolishness. To add to his problems the seas had now become strangely empty of targets and, seeking fresh pastures, he returned to the Steffen Strait. It was, in fact, only the calm before the storm, for the Japanese Navy was on the point of launching its Guadalcanal evacuation operation. Gilmore, of course, knew nothing of this dramatic decision, and neither did the US Navy. Had any details of the enemy's intentions emerged, there is little doubt that *Growler* and every other submarine in the area would have been rushed into The Slot to ambush the destroyers on their way to, and from, Guadalcanal.

On the night of 30 January Gilmore located yet another convoy and succeeded in damaging a freighter. But the enemy escorts were on their toes and *Growler* was subjected to a fierce counter-attack. Thanks to Gilmore's skill and patience, however, the submarine finally wriggled clear and escaped from the scene undamaged.

Resting in his cabin the following evening, *Growler*'s captain was aroused from his gloomy reflections on their recent lack of success by the strident squawk of the intercom loudspeaker on the bulkhead above his bunk.

'Captain to the bridge! Captain to the bridge!'

Gilmore was on his feet in an instant and, as he climbed out onto the bridge, the Officer-of-the-Deck informed him that they had picked up a radar contact fine on the port bow at a range of eighteen miles. Gilmore nodded and took over the Watch. With the scent of the enemy in his nostrils he wasted no time.

'Surface battle stations! All ahead flank!' He glanced down at the gyro repeater. 'Steer three-two-zero!'

'Visual contact, Captain.'

Gilmore crouched behind the torpedo sight and scanned the reported bearing. His trained eyes found a faint smudge on the dark horizon and he swung the sight so that it centred exactly on the barely visible object. The range, speed and bearing of the target were passed to the TDC operator in the control room at thirty-second intervals and the men on the bridge waited tensely as Gilmore prepared to make a surface torpedo attack. The target was clearer now – an enemy gunboat of around 3,000 tons – and at 8,000 yards he warned the bow torpedomen to stand by. But, determined to close the range, he held his fire as the *Growler* approached her intended victim.

Six thousand yards . . . five thousand yards . . . four thousand yards. Suddenly the gunboat spotted the sinister shape of the submarine. Its forward gun turret swung in the direction of the would-be attacker and, moments later, the first 5-inch shell screamed through the night and exploded with a loud crash ahead of the bows.

'Fire!'

Two torpedoes leapt from the tubes and arrowed straight at the enemy ship. Gilmore watched their bubbling wakes and grinned with relief. Thank God this pair were running true. Suddenly the grin vanished. The torpedoes were veering off course and doubling back. Moments later they had completely reversed course and were speeding towards the surfaced submarine. There was no time to dive out of trouble and, calling for flank speed and full left rudder, Gilmore threw the submarine sideways. Looking aft, he watched the errant weapons thrash past *Growler*'s stern and vanish into the darkness. They had escaped disaster by no more than inches.

'Clear the bridge! Dive! Dive! Dive!'

Growler had been extraordinarily lucky for she could have easily shared the fate of other submarines who had had the misfortune to fall victim to their own torpedoes. *Tullibee*, for example, was sunk north of Palau when her torpedoes ran wild on 26 March, 1944, and *Tang** had been lost in similar circumstances north-west of

* See Chapter 18.

Formosa on 24 October of the same year. Such incidents were not new. The earliest known occasion when a torpedo returned to strike the ship from which it had been launched occurred on 27 August, 1879, when a Lay dirigible torpedo doubled-back on the Peruvian corvett *Abtao*. Fortunately the last-minute bravery of Lieutenant Diez Canseco, who jumped over the side and diverted the the weapon away from the corvette with his bare hands, prevented a tragedy.

Certainly *Growler* had enjoyed a fortunate escape. Gilmore did not share his crew's superstitious belief in the existence of a jinx but he was more than a little unhappy about the reliability of his torpedoes. By way of consolation the submarine had been doubly lucky, for, having narrowly escaped destruction by the errant torpedoes, she was spared further punishment when the enemy gunboat failed to locate her position with its sonar apparatus and laid down a barrage of depth-charges at a safe distance from *Growler*'s correct hiding-place.

On 4 February, the night the Japanese sent their destroyers down The Slot to lift the second batch of troops from Guadalcanal, *Growler* made radar contact with a small convoy a few miles to the south of Steffen Strait. Comprising two 10,000-ton merchantmen escorted by a pair of patrol boats, it was heading towards the Gazelle Channel and, in deference to the weather conditions, Gilmore decided in favour of a surface attack. Withdrawing beyond visual range, he altered course south and increased speed in order to place *Growler* ahead of the convoy. Then, having turned into its path, he waited for the dark blur of the oncoming ships to resolve itself into a group of distinct shapes. Suddenly, and without warning, *Growler*'s evil hoodoo struck again.

The range was down to 5,000 yards when the leading Japanese escort detected the submarine. Searchlights stabbed out of the darkness to probe the black waters and, by unlucky chance, one beam found the exposed conning-tower of the surfaced *Growler*. Within seconds the Japanese had opened fire with every available weapon. The staccato bark of the quick-firers punctuated the steady rhythm of the semi-automatic cannons and the *tak-tak-tak* of the heavy machine-guns added an unholy descant to the terrible symphony of death. Gun flashes lit the horizon and *Growler* shuddered as shells exploded all around her and the tracer bullets hosed out of the darkness like horizontal fireworks.

'Clear the bridge! Take her down!'

A Japanese destroyer, a gleaming bow-wave rising from its stem, hurtled into view intent on ramming the submarine but, somehow, Gilmore forced *Growler* under just in time.

161

'Rig for depth-charges!'

As the submarine angled for the safety of deep water the first depth-charges tumbled from the racks on the fantail of the enemy destroyers. Trapped inside the steel tube of the pressure-hull, their faces pale and drawn with tension, *Growler*'s men stared up at the deckhead. The swish of the depth-charges striking the water was clearly audible and, seconds later, they could hear the sinister and terrifying click of the hydrostatic valves triggering the detonators. Then came the ear-splitting explosion and the concussive hammer-blow of the blast against the hull plating. The submarine jolted violently with each explosion, the near-misses throwing the men off their feet and hurling loose equipment to the deck with a metallic clatter. At 4.02 am a particularly heavy explosion forced the bows down and, as the boat rolled slowly back onto an even keel, an anonymous voice came over the battle-phone to report flooding in the forward torpedo room. Gilmore took the instrument from the talker.

'How bad is it?'

'Not sure yet, Captain. Looks like a ruptured manhole gasket in the main ballast. We're trying to plug it right now.'

Under normal circumstances it was not a serious leak for although the sea was entering the submarine at a rate of fifteen gallons per minute this was well within the capacity of *Growler*'s electric pumps, and the tightly dogged watertight door at the rear of the compartment ensured that the flooding could not extend beyond the bulkhead and into the rest of the boat. But circumstances were *not* normal and the tell-tale noise of the pumps would be quickly targeted by the enemy's listening gear, pin-pointing their position with the certainty of a marker flag. So, while the pumps remained silent, the torpedomen struggled to plug the leak and stem the inrush of water with mattresses and bits of clothing.

On this occasion, however, luck was with them. Under Gilmore's skilful direction *Growler* swung hard to starboard and then turned sharp left in response to the ported helm. One minute she was moving forward at emergency speed with the motors whining with agony, the next she was easing backwards at minimum revolutions. Handicapped by the primitive nature of their sonar gear, the enemy found it difficult to keep track of the target and finally Gilmore gave them the slip and stole quietly away, the rumbling thunder of the depth-charges gradually receding as the distance increased. At 5.30 am *Growler* rose to periscope depth. The Japanese ships, now five miles astern, were still fruitlessly searching for a target that was no longer there. The submarine's malevolent jinx had, it seemed, been finally beaten.

Gilmore remained submerged throughout the following day, except for a brief period on the surface while makeshift repairs were carried out on the damaged manhole gasket with the aid of a rubber sheet and some special clamps. Then the submarine slipped beneath the waves again and continued westwards at slow speed until the onset of darkness allowed Gilmore to return to the surface so that the damage control party could fit a replacement gasket. Restored to fighting trim and with her batteries recharged, *Growler* set off in search of fresh targets.

A thick fog shrouded the Steffen Strait as, running on the surface, the submarine nosed her way westwards sniffing electronically for a scent of the enemy. No contacts were obtained during the evening of the 6th but soon after midnight, during the early minutes of 7 February, a bright grey-green echo flashed onto the radar screen. Gilmore searched the fog ahead of the bows but could see nothing. Lowering his glasses he rubbed his eyes and raised them again. A grey blur on the starboard bow attracted his attention and, bringing it into focus, he could just make out the squat outlines of a 2,500-ton patrol boat. Bending over the voicepipe, he called for full left rudder and, as the submarine began turning to port, he was able to confirm that the enemy vessel was steaming on a reciprocal course to that of the submarine. Her lookouts, at a disadvantage without radar, had so far not sighted the *Growler*, but, on passing astern, her bows rose and fell as she entered the disturbed water of the submarine's wake. Someone on the bridge was alert enough to recognize the probable cause of the pitching motion and, although a wall of impenetrable fog separated the two vessels, the Japanese officer reacted to his hunch. The helm went hard over and, as the gunboat turned sharply to starboard, the repeater bell of the bridge telegraph tinkled in the engine-room. *Full ahead both.*

Growler's radar operator watched the blips change direction as the attack developed and he passed an urgent warning to Gilmore. But, before any steps could be taken to counter the threat, the blunt grey bows of the enemy warship loomed out of the fog.

'Collision stations!'

Gilmore tugged the lanyard of the siren and its banshee wail split the air as, deep inside the bowels of the submarine, the watertight doors were slammed shut. Moments later *Growler*'s bows punched into the side of the gunboat and she came to an abrupt stop. The seven men on the bridge were thrown to the deck by the shock of the impact and, intermingling with the shouts of the equally surprised Japanese, there was an agonised screech of torn metal as *Growler*'s battered bows scraped down the length of the still-moving gunboat. Gilmore had just dragged himself back on to his feet when the enemy opened fire at point-blank range. A salvo of 5-inch shells exploded in the water beyond the submarine while streams of tracer shells from the gunboat's 20-mm semi-automatic cannons howled across the bridge. Somewhere in the fog and darkness a machine gun opened up on the conning-tower with heavy-calibre bullets.

The carnage on *Growler*'s bridge was indescribable. One of the lookouts, Fireman Third-class Kelley, fell back with blood spurting from his chest while Ensign Williams, cut down as he turned to speak to the Officer-of-the Deck, dropped in a crumpled heap. The two remaining lookouts were wounded by shell splinters and Gilmore's left arm hung uselessly, his shoulder smashed by a machine-gun bullet.

'Clear the bridge!'

Having given the command, *Growler*'s captain clung to a periscope standard for support and watched in silence as the Lieutenant and the Quartermaster lowered the wounded men down through the hatch. Then, having transferred their human burdens into the willing hands of the sailors waiting below, they turned to help Gilmore. But he motioned them away. He had been hit again and blood was dribbling down his chin.

'Get below!'

The two men hesitated for a moment as if willing themselves to disobey the order. But discipline prevailed and they returned reluctantly to the hatchway, leaving Gilmore alone on the bridge standing guard over the inert bodies of the dead lookout and the young Ensign and seemingly oblivious to the shell splinters and ricocheting machine-gun bullets that were scything across the top of the conning-tower.

Most of the crewmen inside the submarine were unaware of the drama that was being played out on the bridge, although the heavy thud of gunfire and the ceaseless chatter of the machine-guns and semi-automatics confirmed the fierceness of the battle taking place on the surface. Sealed inside their watertight compartments, with no chance of escape, they carried out their duties with stoic calm. Water was already swilling around on the floor of the control room and the pump room was partially flooded, while, up forward in the fore-ends, the torpedomen were fighting to stem the leaks in the collision-damaged bow section where the force of the impact had forced open the outer doors of two torpedo tubes. Inside the conning-tower *Growler*'s Executive Officer, Lieutenant-Commander Schade, waited at the foot of the ladder as the last two members of the bridge party clambered down the shining steel rungs. Where the hell was the skipper?

Huddled painfully in the lee of the conning-tower screen, Gilmore gauged the distance to the open hatchway. It was no more than eight feet from where he lay. But, unable to walk and with Japanese machine guns sweeping the intervening deck space, he knew he had little chance of reaching it alive. In addition, with the submarine still under heavy fire, any further delay could spell disaster. Bullets were already punching holes in the upper part of the conning-tower and it was clearly only a matter of time before the enemy's guns sent *Growler* to the bottom. Gilmore came to his decision. Summoning his remaining strength, he shouted the fateful order:

'Take 'er down!'

Fighting back his emotions, Schade obeyed. The upper hatch was pulled down onto the rubber bed of its watertight seal and the Quartermaster spun the wheel to secure the dog-latches.

'Hatch shut!'

Schade suddenly realized that he was no longer the Executive Officer echoing the Captain's orders. With Gilmore gone, *he* was now the submarine's captain and, as such, the life of every single crew-member had become his personal responsibility. Taking a deep breath, and praying that the tremor in his voice would not betray his innermost feelings, he repeated Gilmore's last command:

'Take her down! Flood negative . . . flood safety! All ahead full! Let's get to hell out of here!'

* * *

By some miracle *Growler* survived. Thirty-five feet of her fore-casing was crumpled, two torpedo-tubes were open to the sea and there was extensive internal flooding. In addition, the impact of the collision had twisted her bows so severely that she resembled some monstrous hammer-headed shark as she punched her way through the long Pacific swell. But by brilliant seamanship Schade succeeded in bringing the crippled boat safely back to Brisbane, a distance of more than 2,000 miles. Had he survived, there is little doubt that Gilmore would have been proud of his former Executive Officer's achievement.

Howard Gilmore's own selfless heroism was recognised by the posthumous award of the Congressional Medal of Honor, the first to be won by a submariner. By his sacrifice he had become a legend and an inspiration to submarine commanders the world over. Few men would ask more from life.

After lengthy repairs, the *Growler* returned to combat service and went on to send a further 32,607 tons of Japanese shipping to the bottom. In addition she scored a remarkable double when, on 12 September, 1944, she torpedoed and sank two enemy destroyers, the *Hirato* and the *Shikinami*, on the same day. But, sadly, less than two months later, on 8 November, she too paid the ultimate penalty when she was depth-charged by Japanese escorts south-west of Luzon following a combined attack on an enemy convoy in company with the *Hardhead* and the *Hake*.

But although she now rests in an unknown grave on the bottom of the South China Sea, she will never be forgotten. Whenever the exploits of the *Growler* are recalled her name will be forever linked with that of Howard W. Gilmore – the captain who gave his life that others should live.

—THIRTEEN—

*Tenente Di Vaceoll** Luigi Durand De La Penne

'*Cold-blooded bravery and enterprise.*'

Although Captain Kaneji Kishimoto of the Imperial Japanese Navy is usually credited with the invention of the midget submarine and its off-shoot, the human torpedo, the Italians actually beat him to it by more than twenty years; and while five of Japan's Type-A midget submarines failed to sink a single ship during the attack on Pearl Harbor in December, 1941, one lone Italian *Mignatta*, or *Leech*, sank the Austro-Hungarian battleship *Viribus Unitis* on the night of 1 November, 1918, in the course of a spectacular raid on the heavily defended harbour at Pola, an operation that is virtually forgotten.

Small submarines, as opposed to midgets, were the rule rather than the exception in the closing years of the nineteenth century and the decade following 1900, but these vessels were only steps on the evolutionary ladder of general submarine development. Virtually all pioneer submarines were small in modern terms. John Philip Holland's first practical boat scaled only 2¼ tons and measured 14 feet in length. To use a current phrase, the state of the art in technology at that time precluded the successful construction of large underwater vessels.

Lieutenant Godfrey Herbert, a former captain of the Royal Navy's submarine *A.4*, was serving in a cruiser on the China

* *Tenente di Vaceoll* = Lieutenant.

Station in 1908 when he first conceived the idea of a midget submarine designed specifically for attacks on defended anchorages and harbours. His boat, the *Devastator*, never progressed beyond the drawing-board, despite support from both Commodore Keyes and Max Horton, and the little secret weapon, failing to gain Admiralty approval, finally succumbed to the pigeon-holes of Whitehall bureaucracy after the First World War. Although it officially never saw the light of day, some experts have suggested that the plans of the *Devastator* were examined by visiting Japanese officers who used the drawings as a basis for their own subsequent midget submarine development programme.

Unaware of Herbert's brain-child, the Italians actually went ahead and built a pair of one-man submarines, the *Alfa* and *Beta*, at the Venice Navy Yard in 1912. Powered by an electric motor giving a speed of 8 knots, they were 19¾ feet long and proved satisfactory sea boats capable of diving and running submerged without difficulty. The problem of a suitable armament was never solved, however, and as a result they did not enter service with the Italian Navy. But they were, in every respect, genuine midget submarines and, as such, entitle the Italians to pole position in the race to develop these specialist craft.

The *Alfa* and *Beta* were followed by the *A*-class which were fully operational during World War One. Designed by Edgardo Ferrati and completed in 1916, they were 44 feet long and displaced 36 tons submerged. Armed with two 17.7-inch torpedoes carried in dropping-cradles on deck, they had a speed of 6.8 knots and a four-man crew.

By contrast Kishimoto did not design Japan's first midget submarine until 1932 and, although two prototypes were constructed, they were shut away in locked sheds at the Kure Naval Arsenal following the successful completion of their initial tests. The *Type-A* boats used in the attack on Pearl Harbor were developed from similar prototypes built at Kure and tested in the Sea of Iyo in July, 1940. Their submerged displacement of 46 tons was close to that of the Italian boats of the First World War as, too, was their underwater speed of 6 knots and armament of two 18--inch torpedoes – although in the Japanese version the latter were fired from conventional tubes. However, despite being considerably longer at 78½ feet, they required a crew of only two men. Nevertheless they bore a remarkable resemblance to Ferrati's original design and it must be remembered that Japan maintained a considerable naval presence in the Mediterranean during the 1914–1918 war and had had ample opportunity to indulge in some discreet espionage at the expense of her allies!

According to the experts, the *Mignatta* weapons designed by Engineer Major Raffaele Rossetti and used in the attack on the *Viribus Unitis* should be classified as 'human self-propelled mines' rather than human torpedoes – a distinction which is difficult to understand as they were identical in function and conception to the human torpedoes, or 'chariots', subsequently developed during the Second World War, although, naturally, without the latter's technical refinements. Indeed the body and engine of the *Mignatta* weapon was no more than a Mark B-57 14-inch Whitehead torpedo of somewhat uncertain vintage but which probably dated back to the early 'nineties. Fitted with a special 17.7-inch propeller the torpedo's compressed-air engine could drive the weapon at 4 knots for a maximum distance of 10 miles while two 170-kg explosive charges, carried at the bow end, could be removed and clamped to the enemy's keel by means of an electro-magnet – a distinct improvement on Ezra Lee's auger, although a magnet would have been of little use when dealing with the wooden-hulled ships of 1776. There was, however, one direct technical link to Bushnell's *Turtle*, for both machines employed a clockwork-operated delay mechanism to detonate the explosive charge.

The crew comprised two men wearing an early version of a wet-suit who could either swim alongside the weapon in the water or ride astride it, the latter method being a major characteristic of the British 'chariots' and Italian 'pigs' used for similar operations during the Second World War. The design did not include a rudder and the operators had to guide the torpedo towards its target by using their hands in the same way that canoeists steer with their paddles.

The *Mignatta*, known in the Service as the *S-1*, was completed in July, 1918, and its inventor, Raffaele Rossetti, together with his team-mate Surgeon Lieutenant Paolucci, began training in the lagoons surrounding Venice. Nearly four months passed before Rossetti was satisfied that they could handle the weapon under combat conditions and finally, on 31 October, 1918, the *S-1* was taken to the Venice Navy Yard where it was hoisted aboard Torpedo Boat *No 65*. The little assault group slipped out of Venice soon after noon and five hours later, as dusk was closing over the Brionian Islands, the mother-ship arrived off the Austrian base at Pola. The torpedo-boat lowered a motor launch and, with its engines throttled back to reduce the noise of its exhaust, the boat towed the *Mignatta* to within 500 yards of the harbour mole. Here, under cover of darkness, the two Italians clambered onto the weapon and, sitting astride the long cigar-shaped body, they started the motor and disappeared slowly into the night at a steady four knots. The outer defence barrier caused them considerable problems until a gate was discovered. But this was unfortunately closed and the two men had to manhandle the *S-1* over the half-submerged beams while, simultaneously, taking care not to trigger the various alarm devices which were intended to give the Austrian defenders audible warning of intruders.

Having surmounted the first obstacle, Rossetti and his companion had next to tackle two sets of net defences – one double, the other triple. The weather was abysmal with cold rain driving across the black water but the darkness afforded a modicum of cover, although the failure of their compass made this a mixed blessing. The machine capsized twice as they struggled to get it over the nets and the powerful current sweeping out of the harbour compounded their difficulties. Finally they cleared the obstacles and at 4.15 am they came alongside the anchored battleship. Their original plan to drift down on the tide had been upset by the current and Rossetti was forced to swim the final 25 yards in order to attach the mine to the target. The weather deteriorated further and a heavy hail storm slashed their faces as they struggled in the freezing water. To add to their problems the *S-1* capsized again.

A bugle call heralding reveille echoed from the upper deck and, almost simultaneously, a searchlight flared out of the darkness, searched the water for a few minutes and then settled on the Italians. Rossetti swam back to the *Mignatta* and opened the flooding valve while Paolucci released and primed the second explosive charge. Then a picket-boat emerged through the driving sleet and the two men were dragged out of the water and taken back to the Austrian flagship – or, more correctly, the Jugoslav flagship, for the battleship had been handed over to the newly created Yugoslav nation the previous day, following the surrender of the Austro-Hungarian Empire.

Rossetti warned the captain that the vessel was in imminent danger of destruction, without specifying the nature of the threat. When the news reached the crew, the majority promptly jumped overboard and abandoned ship. The sea, however, was uncomfortably cold and, having decided that the Italians were bluffing, they returned on board within a few minutes. But at 6.44 am a rumbling explosion beneath the ship confirmed their worst fears and they once again took to the water. Realizing that the vessel was doomed, the Yugoslav captain, Voukovitch, shook hands with the two Italian officers and indicated a rope hanging over the stern. With the battleship literally sinking beneath their feet, Rossetti and Paolucci shinned down the rope and, swimming to a rowing boat lying astern of the listing vessel, they climbed aboard and watched from a safe distance as the *Viribus Unitis* slowly rolled over and sank, a fate shared by the Austrian liner *Wien* which had fallen victim to the second mine.

With the end of the war in sight, the two Italians only remained prisoner for four days. On 5 November Admiral Cagni's flagship *Saint Bon* entered Pola harbour and Rossetti and Paolucci were released by their Austrian captors. Their attack on the *Viribus Unitis* had been a tremendous achievement and it is, indeed, rare for a new and untried weapon to succeed so convincingly the first time it is used. There could be no dispute that the *Mignatta* had proved the feasibility of the human torpedo.

Rossetti, too, proved that the age of chivalry was not yet passed. For when a grateful Italian Government gave him 650,000 lira in recogition of his skill as an engineer and his bravery as an officer, the Major quietly passed the money over to a fund which had been set up to care for Captain Voukovitch's widow and the dependants of the other men who had died when the battleship sank.

Seventeen years later two young Engineer Sub-Lieutenants serving with the La Spezia Submarine Flotilla, Teseo Tesei and Elios Toschi, drew up plans for a new attack weapon closely based on Rossetti's *Mignatta*. Blueprints were submitted to Admiral Cavagnari in 1935 and, recognizing the potential of the idea, he promptly authorized the construction of two prototypes at La Spezia's San Bartolemo Underwater Weapons Establishment.

Known officially as the slow-running torpedo or SLC (Siluro a Lenta Corsa), the boats were affectionately nicknamed *Maiali* or 'pigs' by their crews – a term of abuse bestowed upon an early model by its inventors following a mishap in tests. *The Maiale* was 22 feet in length and was powered by an electric motor, the first unit, for reasons of economy, being built around a salvaged elevator motor retrieved intact when a dockyard building was demolished. Wearing rubber diving suits and breathing-gear, the two-man crew sat astride the machine like underwater motor-cyclists. The pilot, shielded by a form of windscreen, steered the weapon and was provided with a compass, depth-gauge and other rudimentary instruments, while the second man, riding pillion behind the driver and separated from him by a bulky external ballast tank, controlled the buoyancy. The streamlined nose of the SLC was, in fact, a detachable 300-kg explosive charge which the crew could attach to the keel of a target.

Tesei and Toschi tested the first models in January, 1936, but, as there was no immediate use for the weapons, they were, like the Japanese midget submarine prototypes, carefully locked away and the experimental unit was disbanded. As the war clouds gathered over Europe in July, 1939, however, it was reactivated as the Special Weapons Department and placed under the wing of the First Light Flotilla – finally gaining its independence on 15 March, 1941, as the Tenth Light Flotilla. The two original inventors were re-assigned to the project and among the first batch of volunteers to arrive at the Serchio training centre during the early months of 1940 was a young Genoa-born Sub-Lieutenant, Count Luigi de la Penne.

With Mussolini at the helm, Italy entered the war at one minute past midnight on 11 June, 1940, as an ally of Adolf Hitler, a liaison for which the majority of *Il Duce*'s fellow-countrymen showed little enthusiasm, although, as patriots, they were prepared to carry out their duties as directed by the Government whatever their personal feelings.

The 1st Light Flotilla wasted no time in flexing its muscles and within two months of entering the war the High Command had approved plans for an attack on the British fleet base at Alexandria using four of the SCL human-torpedoes. The *Maiali* were ferried across the Mediterranean aboard the torpedo-boat *Calipso* which rendezvoused with the submarine *Iride*, a specially adapted mother-ship, in the Gulf of Bomba to the west of Tobruk on 21 August. The four human torpedoes were transferred during the morning and several of the *Maiali* operators, including de la Penne and his diver Sergeant Lazzaroni who made up the reserve crew for the operation, remained on board the *Calipso* while *Iride* weighed anchor and headed seawards to carry out submersion tests.

Suddenly and without warning three Swordfish aircraft from the British carrier *Eagle* roared over the sandhills fringing the shore. One launched a torpedo against the submarine while its two companions raked the vessel's deck with their machine guns. Lieutenant Brunetti, *Iride*'s skipper, returned fire with his AA weapons, but as the boat was in shallow inshore waters it was impossible to escape by diving. The torpedo struck the submarine forward of the conning-tower and the explosion virtually tore the unfortunate *Iride* in half. Two men were killed by machine-gun fire while more perished in the shattered wreckage of the forward section, but, by a miracle, fourteen crew-members who had been on deck at the time of the attack managed to swim to the surface. The submarine was lying in only 30 feet of water and, as *Calipso* nosed slowly through the débris picking up the swimmers, the *Maiali* operators stripped off their clothes and dived into the sea to search for other survivors.

De la Penne heard the muffled shouts of the men trapped in the undamaged stern section and, after going back to the torpedo-boat for masks and breathing gear, he and other members of the SCL team returned to the seabed again. Tapping signals were exchanged with the nine imprisoned men but inspection of the submarine's hull showed that the engine-room hatch, the only means of escape, had been distorted by the explosion and could not be opened.

At first light the next morning a steel cable was attached to the hatch cover but when it was finally forced open the two men trapped inside the flooded compartment were found to be dead. Seven survivors remained alive further aft, however, but the only way to get them out was through the bulkhead door, and this could only be unclipped from *inside* the compartment. Instructions were passed to the prisoners to unfasten the watertight door but, like the men on the *Seal*, the survivors were too befuddled by carbon dioxide poisoning to grasp what they were supposed to do. De la Penne and the other divers were powerless to help while the vital door remained shut and, in desperation, they warned the trapped men that they would abandon the rescue operation if the door was not opened within the next thirty minutes. It was a brutally harsh ultimatum but the rescuers had no alternative. They could only hope that the bluntness of the threat would penetrate the confused brains of the imprisoned submariners and prod them into action.

The thirty-minute time limit had almost expired when a sudden rush of air bubbles erupted on the surface and, moments later, the first man to escape from the sunken submarine appeared in the maelstrom of seething white water. The *Maiali* operators immediately dived into the sea to help the remaining survivors and, ignoring the danger, de la Penne actually entered the flooded submarine through the bulkhead hatchway. Inside, and up to their neck in water, he found the last two terrified members of the *Iride*'s crew and, helped by the other divers, he dragged them to safety. It had been a gallant effort by the men of the Special Weapon's Group and each member of the *Maiali* team was awarded Italy's prestigious Silver Medal for bravery.

Just a month after these dramatic events had taken place, de la Penne and other members of the Group set off in the submarine *Scire* to make a human-torpedo attack on Gibraltar. Leaving La Spezia on 24 September they arrived off the Rock on the 29th but, to their disappointment, they were recalled when Intelligence reports indicated that the British Fleet had sailed and the harbour was empty.

The impatience of the *Maiali* crews to get to grips with the enemy is apparent from the fact that the *Scire* left Spezia again for a second strike at Gibraltar on 21 October, less than three weeks after their return from the aborted mission at the end of September. This time no recall signal was received and, having carefully reconnoitred the scene, Prince Borghese, the submarine's captain, decided to enter the Bay of Algeciras submerged and to release the assault crews and their weapons off the mouth of the Guadarranque River where the current would help the *Maiali* pilots to reach the harbour.

Getting inside the Bay proved to be a hazardous business for it was still daylight when the submarine made its first approach and shoals and sandbanks added to Borghese's pilotage problems. Indeed, at one point, the current proved to be so powerful that *Scire* had to move crabwise up the Bay with her bows angled at some 40° in order to maintain her calculated course. As an additional hazard, British motor-launches were patrolling inshore, but, by a miracle, they failed to detect the submerged submarine despite the shallowness of the water, often no more than 50 feet in depth.

The submarine reached the launch point at 1.30 am on 30 October and Borghese briefed the *Maiali* crews in the control room: Birindelli was to attack the nearest battleship while Tesei was assigned the second which was anchored further inside the harbour. De la Penne and his diver, Bianchi, were to search for cruisers or aircraft carriers but, if none were found, they were to use their charge against Tesei's target – the second battleship. Half an hour later, at 2 am, *Scire* surfaced briefly to allow the three crews to get into the water and she then submerged as the men mounted and started their underwater craft.

But Fate seemed to be conspiring against them. De la Penne encountered an early setback when his compass failed and then, twenty minutes after launch, a British anti-submarine motor-boat equipped with a powerful searchlight spotted his machine and he was forced to submerge to 45 feet. A depth-charge exploded in the distance and, almost immediately, the motor stopped. Losing buoyancy, the *Maiale* began sinking until, 130 feet down, the machine grounded gently on the seabed. The situation was verging on the desperate for the pressure of the sea was already beginning to crush the thin-skinned *Maiale* which had never been designed to operate at such depths. When the compressed air in the surfacing tank failed to restore buoyancy de la Penne decided to abandon the machine on the bottom.

His companion, Bianchi, was already waiting for him when he finally broke surface and, discarding their breathing gear, they swam some two miles to the Spanish shore where they removed and buried their diving suits before setting off to find the Agent

174

who was responsible for their escape through Spain and back to Italy. The second crew, Tesei and Pedretti, had trouble with their breathing equipment and they, too, were forced to abort the mission. The flood valve of the *Maiale* was opened and the weapon released southwards to sink. Coming ashore near La Linea at 7.10 am, Tesei and Pedretti also managed to find the Agent and, together with de la Penne and Bianchi, they returned safely to Italy by a secret pre-planned route – an almost unbelievable end to an eventful mission. The third team, Birindelli and Paccagnini, also suffered technical problems with their 'Pig' and their breathing-sets. They actually reached the *Barham* but for various reasons Birindelli was forced to clamp the explosive charge to the boom of the net defences instead of to the keel of the battleship. Then, abandoning the *Maiale*, he attempted to swim to Spain but was taken prisoner by the British, as was his diver Paccagnini. The operation thus ended without any worthwhile success, mainly due to technical faults in both the *Maiali* and the breathing equipment. The Italians were perhaps lucky to have recovered four out of the six frogmen who had set out on the mission.

De la Penne did not participate in the next two operations against Gibraltar in the second of which Gamma Group sank the tankers *Fiona Shell* (2,444-tons) *Denby Dale* (15,983-tons) and a smaller unidentified vessel. The 10,900-ton motor-ship *Durham* was also badly damaged and had to be beached with the aid of tugs. As an added bonus all six operators reached the Spanish shore and returned safely home to Italy in due course.

The sinking of the *Barham* by von Tiesenhausen's *U-331* on 25 November, 1941, reduced Cunningham's fleet to just two battle-ships and, in an attempt to destroy the final vestiges of British sea power in the Eastern Mediterranean, the Italian High Command decided to launch a human-torpedo attack on the Royal Navy's base at Alexandria under the code name *Operation EA-3*. The submarine *Scire* was again selected to carry out the mission and Luigi de la Penne, by now a seasoned veteran, was chosen to lead the three *Maiali* that were to make the assault.

Operation EA-3 was planned with meticulous attention to detail and special attention was given to the accuracy of the charts, the reliability of the meterological reports and radio communications. Air reconnaisance patrols maintained a regular check on the number and types of ships anchored in the harbour and *Regia Aeronautica* bombers were ordered to carry out a diversionary raid while the *Maiali* were being launched. Although the *Scire* was instructed to return to Italy immediately she had disembarked the human torpedoes, another submarine, the *Zaffiro*, was sent to lie off Rosetta to pick up the crews after the attack, for, operating inside enemy territory, the survivors could no longer rely on the blind eye of a friendly neutral to provide cover for an overland escape route. As a final touch, incendiary devices were to be scattered on the water to ignite fuel leaking from the ruptured bunkers of the sinking ships.

The strictest secrecy was observed and, as an additional deception, when the *Scire* left La Spezia on 3 December her pressurised deck cylinders which were normally used to transport the human torpedoes were empty, the three *Maiali* being trans-shipped from a naval lighter at sea. Six days later the submarine, with its deadly cargo, reached Port Lago on the island of Leros and on the 12th the crews for the underwater assault craft arrived by air: Luigi de la Penne and Emilio Bianchi, the diver who had been with him on the Gibraltar raid, Antonio Marceglia and his diver Spartaco Schergat, plus Vincenzo Martellotta and Mario Marino. Spaccarelli and Feltrinelli were embarked as the spare crew.

Together with Borghese, the captain of the *Scire* and by now an old-hand at such clandestine missions, the group studied the latest Intelligence reports and aerial photographs of the harbour as they finalized their plans. It had been decided to make the attack on the evening of the 17th but weather conditions deteriorated and Borghese, who had overall tactical control, wisely postponed the operation until the following evening.

Scire remained submerged throughout the daylight hours of the 18th and, as soon as it was dark, the submarine came to the surface. The doors of the storage cylinders were opened and the assault teams, led by de la Penne, climbed out on deck via the hatch and *Scire* slipped quietly beneath the waves again as they mounted their weapons and started up the motors. The time was just after 6.40 pm, weather conditions were calm and they were close enough to the shore for visual navigation. With the *Maiali* trimmed down and with only their masked heads showing above water, the six frogmen steered south-westwards for the harbour entrance.

First, however, de la Penne and his team had to negotiate a line of explosive obstacles that stretched roughly north-south from the shore batteries. But the obstruction presented few problems and within minutes all three of the 'Pigs' were safely through. As the operational time-table had allowed for a delay in passing through this barrier, the Italians were now ahead of schedule and, with almost unbelievable nonchalance, de la Penne decided to open his ration pack and have something to eat. At that moment the assault group was only 500 yards from the Ras el Tin lighthouse!

The boom and net defences guarding the entrance to the

harbour were reached at midnight and, conscious that the Italians might attempt some form of underwater attack, an armed motor-launch was patrolling off the pier dropping small depth-charges at regular intervals. It was an effective means of protection and similar methods of defence remain in use today when ships are anchored in vulnerable harbours. As de la Penne observed, the depth-charges 'were rather a nuisance to us'.

But all their carefully laid plans for breaching the defences were joyfully discarded when three British destroyers arrived un-expectedly off the entrance and, in response to a series of brief light signals, the gate of the boom swung open to admit them. Seizing the opportunity, de la Penne tucked in behind the enemy ships and slipped into the harbour unobserved, with Marceglia and Martellotta following astern. The great adventure had begun. The British Mediterranean Fleet was at their mercy!

De la Penne's target was the 32,700 ton battleship *Valiant*, a veteran from the 5th Battle Squadron at Jutland whose eight 15-inch guns and heavy armour still placed her among the ranks of the most powerful warships in the world. Moving past the huddled shapes of the demilitarized French squadron, impotent hostages to fortune since the collapse of France in 1940, he steered for the massive bulk of his target. His rubberized diving suit had been leaking ever since the *Maiale* had been launched and the chill of the water was insidiously sapping his strength. But he pressed on and, reaching the battleship's anti-torpedo-net barrier, he wriggled his way through it and at 2.19 am bumped softly against *Valiant*'s armour-plated beam.

Flooding the buoyancy tank, he submerged the *Maiale* so that he could manoeuvre the machine underneath the battleship's keel but the valve failed to shut off properly and the 'Pig' went to the bottom in sixty feet of water. To make matters worse, Bianchi was no longer riding pillion on the back seat and de la Penne rose to the surface to look for him. But the sea was empty and, unable to see his companion, the Lieutenant returned to the harbour bottom. Next he tried to start the motor and steer the *Maiale* under the battleship but a steel cable had fouled the propeller and, with unimaginable determination, he set to work to haul the heavy explosive charge underneath the target. The soft mud made movement an effort and the disturbed sediment swirled upwards to create an impenetrable underwater fog. Despite the cold water slowly flooding his wet-suit de la Penne was sweating with exertion as he strained to drag the heavy charge towards its goal. Unable to see, he relied on the noise of the *Valiant*'s suction pump for direction. Finally, after forty minutes of effort, he had dragged the

177

warhead to a point roughly amidships of his target and some ten feet beneath the battleship's vulnerable unarmoured underbelly. Having activated the time-fuse for six o'clock local time, he kicked himself to the surface with his flippered feet, removed his breathing mask and began swimming slowly away from his victim.

But a watchful sentry on the battleship's deck spotted him and shouted a challenge. A searchlight glared out of the darkness and, more ominously, a burst of machine-gun fire splattered the water yards from his head. De la Penne raised an arm to acknowledge his submission and swam across to the large mooring buoy at the battleship's bows. As he hauled himself up onto the rusting cylinder he was surprised to find the exhausted Bianchi sheltering in its lee. The diver, who had floated to the surface after fainting, explained that he had hidden behind the buoy in case a sentry on the deck of the battleship had spotted him and raised the alarm.

A motor-boat appeared out of the night and, judging by the jeering comments of its crew as they dragged the two Italians to safety, the enemy was clearly of the opinion that the attack had failed. De la Penne smiled to himself and said nothing. The British were in for a nasty surprise. He glanced down at his wristwatch. The time was 3.30. There was not long to wait.

The two Italians were initially taken to the *Valiant* but within minutes they had been bundled back into the motor-boat and were on their way to the shore for interrogation by Intelligence experts. They landed near the lighthouse at Ras el Tin where they were marched to separate huts for questioning, but neither de la Penne nor Bianchi would reveal anything beyond their names, ranks and numbers and, for the moment, there was something of an *impasse*. It was clear that an attack on the fleet was taking place but no one in authority could decide what to do next.

News of the prisoners reached Sir Andrew Cunningham aboard his flagship *Queen Elizabeth* at 4 am and the British C-in-C acted with ruthless expediency. Suspecting that the Italians had planted some form of delayed-action device on or near *Valiant* and that other enemy underwater units were operating inside the harbour, Cunningham was desperate for information. With the two Italians refusing to co-operate, intimidation seemed the only solution. In the Admiral's own words: 'I at once ordered them to be brought back to the *Valiant* and confined in one of the forward compartments well below the waterline.'* By deliberately putting the lives of the prisoners at risk in order to obtain information Sir Andrew was acting in defiance of the Geneva Convention.† But the Admiral

* *A Sailor's Odyssey* Page 433.
† See Oppenheim's *International Law* (Longmans, Green & Co) 7th Edition, Vol II, page 378: 'But no physical or mental torture or any other form of coercion may be inflicted on prisoners to compel them to give information.'

was understandably more concerned with the safety of his fleet than the fine print of International Law.

De la Penne and his diver were therefore taken back to the *Valiant* where they were placed in a store-room deep down in the bowels of the ship and, by coincidence, uncomfortably close to the explosive charge. The two frogmen, however, continued to maintain their silence until finally, ten minutes before the charge was due to detonate, de la Penne asked to speak to the battleship's Commanding Officer, Captain Morgan. On being taken aft under guard the young Italian warned Morgan that the vessel would be blown up within the next few minutes, but he stoutly refused to give any further information and, even while the loudspeakers were braying orders for the crew to abandon ship, de la Penne was returned to his dank and dangerous prison.

Shortly before 6.15 am the *Valiant* shuddered under a mighty explosion. Smoke filled the interior and the lights went out. With the sea pouring through a gaping hole in its keel plating the great battleship listed slowly to port and settled on the bottom – crippled and useless. De la Penne was lucky to escape with his life and he fortunately suffered no more than a graze when some chain shackles fell from the deckhead. His guards hurriedly unlocked the door and he arrived on deck just in time to see the *Queen Elizabeth*, Cunningham's flagship and his only other battleship in the Eastern Mediterranean, suffer the same fate as her sister when the charge left by Marceglia and Schergat detonated. Minutes later the tanker *Sagona* fell victim to Martellotta and Marino, the crew of the third *Maiale*. It was a devastating blow to British sea-power in the Mediterranean and an elaborate bluff was sustained for months in an attempt to persuade the Italians that the ships were not seriously damaged. The ceremony of The Colours was observed every day with traditional ritual and a false waterline was painted around the *Queen Elizabeth*'s waist to conceal the fact that she was excessively low in the water. Incredibly, Britain continued to exercise command of the Eastern Mediterranean with two battleships that were too severely damaged to go to sea!

Martellotta and Marino succeeded in reaching the shore after the attack but were arrested as they attempted to pass through the dockyard gates. Marceglia and Schergat, however, gave the authorities a run for their money. They, too, landed in the dockyard but, avoiding the guards, made their way into Alexandria where they caught a train to Rosetta and stayed at a hotel to await the arrival of the other two crews before making their rendezvous with the submarine *Zaffiro* which was lying off-shore in accordance with the original plan. They were finally arrested at 3 pm on the 23rd, six days after the raid. The *Maiali* crews were obviously just as enterprising on land as they were at sea!

With typical understatement Admiral Cunningham's reference to the incident in his autobiography begins: 'Meanwhile something very unpleasant had happened at Alexandria.' And, fair-minded as always, he concluded his account of the raid: 'One cannot but admire the cold-blooded bravery and enterprise of these Italians.'

There was also little doubt as to Churchill's feelings. In a memorandum to Lord Ismay of the Chiefs of Staff Committee which he dictated on 18 January, 1942, exactly a month after de la Penne's assault, he wrote, 'Please report what is being done to emulate the exploits of the Italians in Alexandria harbour and similar methods of this kind.'

* * *

The downfall of Mussolini led to Italy's surrender on 3 September, 1943, and before many months had passed the Italians were fighting side-by-side with the Allies against the common enemy of Nazism.

On his release from prison camp de la Penne resumed his specialist duties with the Italian Navy and in June, 1944, he became involved in a British plan to attack two ex-Italian cruisers which the Germans had seized and which they apparently intended to use as blockships at La Spezia, the former base of the *Maiali* units. *Operation QWZ* was conceived and executed as a joint venture using two of the Royal Navy's chariots* together with three Italian assault swimmers from the famous Gamma Group equipped with limpet mines who were to make a subsidiary attack on the submarine base at Muggiano.

The operation, which took place on 21 June, proved very successful and resulted in the destruction of the *Bolzano*, the last Italian heavy cruiser to remain in German hands, while the assault swimmers also achieved their objective by planting explosive charges on one of the U-boats in Muggiano. Commander P. E. H. Heathfield of the Royal Navy was in overall charge of the striking force with particular responsibility for the chariots and the attack on La Spezia. His opposite number, in charge of the assault swimmers and the raid on Muggiano, was an officer of the Italian Navy. Who else but Luigi de la Penne?

In March, 1945, Italy's premier *Maiale* pilot finally received the *Medaglio d'Oro*, the Italian equivalent of the Victoria Cross or the Congressional Medal of Honor, for his part in the raid on

---

*Human torpedoes very similar in design to the *Maiale*

Alexandria three years earlier. The Prince of Piedmont attended the ceremonial parade at Taranto to present the decoration but, at the last moment, as the recipient stepped forward and saluted, he asked a British Admiral standing at his side to help him pin the gold cross on to the breast of de la Penne's dark blue uniform, a request that was willingly accepted. The Admiral's name was Sir Charles Morgan. On the night of 18 September, 1941, he had been plain Captain Morgan, the Commanding Officer of the battleship *Valiant*.

—FOURTEEN—

Commander Dudley W. Morton, USN

'Destroyer gunning – Wahoo running.'

The *USS Wahoo* produced at least four of the Navy's finest submarine captains in the course of her tragically brief career. Lt-Cdr 'Mush' Morton, her second skipper, gained immortality as one of America's greatest exponents of underwater warfare. So, too, did her one-time Executive Officer, Dick O'Kane, who scaled the heights of heroism in the equally gallant *Tang*.* In addition her former Third Officer, George Grider, later famous for his exploits in command of *Flasher*, and Fourth Officer Roger Paine, who went on to captain the *Stingray*, were both to carve formidable reputations for themselves during the final months of conflict in the Pacific.

Wahoo, a member of the *Gato* class, was designed before the outbreak of war, although she was not, in fact, completed and accepted into service until the early months of 1942. Built by the Mare Island Navy Yard, New York, and officially numbered *SS-238*, she displaced 2,424 tons submerged and, like her class-sister *Harder*†, mounted a 5-inch 50-calibre deck gun and ten 21-inch torpedo tubes. *Haddo, Flasher, Trigger* and Gilmore's *Growler* were other prominent members of this superb class of submarines which, with the *Balbao*-class boats, a deep-diving variant of the *Gato* design, shared the main burden of the underwater war against Japan. They did so with unusual gallantry and distinction.

* See Chapter 18
† See Chapter 16

After some six months of intensive training *Wahoo* left her temporary base at San Diego and set course westwards for Pearl Harbor under the command of her first captain, Lt-Cdr Marvin Kennedy. She arrived in Hawaii at the beginning of August, 1942, but left almost immediately for an anti-shipping operation in the waters around Truk. Although she sank a Japanese freighter, the patrol proved to be a far from encouraging opening to her career. On the twelfth day of her mission she attacked and missed an enemy merchantman and, a week later, sighted another hull-down on the horizon but too far away to intercept.

But these failures were, in many ways, the least of Kennedy's worries. On the thirty-first day of the patrol a member of the crew, carrying out routine tests in the forward torpedo room, pulled the wrong lever and fired No 6 ready-use torpedo while the outer door of the tube was still shut. The safety mechanism prevented an explosion but inspection showed that the door had sprung and that the warhead of the torpedo was jammed in the narrow opening with the main body of the weapon still lodged inboard. It was impossible to say whether the safety device – a spinner on a threaded spindle which only released the firing pistol after the weapon had travelled some 400 yards through the water – was still in position and, as an added complication, the firing mechanism of this particular model could also be triggered by magnetic influence. A jammed torpedo is hardly the friendliest of companions to sail with but, despite strenuous efforts to free it, the weapon refused to budge and *Wahoo*'s crew were forced to live with the threat of instant destruction hanging over their heads for the rest of the patrol.

Shortly after this mishap the bow buoyancy vent jammed in the shut position, a malfunction which effectively prevented the submarine from diving. Repairs were put in hand immediately but the fault proved too serious to be rectified at sea and the engineers had to rig a makeshift alternative to enable the submarine to dive in an emergency although, as they readily admitted, returning the boat to the surface in such circumstances posed an even greater problem. Finally, and probably the most bitter pill of all, *Wahoo* encountered the seaplane carrier *Chiyoda* and the carrier *Ryujo* towards the end of the patrol, but the range of the enemy ships was too great and they were moving too quickly for an attack to be made. It was a galling disappointment and both officers and men were thoroughly dejected by the time they reached Pearl Harbor on 17 October.

When the *Wahoo* set out on her next mission she was carrying a passenger, Lt-Cdr Dudley Morton. Morton, a Kentucky-born

183

career officer, was known throughout the submarine service as 'Mush', short for mushroom, a nickname bestowed upon him for his drawling Southern accent and his skill at telling improbable stories. Morton had come from the Atlantic where he had been in command of an old R-class boat, but he had seen virtually no combat and on the only occasion when he encountered an enemy U-boat the veteran submarine had proved to be too slow to reach an attacking position and the German vessel had escaped. He was, however, now the captain-designate of the *Wahoo* and was accompanying Kennedy on a routine patrol so that he could familiarize himself with both the submarine and the different operational conditions in the Pacific.

Although he had no specific duties to carry out, Morton's happy-go-lucky presence quickly renewed confidence and raised spirits. And more importantly he also brought the submarine that most essential ingredient for success, good luck. For on her second war patrol *Wahoo* sank a freighter, survived a counter-attack with forty depth-charges and sank a surfaced Japanese submarine, a record sufficient to satisfy any captain. It was a joyful crew that brought her back to Brisbane, Australia, on Boxing Day, 1942, just in time to enjoy the tail-end of the Christmas festivities.

Morton was formally appointed in command on 1 January, 1943, and it was quickly apparent to the officers and crew that Mush was no ordinary captain. 'Built like a bear and as playful as a cub' was George Grider's description of his new Commanding Officer. The silhouettes and recognition photographs of Japanese warships and aircraft that had adorned *Wahoo*'s deckhead and bulkheads were stripped away to be replaced by wholesome, if saucy, pin-up pictures, a change warmly welcomed by the enlisted men. Jokes and laughter became commonplace in the wardroom and mess-spaces alike and Mush was constantly moving around the boat chatting to, and getting to know, his crew. The men loved him and, as Grider wrote later, they were ready and eager to follow him anywhere.

Wahoo's third patrol – and her first with Morton in the driving seat – began when she left Brisbane on 16 January. Although the submarine's combat orders were to seek out and destroy the enemy in the traditional manner, Morton's instructions initially required him to carry out a reconnaissance of the Japanese anchorage at Wewak on the northern coast of New Guinea. This sounded a reasonable assignment except for two difficulties: firstly Wewak was not marked on the Navy charts issued to the submarine and no one seemed to know its exact location. Secondly, Morton had his own idea about the meaning of reconnaissance. In the considered opinion of the wardroom officers their orders meant taking 'a cautious look at the area, from far out to sea, through the periscope, submerged'. But that did not match up with Morton's aggressive conception of the task. 'Hell no,' he told them, 'the only way you can reconnoitre a harbour is to go right inside it and see what's there.' Even with detailed large-scale charts available, it was a somewhat impetuous interpretation of the orders he had been given by the Flotilla Staff before leaving Brisbane. Without charts of any description and lacking the most rudimentary navigational information about the anchorage, it was little short of suicidal.

The first step, however, was to locate Wewak. Once again luck came to Morton's aid in the shape of a Motor Machinist's Mate who had bought a High School atlas while ashore in Australia. Browsing through its pages while off-duty, he was surprised to find Wewak marked on a map of New Guinea. He immediately showed it to an officer and with the assistance of Grider's Graflex camera the vital map was enlarged to match the scale of the official charts and the relevant details were sketched in on the blank spaces. But although they now knew Wewak's approximate position they still had little precise knowledge of the anchorage itself, especially the depth of water both inside and outside the reef. But Morton was unconcerned about what he termed 'minor details', and, without further ado, *Wahoo* altered course for that vague dot on a schoolboy's highly coloured and probably highly inaccurate map.

The submarine reached the entrance to the anchorage on 24 January and, running submerged, headed for the channel between the two islands that guarded the harbour. With razor-sharp coral only a few fathoms beneath the keel, Morton pushed down the 9-mile dog-leg passage that led to the inner harbour. With character-istic aplomb he remained in the control room and left his Executive Officer, Dick O'Kane, at the periscope in the conning-tower with instructions to pilot the *Wahoo* through the narrow unmarked channel. It was a nerve-wracking experience for a young Lieut-enant but the responsibility Mush had thrust upon O'Kane no doubt served to increase his self-confidence. This ability to rely on his own judgement was to stand him in good stead when, on Morton's recommendation, he was given command of his own boat.

O'Kane kept up a running commentary as the submarine penetrated deeper into the harbour and the leading marks he reported were noted on the chart, together with the varying depth of water in the main channel as revealed by the submarine's echo sounder. But the harbour proved to be empty of worthwhile targets and the only boats in sight were a tug and two patrol launches, none large enough to merit a torpedo. At around noon O'Kane saw the masts of a large ship rising above the palm trees, but investigation revealed that a reef prevented *Wahoo* from getting in close enough. Running the motors in reverse, he backed the submarine into the main channel and pushed ahead once again. Rigged for silent running and with her crew closed up at Submerged Battle Stations, *Wahoo* rounded the tip of the reef and edged towards her target. When the range had closed to 6,000 yards, Morton passed an order for the bow tubes to stand by, but the next time O'Kane raised the periscope the situation had changed dramatically. The enemy ship, a destroyer, had apparently spotted the submarine in the crystal-clear waters of the lagoon and was already steering out to sea.

Morton swung *Wahoo* to starboard, hoping to fire his stern tubes but at the next periscope check O'Kane reported that the target had turned with them and was now moving across the submarine's bows. With the range down to 3,000 yards Morton fired three torpedoes but they all ran astern of the enemy vessel, which was obviously moving faster than he had estimated. The target speed was up-rated on the Torpedo Data Computer and a fourth weapon shot from its tube seconds later. This, too, missed and, with the destroyer now heading straight at the submarine and clearly intent on ramming, the situation was becoming dangerous. Another torpedo, fired 'down the throat' at 1,800 yards, ran wide of the target and the destroyer's sharp steel bows hurtled towards them at flank speed. O'Kane stood his ground at the periscope and mentally measured off the divisions – a series of graticule lines etched on the lens – which were used to estimate range.

'When do I fire, sir?' he asked Morton.

'When it fills four divisions,' Mush replied casually.

'It's already filling eight!'

'Goddam it! What are you waiting for? *Fire!*'

O'Kane's thumb pressed the firing button and, as the torpedo streaked from the tube, he pushed *Wahoo* down into a steep dive in anticipation of an immediate depth-charge attack. But apart from a single heavy explosion nothing else happened. Mush raised his eyebrows and looked at O'Kane. Surely they couldn't have been *that* lucky? Morton decided to find out for himself and he ordered his Executive Officer to take the submarine back to periscope depth. As the top lens emerged above the surface he found the destroyer and carefully focused his eye-piece. The enemy ship had broken into two halves and the bow section was already sinking. Japanese sailors were scrambling wildly in all directions but the

186

sight of the submarine's periscope column breaking surface restored discipline in an instant. Seizing this unexpected chance to hit back, they ran to their battle stations and turned the guns on *Wahoo*. Their own lives counted for nothing. If they were to die for the Emperor they would, at least, take the enemy with them. They were still serving their weapons as the two halves of the destroyer vanished from sight. Not a single man survived.

Two days later, on 26 January, Morton fought one of the most determined battles against an enemy convoy ever recorded in the history of submarine warfare. He did not sink as many ships as Otto Kretschmer had done during his famous attack on SC-7 in October, 1940. Neither did he come near to beating the score set up by O'Kane and *Tang* some four years later. But few other commanders have ever demonstrated such single-minded perseverance in pursuit of an objective.

On leaving Wewak, Morton steered a north-westerly course towards the main Japanese supply route from Palau to the Bismarck Sea – the staging area for the ships shuttling stores, ammunition, and troops to Guadalcanal and New Guinea. With typical high-spirits, and taking a few hours out from the grim reality of war, he insisted on observing the time-honoured ceremony of Crossing the Line when *Wahoo* reached the Equator. He wisely left the detailed arrangements to Chief Torpedoman Russell Rau and with due dignity and ritual the unfortunate Polliwogs were subjected to the traditional humiliations. As Third Officer George Grider soon discovered, not even wardroom rank could offer protection from the indignities of King Neptune's Court.

Soon after breakfast the following day, 26 January, the bridge lookouts sighted smoke on the horizon. It was a fine clear morning with a calm sea and excellent visibility and, disdaining to submerge, Morton steered towards the smoke until he was able to identify the masts of two freighters moving in an easterly direction. Speeding ahead of his targets he worked *Wahoo* into a good attack position and then submerged to await his unsuspecting prey. It all seemed ludicrously easy. The cargo ships were only steaming at 10 knots and they were holding a straight course with no attempt to zig-zag. The officers gathered on the submarine's bridge concluded that the two vessels were probably loitering in the area in order to rendezvous with an escort destroyer before proceeding to New Guinea or the Solomons. It occurred to several of them that the ship for which they were waiting was the destroyer that *Wahoo* had sent to the bottom two days earlier at Wewak.

But despite these tactical advantages the attack started badly.

Morton planned to launch his torpedoes at 1,000 yards – virtually point-blank range – firing the three starboard tubes at the leading vessel and the three port tubes at the other. But a wrong estimation of target speed found *Wahoo* too close to the oncoming ships at the crucial moment and Mush had to swing the submarine rapidly away and deploy for an alternative line of attack. The change in plan meant using the stern tubes and this would result in firing only four torpedoes instead of six – a one-third reduction in their chances of obtaining a hit. But Morton had little choice as the alternative would mean withdrawing and starting the attack all over again.

'Fire'

All four tin-fish hissed from the stern and, after a brief interval, the hydrophone operator confirmed that they were running. O'Kane watched the bubbling white tracks of the torpedoes through the periscope and a tense silence fell over the control room as Morton and the attack team waited anxiously for the sound of success. Their eyes were fixed on the hands of the brass-rimmed clock on the bulkhead and their lips moved soundlessly as they counted off the seconds.

The echoing boom of the first explosion was clearly audible inside the submarine and Morton's frowning concentration dissolved into a broad grin as O'Kane took up a running commentary of the events on the surface.

'Nice shooting! We've hit her smack bang in the bows. Plenty of smoke and steam. Where's Number Two?' The attack team slapped each other on the back as they heard the rumble of another underwater explosion. 'Same target – in the stern. This baby sure won't be with us much longer.' There was a pause as O'Kane moved the periscope and searched to the right. 'Sorry, guys, looks like Number Three's missed. Must have run astern. I can see another track . . . its going for the second boat. It's a hit! It's a hit with Number Four!'

The periscope slid down as *Wahoo* began to turn. With her stern tubes empty Morton was reversing the course of the submarine through a full 180° to bring the bow torpedo room into action. Four minutes later, as *Wahoo* steadied on to her new bearing, the periscope poked up above the surface again. The leading ship was listing to port and sinking by the stern and O'Kane concentrated his attention on the other vessel. Despite the torpedo hit the second ship was steering towards the submerged submarine and, anxious to dispose of her before she posed a threat, O'Kane passed the necessary attack data to the TDC operator.

'Bearing – *mark*! She's coming right at us but she's going slow.

188

Hell, there's another son-of-a-bitch. Bearing – *mark*! Angle on the bow ninety starboard! Range eighteen hundred!'

A *third* ship? Surely not. Perhaps O'Kane had got it wrong. But Mush didn't think so. He had implicit faith in his Exec and, on the basis of the periscope information, he quickly formulated another plan.

'It's a big one,' O'Kane reported. 'Could be a transport.'

'Okay, Dick – let's get him!'

The TDC had already given the deflection angle for the new target and, as the settings were passed to the forward torpedo-room, the green lights on the firing panel in the control room sparkled to life one by one.

'Green all the way.'

'Stand-by Bow One, Two and Three. *Fire*!'

Once again there was the inevitable gut-gnawing eternity of anticipation as the weapons thrashed towards their target at 45 knots. A double explosion confirmed two hits. But despite this new success *Wahoo* was standing into danger.

'That other guy's still coming at us – slow but sure. Down the throat, sir?'

'Down the throat, Dick,' Morton confirmed.

O'Kane passed a new set of bearings, ranges and speeds to Roger Paine at the TDC and the machine whirred and clicked as it digested the information.

'Solution!'

'Stand-by Bow Four and Five. *Fire*!'

This time one torpedo struck home and the other missed. Undeterred, the captain of the Japanese freighter kept on coming. It was obvious that he intended to ram the submarine or die in the attempt.

'Take her down. Depth 100 feet! Full left rudder!'

Wahoo turned aside and plunged to safety as the crippled cargo ship rumbled overhead.

'Reload bow tubes!'

When Otto Weddigen first began training *U-9*'s crew to reload the torpedo tubes while submerged in 1914 many officers regarded the exercise as an evolution rather than a practical drill. But by 1943 it had become a regular part of a submarine's combat routine. The gleaming steel cigars, each weighing some 1½ tons, were swung down from their storage racks and brawny arms thrust them quickly into the empty tubes, pushed them tight up against the locking pins, then shut and dogged the inboard loading doors before flooding the tubes ready for firing. It was tough work. But *Wahoo*'s torpedomen were veterans.

'Five tubes loaded, sir. Number Six empty.'

The submarine had expended half of her outfit of weapons already. She was running short of hardware. Morton shrugged. That meant he could not afford any more wasted shots. The loading routine had taken exactly eight minutes – a time that would have undoubtedly impressed Weddigen – and, ready for action once again, *Wahoo* returned cautiously to periscope depth. The first ship had by now sunk while the second, their erstwhile attacker, was limping slowly from the scene on an erratic course which suggested that torpedo damage to her rudder was causing serious steering problems. The third vessel, now positively identified as a troop transport, was lying stopped in the water although she seemed in no immediate danger of sinking. O'Kane relayed his observations to Morton who responded with enthusiasm.

'Let's finish off the bum!'

Having made his decision, Mush now concentrated on bringing *Wahoo* into a favourable position for delivery of the fatal shot, but the troops lining the decks of the transport did not intend to go down without a fight and a hail of rifle and machine-gun bullets greeted the submarine's periscope each time the upper lens broke surface. Undeterred, *Wahoo* closed to 1,000 yards and fired a single torpedo. It should have been an easy kill. The target was stationary and the range was virtually point-blank. But torpedoes can be contrary beasts and this particular one turned out to be a dud. Although it struck the transport fair and square it failed to explode.

Morton told O'Kane to fire another. The next torpedo performed to perfection and the Executive Officer watched it streak towards its target. The crash of the exploding warhead echoed through the submerged submarine like the rumble of distant thunder.

'There she goes!' O'Kane shouted. 'The son-of-a-bitch – what a hit!'

There was good reason for his jubilation. The torpedo had struck the transport directly beneath her solitary funnel and a column of smoke and flame rose high into the air. Moments later the vessel rolled violently and the Japanese soldiers lining the decks tumbled over her canted side in a wild effort to escape from the sinking ship. Less than a minute after the torpedo had struck the transport's stern lifted and she slid to the bottom bows-first leaving several hundred men swimming in the water. O'Kane could see the terror in their faces through the high-magnification lens and their fear was understandable. In these shark-infested waters their chances of survival were precisely nil.

Having paused while Grider took a series of periscope photographs as evidence of their success Morton set off in pursuit of the

190

last remaining ship which, despite two torpedo hits and a damaged rudder, was still making a commendable six knots. But with *Wahoo*'s batteries nearly exhausted the Japanese freighter had a clear edge over the submarine's maximum submerged speed and, to Mush's irritation, she was gradually pulling clear. At this moment a fourth vessel appeared somewhat unexpectedly on the horizon. In the excitement she was at first incorrectly identified as a light cruiser but, as she grew nearer, O'Kane realized that she was a tanker. Not quite such a glittering prize as a major warship but still a worthwhile victim. Having steamed to within five miles of the waiting submarine, however, the tanker suddenly altered course and began steering towards the crippled freighter, the change of direction no doubt taking place as the result of an exchange of signals which the submerged *Wahoo* had been unable to intercept.

Thanks to their speed advantage both ships soon melted into the haze of the horizon and Morton brought *Wahoo* to the surface so that he could use the submarine's powerful diesel engines to continue the chase on a more equal footing. He also made use of the opportunity to recharge his depleted batteries. Although the chase had begun at noon it was 3.30 before Morton caught up with his prey and a further two hours elapsed before *Wahoo* had taken up station ahead of the fleeing ships. But even now, with the ambush set, the Japanese still held a number of trump cards. Dusk was due in thirty minutes, both vessels were maintaining a zig-zag course and the submarine was down to her last seven torpedoes.

At 6.30 pm O'Kane fired a salvo of three torpedoes at the tanker and there was a sudden flare of flame in the darkness as one struck the target and exploded. But, despite the damage, the oiler showed no sign of slowing and Morton realized that he would have to come topsides to finish off the fight.

'Surface!'

Wahoo rose upwards in a seething foam of air bubbles as the water ballast was vented from her tanks. Her conning-tower emerged through the cauldron and the Quartermaster reached up to undog the upper hatch.

'Open main induction . . . all ahead flank!'

The guns on the crippled freighter opened fire the moment the submarine broke surface but it was difficult to aim accurately in the darkness and her weapons posed no immediate threat. Morton decided to concentrate on the tanker. Careful observation had revealed that she was steering a predictable and regular zig-zag pattern based on a series of 90° turns. Her damaged but more cunning companion, on the other hand, was following an erratic course that made a successful attack almost impossible. Never-

191

theless an hour and a half passed before *Wahoo* had been jockeyed into a suitable position to administer the *coup de grace* and Morton once again demonstrated his considerable skill as a tactician by placing the submarine in exactly the right place at the right moment. As the oiler turned through 90° to begin the next leg of her zig-zag Morton used full left rudder to bring *Wahoo*'s stern tubes to bear. Two torpedoes cut through the water and everyone kept their fingers crossed as they covered the 1,850 yards to the target. The first weapon missed but the second struck home and, finding a weak point in the hull structure, the tanker broke in two and sank as the warhead detonated.

Morton turned away and once again set off in pursuit of the freighter, a chase that had by now lasted twelve hours. Once again the Japanese deck guns opened fire, this time with disconcerting accuracy. Exploding shells bracketed the submarine and splinters of jagged steel screamed through the darkness. Things were getting unpleasantly hot and Mush wisely took *Wahoo* down to 50 feet until things became quieter. Fifteen minutes later the submarine returned to the surface ready to renew the chase and continue the duel.

A short while later the powerful beam of a warship's searchlight appeared on the horizon and Morton cursed at the thought of losing his prey at such a late stage of the game. But at that moment the Japanese captain made his first and only mistake. Realizing that help was at hand he abandoned his baffling zig-zag pattern and headed straight towards the glare of the distant light.

'Full ahead flank'

Wahoo's four 10-cylinder Fairbanks Morse diesel engines roared to maximum power and Morton, sizing up the situation in a matter of seconds, swept past the freighter in the darkness. Once ahead of his target he turned across its path and submerged. Just three minutes later *Wahoo* fired her last two torpedoes. Both hit the gallantly handled cargo ship and she sank like a stone. The long chase was over. Morton had won. Without torpedoes there was no possibility of attacking the destroyer as it closed the scene to search for survivors so, with the satisfaction of a job well done, the submarine moved quietly away. Although *Wahoo* still had plenty of fuel aboard course was set for an early return to Pearl Harbor. A short while later Morton's combat report was transmitted to Vice Admiral Lockwood, the US Navy's submarine Commander-in-Chief for the Pacific:

In ten-hour running gun and torpedo battle destroyed entire convoy of two freighters, one transport, and one tanker. All torpedoes expended.

Lockwood's reply was typical of the good-humoured camaraderie that welded the Pacific Submarine Force together:

'Come home, Mush. Your picture's on the piano.'

Despite the submarine's lack of torpedoes Morton continued to look for opportunities to strike at the enemy. The very next morning *Wahoo* sighted another convoy. Morton was called to the bridge and, having weighed up the situation, he agreed with the Officer-of-the-Deck, George Grider, that there was little they could do beyond observing the convoy's course and speed and transmitting a shadowing report to other boats in the area.

Morton, however, was chafing at the bit as the convoy slid past his periscope. Suddenly he noticed that the rear ship of the group mounted no defensive deck armament and was steaming more slowly than its companions. Perhaps she was the proverbial lame duck. Mush called his senior officers into the conning-tower to explain his theory. If, he pointed out, *Wahoo* surfaced astern of the rear ship the remaining vessels would probably take fright, pile on speed and get to hell out of it. The lame duck, left behind in the general panic and unable to defend itself, could then be polished off by the submarine's 5-inch deck gun. How, he asked, did they feel about it? His officers shook their heads. Much as they admired Morton's guts, this was one caper too many.

But the Captain had the last word. *Wahoo* broke surface astern of the trailing tanker and, as predicted, the other two ships began steaming hard for the shelter of a rain squall which was visible on the horizon ahead. Mush gave chase more for effect than effectiveness and, as the Japanese vessels ran out of gun range and vanished into the low pressure system, he swung the submarine around and called the gun team to their battle stations as he closed the straggler. The lame duck was about to become a sitting duck. And, with luck, after a few well-placed shells, a dead duck!

In the event Morton's plan was doomed to disappointment. An enemy escort suddenly appeared out of the squall and *Wahoo* was forced to turn away from her intended victim and run for it. Mush, as usual, was wildly optimistic and insisted that the pursuing ship had insufficient speed to catch the submarine. But even with *Wahoo* clocking a record 21 knots, the Japanese vessel was still closing the gap and, coming within range, it veered to one side, brought its guns to bear and opened fire. Morton's 'antiquated coal-burning corvette' was, in fact, a modern and very fast destroyer and Mush's face was a picture of innocent astonishment as the first shells exploded around the submarine.

Wahoo dipped beneath the surface in double-quick time and was already at a safe depth when the counter-attack started. Fortunately the destroyer had no clear idea of where the submarine was lurking and the exploding depth-charges posed no threat. The attack was only a short-lived affair and, anxious to rejoin the convoy, the enemy warship soon lost interest in the hunt and steamed away. *Wahoo* cautiously returned to the surface some while later and, in the radio room, the operator was tapping out Morton's latest action report to Admiral Lockwood:

Another running gun battle today. Destroyer gunning. Wahoo running.

Dudley W. Morton returned to Pearl Harbor in style and, taking inspiration from the 17th Century Dutch Admiral Marten Tromp, *Wahoo* had a brush lashed to her periscope standard as she nosed her way into the submarine basin at the beginning of February – a symbol that she had swept the seas clear of the enemy and a piece of flamboyance much appreciated by her crew.

Wahoo's fourth war patrol took her to the Yellow Sea and deep inside Japanese home waters. It was a dangerous mission but Morton revelled in the wealth of targets and opportunities and by the time he returned to Pearl six weeks later he had sunk eight freighters and a troop transport. The fifth patrol, in April, 1943, yielded three more merchantmen sunk plus another two damaged and confirmed Morton's ranking as one of the US Navy's top submarine commanders.

On her return to Hawaii, and to Morton's annoyance, *Wahoo* was ordered back to the Mare Island Navy Yard at San Francisco for an extensive two-month overhaul. Dick O'Kane was relieved as Executive Officer to take over command of the brand-new *Tang*, in which he was destined to gain a fighting reputation fully equal to that of his mentor,* and George Grider was transferred as second-in-command of the *Pollack*. Roger Paine also left the submarine soon after her return to Hawaii when he was hospitalized with appendicitis. Morton missed his old shipmates. Together they had constituted an unbeatable team. But he did not begrudge them the promotions which they so richly deserved and he realized that in wartime such upheavals were inevitable. He had little doubt that, after serving beside him for a few months, his new team would be equally efficient.

The next patrol began on 2 August and took *Wahoo* to the Sea of Japan, probably the most hazardous of all operational areas. Patrolled by surface ships and watched by aircraft, it was scattered with uncharted minefields and could be transformed into a hornet's nest the moment a submarine tried to attack. To add to

* See Chapter 18.

the dangers Morton fell victim to a series of technical problems with his torpedoes. The entire outfit proved to be faulty and in nine attacks on enemy merchant ships in a single four-day period, all ten of the torpedoes he fired failed. Some suffered gyro defects which made them wander off course. Faults in the balance chambers of others led to erratic depth-keeping, and when the remainder managed to reach and strike the target they failed to detonate, a situation that would have evoked a sympathetic response from Otto Kretschmer who had suffered from similar difficulties in 1940.

Although the torpedoes failed to blow up, the same could not be said of Morton who, not surprisingly, exploded with fury. A blistering report was transmitted to ComSubPac and within hours *Wahoo* received a recall signal. It had been a disappointing mission, especially with a new team of officers aboard, but the irrepressible Mush did not return empty-handed. He surprised and sank two fishing sampans while leaving his patrol area and arrived in Pearl on 29 August with six rather bewildered Japanese fishermen whom he had taken prisoner.

After unloading her remaining torpedoes *Wahoo* was supplied with a batch of the new Mark 18 electric weapons. Mush went straight to Vice Admiral Lockwood's office where he gave vent to his feelings. Uncle Charlie, as Lockwood was affectionately known, listened sympathetically, for Morton was not the first captain to complain about the quality of the torpedoes which were being received from the Board of Ordnance. As a veteran submariner himself he could understand the frustration behind Mush's anger. He recognized, too, the first symptoms of combat fatigue – not serious as yet but potentially dangerous in the future. He wondered whether *Wahoo*'s skipper should stand down from the next patrol so that he could have an opportunity to relax and cool off. He asked Morton if he would like some recuperative leave.

'Admiral,' Morton replied quietly, 'I want to go right back to the Sea of Japan. But this time I'd like to have some live fish in the tubes.'

A few days later, with Morton still in the driving seat, *Wahoo* left Pearl Harbor for Midway where she topped up her fuel bunkers in readiness for the long voyage ahead. On 20 September the submarine entered the La Perouse Strait between Sakhalin and the northernmost Japanese island of Hokkaido. No further signals were ever received but post-war records show that Morton sank four more ships during the next twenty-one days – one being a troopship with 500 soldiers aboard. On 11 October a Japanese seaplane sighted a submarine on the surface in the La Perouse Straits and, although the vessel dived as soon as she realized that she had been spotted, she had not reached a safe depth when the aircraft dropped its three depth-charges. The surface of the sea heaved as the charges exploded but the pilot sighted neither oil nor wreckage and did not claim a kill.

Wahoo's loss was announced on 9 November, 1943. Commander Mush Morton, the legend of the Pacific, had completed his last patrol.

—FIFTEEN—

Lieutenant-Commander Malcolm David Wanklyn, RN

'I think it's time for a mug of tea.'

According to British Admiralty records the submarine *Upholder* was sunk as the result of a depth-charge attack by the Italian destroyer-escort *Pegaso* north-east of Tripoli during the late afternoon of 14 April, 1942. Many experts, however, do not accept these 'official facts'. Various theories have been advanced concerning the true cause of *Upholder*'s destruction.

Pegaso's attack was brief – almost too brief to be successful – and no oil or wreckage was observed on the surface when the tumult of underwater explosions had died away. In addition the attack took place some 100 miles north of *Upholder*'s patrol area and, even more significantly, although *Pegaso*'s captain, Lt-Cdr Francesco Acton, reported attacking an unidentified submerged submarine with depth-charges he did not claim to have sunk it.

One alternative theory, backed by a wealth of circumstantial detail, suggests that *Upholder* was sunk in the mine defences covering the seaward approaches to Tripoli and, indeed, there are confirmed reports that a submarine had been sighted close to the minefield two nights earlier. But the existence of this deadly barrage was common knowledge among the submarine captains of the Malta Flotilla and it is extremely unlikely that *Upholder*'s skipper, Lt-Cdr Wanklyn, would have been guilty of such a fatal navigational error. Another theory maintains that *Upholder* fell

197

victim to a second and quite separate depth-charge attack close inshore, an attack reputedly heard by other British submarines in the area, although Italy's naval archives contain no references to any incidents at the relevant time.

Wanklyn's ability to survive enemy depth-charges had already made him a legend in his own lifetime. Many instances are on record where he correctly predicted the precise bearing and range of the next explosion, an uncanny gift that enabled him to steer the submarine well clear of the danger point before the depth-charge actually detonated. Indeed Wanklyn's friends and fellow officers were so confident of his skill that many refused to accept that *Upholder* had been destroyed by the enemy and claimed, instead, that the submarine had become entangled with one of the many uncharted wrecks that littered the seabed off the North African coast and, damaged, or helplessly trapped in the depths, had been unable to return to the surface. In the relatively shallow waters of the Mediterranean an accident of this nature need not be fatal and, in normal circumstances, a proportion of the crew should be able to make good their escape from the crippled vessel with the aid of their DSEA equipment.* When critics drew attention to the lack of survivors supporters of the accident theory were quick to point out that, in wartime, many submarine captains had the escape hatches welded down to prevent them from bursting open during a depth-charge attack. Although there is no evidence that Wanklyn followed this practice it is highly probable that *Upholder*'s escape hatches received the same treatment.

The deaths of the First World War air aces Albert Ball, Georges Guynemer and Manfred von Richthofen are surrounded by similar myths. For the aura of mystique and invincibility that surrounds such legendary heroes seems to demand a god-like immortality. When the reality of death reveals them to be mere mortals, an element of mystery helps to perpetuate the legend they have created in their lifetimes.

Wanklyn was the first British submarine captain to win the Victoria Cross in World War Two. He was also the Royal Navy's most successful underwater commander in terms of mercantile tonnage sunk, not to mention the destruction of an enemy destroyer and three Italian submarines. Judged by any criteria he was a hero and, in Churchill's own stirring phrase, a true Captain of War. What, then, elevated him from the status of hero to that of legend?

* Davis Submerged Escape Apparatus – a self-contained breathing kit designed to assist survivors to escape from a sunken submarine.

Although Malcolm David Wanklyn was born in London in 1911 the blood of Scotland coursed through his veins and he never lost the soft Scottish burr he acquired from his parents. Educated at a small private school at Haywards Heath in Sussex he passed the highly competitive public examination for the Royal Naval College at Dartmouth at the age of thirteen and began his studies in January, 1925. He found his niche almost immediately and after passing out with honours in 1928, including second prizes in mathematics and science, he joined the battleship *Marlborough* as a cadet. Promoted to Midshipman the following year, he gained a First Class Certificate for Seamanship while serving in the *Renown* and went on to obtain four more 'Ones' on completion of his Sub-Lieutenant's Course at Greenwich. By 1933, the year in which Hitler became Chancellor of Germany, he was a full-fledged Lieutenant and in May he proceeded to *HMS Dolphin* to qualify as a submarine officer.

Graduating with high marks, he was posted to the *Oberon* for a spell of duty in the Mediterreanean, an experience he enjoyed to the full. Various appointments followed and in May, 1938, he married Elspeth Kinloch whom he had met while on a fishing holiday in the Highlands. Fishing was Wanklyn's overwhelming passion in life, ranking second only to his enthusiasm for stamp collecting – a seemingly unexciting hobby for a submariner – and pig farming!

The early months of the war were spent in command of the submarines *H.31* and *H.32* in which he carried out a number of secret operations the nature of which have never been disclosed but which were probably connected with early experiments with radar or sonar. In August, 1940, while the Battle of Britain was literally raging overhead, he was appointed to command the submarine *Upholder* which, at the time, was still under construction at Barrow. Wanklyn supervised the final stages of her construction and fitting out, carried out her acceptance trials, and, after commissioning her into the Royal Navy, he left England on 10 December, 1940, en route for the Mediterranean. Reaching Gibraltar on 23 December, he remained at the Rock long enough to enjoy both the Christmas and the Hogmanay festivities and did not leave until 3 January, 1941. He arrived at Malta nine days later.

The Malta Submarine Force, an off-shoot of the 1st Submarine Flotilla in Alexandria and commanded by 'Shrimp' Simpson, was based in Lazaretto Creek close to the island's Grand Harbour where it offered a tempting target for Mussolini's bombers as they swooped over Valetta. Most buildings were in ruins and the HQ

Staff frequently had to work from cellars and holes in the ground as the blitz continued. When the air offensive was at its peak in 1942, the submarines were often forced to seek shelter from enemy bombs by submerging in the Creek during raids and the near-siege conditions in Malta offered little opportunity for relaxation or rest to the submariners when they returned from patrol. It was officially accepted that fifteen war patrols was the maximum number a captain could withstand without breaking down either mentally or physically. Yet in the course of his career with the Malta Submarine Force Wanklyn was to carry out no fewer than *twenty-five* combat missions!

His first operational patrol in *Upholder* gave an early indication of the promise that lay ahead and its success was duly noted by Commander Simpson. Leaving Lazaretto Creek on 24 January Wanklyn set course for Cape Bon, an important landmark on the Axis convoy route from Italy to North Africa, and two days later made his first contact with the enemy – a small convoy comprising two supply ships, the German *Duisburg* and the Italian *Ingo*, escorted by the armed auxiliary *Caralis*. The submarine fired a salvo of four torpedoes but their bubbling wakes were spotted by the enemy lookouts and all were safely avoided. Wanklyn swallowed his disappointment and, despite *Upholder*'s inferior speed while submerged during the day, he set off in pursuit of his erstwhile victims.

The convoy was sighted by a Sunderland flying-boat at noon the following day and a group of Malta-based aircraft belonging to the Fleet Air Arm took off to launch an attack on it. A torpedo from one of the Swordfish sent the *Ingo* to the bottom but, after stopping to pick up survivors, the remaining two ships resumed course for Tripoli. Shortly before dawn the next morning Wanklyn finally caught up with the vessels and, at 5.38 am, launched a submerged attack as they slowed and turned into the swept channel leading to the North African capital. Two torpedoes struck the *Duisburg* inflicting serious damage below the waterline and only the hasty intervention of a tug which hurried out of the harbour and towed the sinking freighter back to Tripoli stern-first saved her from total destruction. Even so, she remained under repair for several months and when she finally emerged she quickly fell victim to the cruisers of Malta's Force K.

Wanklyn met up with another convoy a few days later and sent one of the heavily-laden merchantmen to the bottom with his last two torpedoes. On this occasion the escort ships counter-attacked and Wanklyn had his first taste of being depth-charged. It was a frightening and unpleasant experience, but *Upholder*'s captain found little difficulty in outwitting the enemy and the submarine escaped undamaged. Returning to Malta on 1 February, Wanklyn was greeted by a typically laconic signal from Simpson: *Patrol well executed.* For a member of the Malta Submarine Force it was quite an accolade.

But the promise of Wanklyn's first war cruise was not maintained. *Upholder*'s next four patrols all ended in failure and the fifth, in early April, resulted in three abortive attacks and eight wasted torpedoes. There was, however, one small gleam of encouragement. While returning to Malta from its fifth patrol, the submarine chanced upon a small Tripoli-bound convoy on the night of 13 April. *Upholder* had expended her full outfit of eight torpedoes and was in no position to attack but, turning the darkness to his advantage, Wanklyn surfaced and fired a star-shell from the boat's 12-pdr deck gun. The Italian convoy commodore, mistakenly thinking that the flare heralded an attack by British surface warships, promptly turned his ships around and made for the safety of home waters.

Despite the initiative which Wanklyn had demonstrated on this occasion, Simpson was seriously worried about *Upholder*'s captain. He could not afford to use commanders who wasted torpedoes or who returned from patrol time and time again empty-handed. He passed his misgivings back to the Admiralty in London.

Wanklyn put on a brave face but it was difficult to hide his disappointment. Never a man to suffer from self-doubt, he *knew* that his luck would change shortly. He prayed that the Admiralty would give him time to find his feet. Meanwhile he struck up a friendship with Lt-Cdr Collett, a fellow submarine captain who shared his enthusiasm for pig breeding, and the two officers were often to be seen driving along the dusty bomb-ravaged streets of Valetta in a small pony and trap which they had somehow managed to acquire. Their mutual interest was soon to pay dividends. Joined by another enthusiast, Lt-Cdr Dick Cayley of *Utmost*, they bought a number of pigs from local farmers and set up Submarine (Malta) Piggery Ltd. Fed on swill from the Messes, and tended by the men of the Malta Submarine Force, the initial handful of animals soon grew in numbers and Wanklyn's personal pet sow, Snow White, delighted her proud owner by producing a litter of seven healthy porkers. The Piggery did much to maintain morale at a difficult time and the stock was soon fetching a high price in Valetta's war-starved market, all profits being donated to naval benevolent funds and particularly those set up to help the families of submariners lost in action.

Wanklyn's sixth patrol was a rip-roaring success and it did much to remove Simpson's doubts about his ability. Leaving Malta on 21 April, the *Upholder* met up with a convoy in the Lampedusa Channel three days later and, closing to 700 yards, Wanklyn sank the *Antonietta Laura* (5,428 tons) with his first shot. In fact the torpedo struck the transport before the third weapon of the salvo had left its tube and he was able to countermand his firing orders and thus save the third and fourth torpedoes for another occasion. A few hours later Wanklyn received a radio signal ordering him to locate and sink an Italian destroyer and a German merchant ship that had run aground on shoals in the area of the Kerkenah Bank, following an attack by surface units of the Malta Striking Force.

Upholder herself ran aground while trying to approach the abandoned destroyer – a dangerous predicament for a submarine in enemy waters – but Wanklyn persuaded her off the mudbank by running the motors full astern and, having aborted his attempt to sink the destroyer, he turned his attention on the German-registered *Arta* and her cargo of army trucks and equipment destined for Rommel's *Afrika Korps*. Bringing the *Upholder* alongside the freighter, Wanklyn sent Lieutenant Read and a boarding-party up over the side. After searching for confidential books and papers, the submariners laid explosive demolition charges in various parts of the deserted vessel and then returned to *Upholder* laden with loot. As the submarine reversed away from her pillaged victim, the demolition charges began to detonate and the huge fires which they started soon linked together and engulfed the *Arta*. Satisfied that the burning freighter would never sail again, Wanklyn submerged and resumed his patrol.

He remained in the vicinity of the Kerkenah Bank for five days and his patience was rewarded by the appearance of a five-ship convoy escorted by four destroyers en route for Naples from Tripoli. Diving beneath the destroyer screen, Wanklyn fired a salvo into the convoy and hit the 7,000-ton *Bainsizza* plus two German ships, *Arcturus* and *Leverkusen*. The first two vessels sank almost immediately, but the badly damaged *Leverkusen* was taken in tow by a destroyer which headed back towards Tripoli. Ignoring the savage depth-charge attack that followed, Wanklyn went deep to reload his tubes and then, with his final two torpedoes ready for action, he set off in pursuit of the cripple. He found her some hours later wallowing astern of the destroyer. The last two torpedoes streaked from the submarine's bow tubes and the *Leverkusen* went to the bottom like a stone.

Upholder caused something of a sensation when she returned to Malta. A large Swastika flag was flying from the conning-tower's diminutive masthead, surmounted by an even larger White Ensign. When Simpson came on board to inspect the submarine, her crew paraded on deck wearing German steel helmets and presented arms with genuine *Afrika Korps* tommy-guns. It was, in fact, the loot taken off the *Arta*, but a rumour persisted in Malta for weeks afterwards that a German U-boat had entered Lazaretto Creek to surrender personally to Commander Simpson!

If the sixth patrol had been a resounding success, the seventh proved to be a veritable triumph, despite its unpromising beginning. On the second day out one of *Upholder*'s torpedoes developed an air leak, a fault that required the weapon to be drawn out of its tube so that a spare could be loaded in its place. It was a tricky operation for the fore-ends compartment was cramped and crowded and *Upholder* still had her full complement of four reserve weapons in the racks. But with much sweating and swearing the task was accomplished and Wanklyn was able to continue towards his hunting grounds off the south-eastern coast of Sicily in a happier frame of mind.

On 20 May he carried out a long-range attack on a small coastal convoy and, although the torpedoes missed, he was subjected to a violent counter-attack which wrecked the submarine's Asdic apparatus and hydrophone listening gear. Once below periscope depth, a submarine captain has to rely on his mechanical 'ears' in much the same way as a blind person relies on sound as he feels his way across an unfamiliar room. The loss of his listening equipment meant that Wanklyn would have to operate under very unfavourable conditions if he was forced to dive below periscope depth, but, shrugging off a handicap that would have persuaded many captains to return home, he remained on patrol.

His dogged persistence was rewarded three days later when he torpedoed and sank the *Daniani*, a Vichy French tanker on charter to the Germans. But he again found himself on the receiving end of a vicious depth-charge attack and, unable to follow the movements of the enemy ships on the surface with his hydrophones, he was forced to lie doggo and sweat it out.

With only two days of the patrol period remaining, *Upholder*'s complement of servicable torpedoes was now down to two. But, ever optimistic, Wanklyn moved to the western end of the Messina Straits and waited hopefully for an enemy convoy to appear. At sunset on the 25th, while *Upholder* was cruising slowly at periscope depth and Wanklyn was scanning the horizon preparatory to surfacing and recharging his batteries when darkness fell, he suddenly sighted an aircraft low down on the horizon to the north-west. Guessing it to be part of a convoy's air cover, he steered towards his still invisible prey.

A short while later he picked out the massive bulk of a twin-funnel liner showing darkly against the afterglow of sunset. Gradually more ships emerged from the dusk until finally he could see four large passenger liners, the *Conte Rosso, Marco Polo, Victoria* and *Esperia*, screened by four destroyers. The strength of the escort force confirmed that this was a valuable convoy and with only two torpedoes left Wanklyn knew he could not afford to risk a long-range attack. It would not be easy, for without listening-gear everything would depend on the accuracy of his periscope observations. But despite the enormous pressure of the situation he showed no sign of stress as he quietly ordered the tubes to be flooded. The convoy had moved closer and a sudden turn at the end of a complex zig-zag movement reduced the range even further. *Upholder* was now right in among the destroyer escort and Wanklyn hardly dared to use the periscope in case a lynx-eyed lookout spotted the slender column cutting through the water.

'Torpedo room stand by . . . Fire both!'

There was a slight jolt as the torpedoes streaked away in a flurry of gaseous air bubbles and Wanklyn ordered the planesmen to take the boat to 150 feet, at the same time warning the crew to secure for depth-charges. It was 8.40 pm.

The wakes of the two torpedoes were sighted by a lookout on the destroyer *Freccia*. The vessel's captain swung his ship out of danger and fired two flares from the bridge as a warning to the convoy. But he was too late. The 17,879-ton *Conte Rosso*, a former Lloyd-Triestino liner built for the Far East run and now, converted for transport duties, carrying 2,729 soldiers and crew, staggered like a wounded elephant as both torpedoes slammed into her hull and exploded beneath the waterline. The great ship sank quickly and there was not even time to launch the lifeboats. It was a nightmare disaster and the Italian army lost more than 1,300 troops as the *Conte Rosso* lifted her bows and vanished beneath the waves.

After such an assault a retributory depth-charge attack was inevitable and the enemy wasted no time. The first explosion came just two minutes later and, without the submarine's listening gear, Wanklyn was powerless to assess or predict the development of the merciless counter-attack. For the third time in five days he and his ship's company had to sit passively while the escorting destroyers did their worst.

The depth-charges were closer now and each explosion was like a gigantic hammer-blow against the hull. Moving at silent speed and keeping deep, Wanklyn tried to escape the onslaught as *Upholder* dived and twisted like a trapped fish. The frightening crash of the detonating depth-charges continued without respite. The submarine shuddered violently, light bulbs shattered, loose items of equipment were thrown to the deck and cork insulation scattered from the strained seams of the deckhead. One man, a telegraphist, broke under the strain and tried to open the conning-tower hatch until he was forcibly restrained by his shipmates. It was a moment of high tension but Wanklyn seemed unperturbed by the incident and the excellent morale of the submarine's crew quickly dispelled any further symptoms of panic.

The attack lasted a full two hours and *Upholder*'s Petty Officer Telegraphist, the submarine's official tally-man, had marked off forty-four separate explosions in his notebook before it ended. Wanklyn suddenly smiled and stifled a yawn.

'I think it's time for a mug of tea.'

His words brought an instantaneous easing of the tension. Colour returned to pallid cheeks. The men grinned at each other. The skipper's call for a mug of tea was the traditional signal that the attack was over. And he'd never been wrong yet. *Upholder* rose slowly to the surface to survey the scene. The acrid stench of fuel oil made their eyes water. Small items of wreckage and an occasional empty raft were all that remained to mark the grave of the *Conte Rosso*. Wanklyn had done his job well. And so, with no torpedoes left, a jammed bow cap, considerable internal damage, and without either Asdic or hydrophones, the *Upholder* returned triumphantly to Malta.

Some weeks later the *London Gazette* announced that Malcolm David Wanklyn had been awarded the Victoria Cross for his part in sinking the Italian troopship, *Upholder*'s captain being the first submariner to win the decoration in World War Two. By an odd coincidence Norman Holbrook, the commander of the *B.11* and the first underwater VC of World War One, was also a member of the Malta Flotilla.

But Wanklyn was given no time to rest on his laurels. Malta was under siege, the campaign in North Africa was not going well, and the handful of submarines operating out of Lazaretto Creek were kept hard at it. And none, it seemed, harder than the *Upholder*.

Between the end of May and the middle of September Wanklyn scoured the length and breadth of the central Mediterranean like a rampaging bull. On his tenth patrol he sank an escorted freighter, the 6,000-ton *Laura C*, and survived a counter-attack of nineteen depth-charges. On his next foray he put down another supply ship and escaped an equally ferocious underwater attack. He also secured two torpedo hits on a cruiser of the *Condottiere*-class while it was travelling at 28 knots – possibly one of the finest shots ever achieved by a submarine captain. Wanklyn was credited with a 'probable' sinking and the general feeling in the Flotilla was that the cruiser 'almost certainly sank', but post-war records reveal that the ship, although damaged, staggered back to harbour and lived to fight another day.

Following the tradition begun by Max Horton in 1914, British submarines returning from patrol fly a Skull & Crossbones ensign on which are stitched various symbols representing sinkings, gun bombardments, aircraft destroyed and other more clandestine operations. Merchant ships which have fallen victim to the submarine usually appear in the shape of a plain white bar but when *Upholder* returned to Malta after her twelfth patrol her Jolly Roger flag had a particularly large bar stitched on it. A fellow captain, greeting Wanklyn as he stepped ashore at Lazaretto Creek, cocked an eye at the pirate ensign and asked: 'What the hell are you celebrating this time? Sinking a floating dock?'

Wanklyn shook his head. 'Good heavens, no. It was just a whopping great tanker which we sunk by a whopping great fluke. So we stitched on a whopping great bar!'

The whopping great tanker turned out to be the *Tarvisio*, full of priceless oil for the *Afrika Korps* in Libya, and heavily escorted by no less than three destroyers. With dense clouds of black smoke billowing from the sinking ship the escorts launched a furious counter-attack. Depth-charges rained down like rocks in an Alpine avalanche – forty-eight in just eight minutes and a total of sixty in all! But, as was now becoming customary, Wanklyn bore a charmed life and *Upholder* emerged from the maelstrom of explosions with little damage to show for her ordeal. The legend of his invincibility was growing fast.

In mid-September air reconnaissance reported that an important troop convoy was assembling at Taranto and four Malta-based submarines, *Unbeaten, Ursula, Upright* and *Upholder*, were ordered to intercept it. Wanklyn's gyro compass failed within hours of his departure and he was forced to rely on the submarine's small magnetic compass, a far from reliable instrument.

Unbeaten sighted the convoy at 3.30 am on the 18th but the range was too great to allow an attack and Woodward radioed details of its position, course and speed to the other three boats. Wanklyn picked up the message and, running on the surface, steered to intercept. Exactly ten minutes later the men on *Upholder*'s bridge caught their first glimpse of the enemy – a series of indistinct black shapes moving against the darkness of the night sky. A few more minutes and the convoy was clearly visible through binoculars: three large troop transports, the former luxury liners *Oceania, Neptuna* and *Vulcania*, escorted by five fast-moving and well-armed destroyers.

The sea was extremely choppy thanks to a strong cross-wind and *Upholder*'s bows yawed from side to side as Wanklyn lined up for an attack. It was impossible to shorten the range any further for the targets were moving too fast and Wanklyn was forced to fire his torpedoes at 5,000 yards, carefully timing each shot so that the weapons left the tubes at the precise moment the submarine's bows swung across the line of the firing axis. As soon as the fourth Mk VIII had been launched he ordered the bridge party below, slammed the upper hatch shut and pushed *Upholder*'s bows down in a steeply angled dive.

Wanklyn's skill on this occasion was quite incredible. The submarine was yawing badly, he had no gyro compass and the targets were nearly three miles away. Yet one torpedo slammed into the stern of the *Oceania* wrecking her propellers and bringing her to a standstill, while two more struck the *Neptunia*. The surviving transport, the *Vulcania*, did not wait to find out what was happening. Flanked by one of the destroyers, she made for Tripoli as if the Devil himself was at her heels. *Upright* witnessed her flight but the Italian ship had already run out of range by the time the submarine could reach an attacking position. *Ursula* also saw her and launched a salvo of torpedoes, but all missed. There is little doubt that, had Wanklyn not been part of the attacking force, the convoy might well have escaped scot-free.

But the night was not yet over. Taking advantage of the confusion and with unexampled audacity Wanklyn brought *Upholder* to the surface at 4.45 am and, incredibly, despite the brightness of the moon, the Italians were too preoccupied with the aftermath of the disaster to notice the British submarine lurking in the background. Having taken stock of the situation, Wanklyn submerged again to await the first light of dawn and, using the intervening interval to reload his empty tubes, he steered *Upholder* into a position east of the enemy ships so that the rising sun would be behind him at the moment of attack.

Meanwhile, and unknown to Wanklyn, *Unbeaten* had finally caught up with the convoy. As Woodward prepared to attack the crippled *Neptunia* at dawn, he was equally unaware that *Upholder* was still on the scene. But Fate denied him his victim, for, within minutes of sunrise, *Neptunia* finally succumbed to Wanklyn's initial salvo and slid beneath the waves. Shrugging off his disappointment, Woodward turned his attention to the *Oceania*.

Once again the sights were lined up on the target and Woodward warned his crew to stand by. He was just about to begin his countdown when, suddenly, two columns of water shot high into the air on the far side of the enemy ship and she immediately listed to starboard with the sea flooding in through two gaping holes beneath her waterline. *Upholder*'s final salvo of torpedoes had sent the 19,500-ton *Oceania* to the bottom bare moments before Woodward could fire. *Unbeaten* had been beaten to the draw! Wanklyn had done it again!

Upholder's seventeenth mission was to bring further successes – an Italian submarine and a destroyer – although the circumstances of this latter sinking were to cast an unfortunate shadow over the Wanklyn legend.

An important convoy of seven supply ships with a close escort of six destroyers and supported by two heavy cruisers and a further four destroyers emerged from the Straits of Messina at noon on 8 November en route for Tripoli with vital supplies and equipment for the *Afrika Korps*. Malta's *Force K*, two cruisers and two destroyers under the command of Captain W. G. Agnew, was despatched to intercept it and contact was made just after midnight at a range of six miles. Thanks to the Royal Navy's use of radar the Italian admiral was caught completely by surprise and, despite being outnumbered and out-gunned, *Force K* tore into the convoy like ravaging terriers attacking a flock of sheep. By the time the British squadron withdrew, all seven merchantmen had been sunk and the destroyer *Grecale* badly damaged.

Shortly before dawn *Upholder* chanced upon the shattered remains of the convoy. Wreckage, sinking ships, empty lifeboats and the bobbing heads of swimming men littered the oil-polluted sea in the aftermath of the massacre. The *Oriani* was trying to take the crippled *Grecale* in tow while the other destroyers circled cautiously, picking up survivors. One, the *Libeccio*, had stopped and her crew were lining the sides dragging the exhausted swimmers from the sea. Wanklyn must have been aware that the three enemy destroyers were engaged on an errand of mercy, but with ruthless efficiency he brought the stationery *Libeccio* into his sights and sank her.

Many British accounts of the attack ignore the fact that the Italian ship was saving life and many refer to the destroyer as being already damaged. The Italians, however, make no secret of their feelings and nearly every one of their reference books lists the *Libeccio* as being sunk 'while picking up survivors!' In *The World Crisis* Churchill emphasized that Otto Weddigen had sunk both the *Hogue* and the *Cressy* while they were trying to rescue survivors from the *Aboukir*. However, no such implied criticism was ever levelled at Wanklyn for doing exactly the same thing. In the heat of war many regrettable incidents occur and it is therefore only fair to pass over this episode without further comment. In justice a similar forbearance should be extended to German and Japanese submarine captains who have been accused of committing war crimes for attacking rescue ships in similar circumstances.

Meanwhile, back in Malta, the pig farm was flourishing. Aside from the relaxation it afforded the officers and men after the stress of combat patrols deep inside enemy waters, the profits helped to swell the benevolent funds set up to assist the families of those who did not return. Three of the boats that had made up the original Malta Submarine Force – now promoted to the 10th Submarine Flotilla with Simpson as Captain (S) – had already gone and others were to follow. Casualties were high and the assistance of the charitable funds that benefited from the piggeries was greatly appreciated by those who found themselves in need.

Wanklyn was a frequent visitor to the pig farm whenever *Upholder* was in harbour and he was often seen clattering over the dusty roads of the island in his pony and trap during off-duty periods. When ashore Wanklyn wore his 'respectable uniform', but at sea he was not exactly noted for his sartorial elegance. When friends chided him about the frayed monkey jacket, its gold rings mildewed and green with age, and his equally shabby trousers and dirty oil-stained sweater which he habitually wore at sea, he simply shrugged off their comments and explained that he 'liked to be comfortable'.

But, if Wanklyn was comfortable, the Axis High Command responsible for keeping Rommel's *Afrika Korps* supplied with war materials did not share his sense of well-being. During September, 1941, no less than 28% of all cargoes shipped to North Africa were lost to British surface, air and submarine attack and, although this figure fell to 21% the following month, it shot up to a disastrous 63% in November, thanks, in part, to the activities of *Force K* and *Upholder*. The situation was, in fact, far more serious than that facing the Allies in the Atlantic and, in desperation, the Italians employed smaller convoys and sent high-speed single ships on supply missions – even, on occasions, using valuable cruisers to carry aviation fuel destined for the *Luftwaffe* and the *Regia Aeronautica*. But the losses still continued and the German High Command reported that 'a very severe supply crisis must occur relatively soon.'

Determined not to relinquish his tenuous grip on North Africa, Hitler intervened personally and German Navy technicians with anti-submarine equipment were hurriedly diverted to the Mediterranean. Fresh *Luftwaffe* squadrons followed in their wake and in December the bombing onslaught on Malta was renewed. This time the main attack was aimed at the submarines. Boats returning from patrol had to run the gauntlet of cannon and machine-gun fire as they surfaced to come into harbour and Simpson was forced to restrict entry and exit to and from the Flotilla's base to the hours of darkness, despite the additional navigational hazards this posed on the exhausted submarine captains. Repair and maintenance work had to be carried out at night and the Malta submarines were forced to remain submerged on the bottom of the anchorage during the hours of daylight, a tactic which the Japanese were to copy at Rabaul later in the war.

The German air attacks were devastating. *P.31* had to be written off after damage sustained in dock on 6 January, 1942, and the Greek *Glavkos* and the British *Pandora* were both sunk while unloading stores. The Polish *Sokol* was hit by bombs and four other boats, including *Upholder*, suffered moderate damage. So intense was this offensive against the Malta submarines that the *Luftwaffe* even bombed and machine-gunned the Flotilla's rest camps at the opposite end of the island. Realizing the strain under which his captains were operating, Simpson decided that fifteen successive patrols was the maximum number they could stand without breaking down.

Wanklyn had by now completed nineteen war patrols, but, miraculously, he seemed unaffected by the stress and the legend of invincibility grew stronger. His first patrol in 1942 was an eventful affair. Leaving Malta on New Year's Eve *Upholder* made for the west coast of Sicily where, some four days later, she intercepted a tanker. Two torpedoes from the first salvo proved to be duds but, fortunately, one of the others struck the enemy ship, inflicting severe damage. When Wanklyn realized that the tanker was not likely to sink, he brought *Upholder* to the surface with the intention of finishing her off with the submarine's 12-pdr deck gun. But on this occasion the Italian crew were made of sterner stuff. The tanker proved to be well-armed and she hit back so hard that Wanklyn was forced to dive and make his escape before he was sunk by his erstwhile victim.

By the time *Upholder* withdrew from her patrol area and set course for home she had only one torpedo left in her tubes, but Wanklyn ensured that it was not wasted. While running on the surface the following day, *Upholder*'s lookouts sighted a large enemy submarine a mile or so astern. Wanklyn dived immediately and, taking a snap shot at a range of less than a thousand yards, he scored a direct hit which sent the Italian boat plunging to the bottom in a sheet of flame. Three survivors were dragged from the sea and from these Wanklyn learned that he had sunk the 2,170-ton *Ammiraglio Saint-Bon*, one of the largest submarines serving in the Italian Navy. He also discovered that the enemy boat had spotted *Upholder* and was preparing to fire its deck guns when the British submarine had dived out of sight to launch its submerged torpedo attack. It had been a narrow escape, the second in as many days.

On Wanklyn's return to Malta 'Shrimp' Simpson insisted that Wanklyn must take a brief rest, and, when the submarine left on her next patrol, her First Lieutenant, Norman, was in temporary command. He proved to be an apt pupil and, after sinking an Italian merchant ship and surviving a depth-charge attack, he brought his charge back to Lazaretto Creek safe and sound.

But the writing was on the wall. On his return from his 23rd patrol on 5 March Wanklyn was ordered to report to the Flotilla Captain's office. Simpson wasted no time on preliminaries and he told *Upholder*'s commander that he was to be sent back to England for a prolonged rest on completion of his 25th patrol. Wanklyn pleaded for an extension but 'Shrimp' was adamant. No amount of talking would persuade him otherwise.

Upholder's twenty-fourth and penultimate patrol began on 14 March, 1942. With black diesel smoke curling from her exhausts, the submarine steered for the waters around Brindisi, always one of Wanklyn's happier hunting grounds. On the 18th, while cruising at periscope depth, he sighted a supply ship moving slowly down the swept channel towards the harbour but for some reason he decided against attacking her. Half an hour later his forbearance was rewarded by the unexpected appearance of a large *Settembrini*-class submarine. Taking *Upholder* deep to avoid being sighted by some small boats that were hovering in the vicinity, Wanklyn ordered the torpedoes to be set for shallow running, his experienced eye having noticed that the enemy submarine was riding high out of the water at maximum buoyancy. Raising the slender column of the attack periscope, he found the *Tricheco* only 600 yards away and almost broadside on. Four torpedoes streaked from *Upholder*'s bow tubes at eight-second intervals. The first struck the target amidships with a tremendous explosion. The second hit the submarine in the stern sending water and wreckage high into the air as the warhead detonated. By the time the third and fourth weapons arrived *Tricheco* was already spiralling to the bottom. It was a copy-book attack by an acknowledged master.

Having reloaded *Upholder*'s empty tubes, Wanklyn surfaced at nightfall to charge the batteries and ventilate the stuffy interior of the submarine. The night passed peacefully and next morning, unwilling to waste a torpedo on a minnow, he brought *Upholder* to the surface to sink a passing trawler by gunfire. It was, had he but known it, his last kill.

The storm clouds that had been gathering threateningly throughout the morning suddenly broke with violent fury and, lashed by a south-easterly gale, the submarine rolled and pitched in a seething maelstrom of tumbling white water and crashing breakers. Rain reduced visibility to nil and, with over half of the crew prostrate with sea-sickness, Wanklyn submerged to periscope depth in an attempt to reduce the nauseating motion of the sea. In the midst of these appalling conditions he sighted an Italian battleship beating her way through the pounding waves with spray spuming upwards as the seas smashed over her bows on to the forward gun turrets. Wanklyn fired his remaining four torpedoes from a range of 4,000 yards. Not surprisingly, they all missed.

After a ten-day rest period, Wanklyn left Malta for *Upholder*'s 25th patrol on 6 April. He knew that on his return he would be given a one-way ticket back to England and he was determined to end his period in the Mediterranean with one final outstanding success. *Upholder* had already sunk 129,529 tons of enemy shipping plus two destroyers, an armed trawler and two submarines, not to mention damaging a cruiser. It was a record to be proud of and was never to be surpassed by any other British submarine commander. But Wanklyn thirsted for more scalps and, having landed two agents from the Special Operations Executive on the North African coast and transferred their Controller, Captain Wilson, to the safe-keeping of *Unbeaten* which was en route for Gibraltar, he set course for his new patrol area west of Tripoli.

On 12 April *Upholder* received and acknowledged radio orders to join up with the submarines *Urge* and *Thrasher* and to intercept a Tripoli-bound convoy which was expected to pass through the area on the 15th. It was Wanklyn's last contact with the outside world. During the afternoon of the 14th the *Thrasher* heard the noise of a prolonged depth-charge attack and attempts to establish radio contact with *Upholder* a few hours later failed to obtain a response. That same afternoon the Italian escort-destroyer *Pegaso* launched a depth-charge attack on an unidentified submerged submarine some 100 miles further to the north. But her Captain did not claim a kill and reported rather inconclusively that 'there had been no wreckage or survivors'.

News of Wanklyn's death and the loss of *Upholder* was withheld from the British public for several weeks although Mrs Wanklyn was advised that the submarine 'is seriously overdue and (is) considered to have been lost' on 1 May. She was, however, asked to keep the information secret until the loss was officially announced at a later date, a painful duty which she discharged in the best traditions of the Service to which her husband had dedicated his life.

When the public announcement was finally made, however, the Admiralty took the unprecedented step of paying tribute to the submarine, her crew and her captain. Having briefly touched upon *Upholder*'s achievements it concluded:

'Such was the standard of skill and daring that the ship and her officers and men became an inspiration not only to their own flotilla but to the fleet of which it was a part, and Malta, where for so long *HMS Upholder* was based. The ship and her company are gone, but the example and inspiration remain.'

It was an appropriate and fitting epitaph for Lt-Cdr Malcolm David Wanklyn VC, DSO, RN, Britain's most successful exponent of underwater warfare, and for the equally gallant crew of His Majesty's Submarine *Upholder*.

213

—SIXTEEN—

Commander Samuel David Dealey Jr USN

'Hit 'em Harder!'

When Roger Keyes described Max Horton's attack on the *S-116* in his *Memoirs*, he likened the sinking of a destroyer by a submarine to 'shooting snipe with a rifle'. Indeed, any submarine commander who could boast a destroyer amongst his tally of kills had reason to be proud. Sam Dealey sank five in the course of a single patrol plus another a few months earlier. Six in all! More than enough to guarantee his place in the records books.

But Dealey had other, and equal, claims to fame. He was one of only seven submarine captains to be awarded the Congressional Medal of Honor. He won the Navy Cross no less than three times, and he was decorated with the Army's Distinguished Service Cross on the personal recommendation of General Douglas MacArthur. In addition his submarine, *Harder*, received a Presidential Unit Citation.

Born in Dallas, Texas, of Irish-American parentage, Dealey graduated from the United States Naval Acadamy in 1930 and spent his next four years on the *Nevada*, a battleship destined to fall victim to Japanese torpedoes at Pearl Harbor, although she was later raised and rebuilt and saw service during the Normandy landings and at Iwo Jima and Okinawa where she was hit by a *kamikaze*. Having completed his enforced stint of big-ship routine, Sam joined the Submarine School at New London and, after further training, served in various S-boats as a junior officer.

Promoted to Lieutenant in 1940, he was given more surface ship experience in the four-stacker destroyer *Reuben James*, a period during which he absorbed much of the anti-submarine knowledge that was to stand him in such good stead in his subsequent career. By the end of that year, which had seen the destruction of the *Orzel* and the surrender of the *Seal*, he was back with submarines and in command of the 850-ton *S.20*, a twenty-year-old veteran which was being used as a guinea-pig for sonar trials and other tests. When war came to the Pacific Dealey naturally expected to join a combat flotilla, but, to his disgust and despite numerous requests, he remained with *S.20* carrying out a series of routine experiments in home waters. Finally, however, his wish was granted and he was given command of the brand-new *Harder*, a member of the famous *Gato* class, built, like Gilmore's *Growler*, by the Electric Boat Company and launched on 19 August, 1942. By European standards she was a large boat displacing 2,424 tons in submerged trim – Kretschmer's Type VIIB *U-99*, by contrast, scaled only 857 tons – with an overall length of 311 feet, 9 inches. It is interesting to note that these dimensions almost exactly equalled those of von Arnauld de la Perière's giant First World War U-cruiser *U-139* which displaced 2,483 tons on a length of 311 feet.

Equipped with a single 5-inch deck gun, 40-mm anti-aircraft weapons and ten 21-inch torpedo tubes, six forward and four aft, *Harder* packed a considerable punch. Her fighting ability was enhanced by her sonar apparatus, Torpedo Data Computer and sky and surface search radar systems. Four H.O.R. diesel engines provided a top surface speed of 20¼ knots, while the electric motors, powered by a 252-cell Exide battery, were capable of 8¾ knots submerged. Large oil bunkers gave her a range of 11,800 miles at 10 knots, an operational necessity in the vastness of the Pacific theatre, and her authorized complement comprised eighty officers and men.

Dealy and his new command left New London on 26 April, 1943, and, having passed through the Panama Canal, headed out into the Pacific en route for Pearl Harbor, a total passage distance of nearly 7,000 miles. After shore leave and a further period of training, *Harder* sailed from Pearl on her first combat patrol during early June and arrived off the Japanese home island of Honshu on 20 June. There is little doubt that Sam Dealey was being thrown in at the deep end for he had no previous operational experience, not even as a junior officer, so it is clear that the US Navy's top brass had the utmost confidence in his abilities.

Although they were sitting astride the main shipping route out of Tokyo Bay there was virtually no traffic and Dealey, correctly guessing that the enemy was routeing its commercial shipping

215

inshore where shallow waters made submarine operations more difficult, decided to move closer to the Japanese mainland – so close, in fact, that he reported that 'the headlights of the cars moving along the nearby highway reminded us of Riverside Drive along the Hudson'. That night he sighted a small convoy of two merchantmen protected by a single warship. Dealey fired a fan of six torpedoes but one of the salvo detonated prematurely attracting the attention of the escort and *Harder* had only reached 100 feet when the first depth-charge exploded. Lacking combat experience, the crew did not react with the cool efficiency which they were to demonstrate on later patrols. Someone admitted too much water into the ballast tanks and the submarine arrowed down in a virtually uncontrolled dive. She struck the bottom at 300 feet – her own maximum safety depth – and the force of the impact threw the men off their feet and sent loose equipment crashing down on to the steel decks. More seriously, it crushed the sonar dome and deprived Dealey of his sound-ranging apparatus. But it could have been worse. There was no structural damage, they were too deep for the depth-charges to be effective, and they had drawn their first blood by sinking one of the freighters, always a boost to morale for a new crew. With dawn less than an hour away, Sam Dealey had to act fast before reinforcements arrived. Gambling that the enemy had used up all his depth-charges, he put the motors on full power and blew the ballast tanks in an effort to pull *Harder* out of the mud. It took forty-five minutes of concentrated effort to extricate the submarine from the sea-bottom but, finally, with a reluctant lurch, the boat came free and Dealey crawled quietly out of the danger zone.

The following night *Harder*'s radar picked up the echoes of a large cargo ship and Dealey hit the vessel at dawn with a single well-placed torpedo. His victim, the 7,189-ton *Sangara Maru*, listed to starboard but remained afloat and, in a desperate attempt to save his ship, her Captain steered for the shore. With the Japanese mainland so close, Dealey did not dare to follow and finish her off and he was forced to cut his losses and let her go.

On the very next day, 24 June, he torpedoed a transport and, less than twenty-four hours later, he tried a double-ended attack on a small convoy – the torpedoes from the bow tubes striking one freighter while those fired from *Harder*'s stern tubes hit another. With only two torpedoes left, Sam Dealey set off in pursuit of fresh prizes but found, instead, his earlier victim, the *Sangara Maru*, hard aground with only her upperworks showing above the surface. However, as the *Harder* picked her way through the shoaling waters to administer the *coup de grace* a three-ship

216

convoy appeared over the western horizon. This new target seemed an obviously better proposition than the stranded merchantman, but, as Dealey turned towards it, yet another ship, a freighter, appeared on the eastern horizon steaming in the opposite direction. Five targets – but only two torpedoes. Dealey had to choose quickly. He decided to hit the convoy and the last two tin-fish streaked from *Harder*'s bows. The first struck a transport in the centre of the group. The second weapon missed, but it was not wasted. Passing astern of the sinking troopship it ran on and slammed into a well-laden tanker on the far side of the group.

Although Dealey heard the torpedoes explode he did not dare to remain at periscope depth for visual confirmation of his success. The convoy had an aerial escort and, as he drove the submarine down, a Japanese aircraft hurtled towards the wisp of spray left by *Harder*'s periscope. The bomb was a big one and the underwater blast that followed its detonation shook the submarine far more severely than the earlier depth-charge attacks. But fortunately, thanks to Dealey's instant response, *Harder* was now too deep to be in danger from any further attacks and, levelling off at 200 feet, her captain passed the welcome order to set course for home.

It had been a more than satisfactory first combat patrol and Sam Dealey was, in due course, to collect the first of his three Navy Crosses. Two equally successful patrols followed in quick succession and during the first of these he had the temerity to come to the surface and engage in a gun battle with a group of Japanese anti-submarine trawlers. By the time the *Harder* returned in triumph from her third patrol she had sunk a total of twelve merchant ships and damaged two others. A few days later she sailed for her home base for refitting and a spell of leave for her crew.

Dealey was back in the Pacific by the Spring of 1944 and *Harder*'s fourth patrol brought her skipper fresh laurels. The emphasis of the naval war was now changing and on 13 April a Directive from the C-in-C rated enemy destroyers as higher priority targets than merchant ships. It also made the game more dangerous. But it was a change of tactics that suited Sam Dealey down to the ground. The day after details of the Directive were received by radio, the submarine claimed her first scalp.

The opening days of the patrol had given no hint of the glories that lay ahead. The waters around the Caroline Islands were disappointingly empty and even the main shipping route from Guam to Woleai proved unexpectedly bare of targets. The humid tropical heat made life unbearable inside the cramped and airless interior of the submarine and, in an attempt to give the crew some relief, *Harder* was running on the surface in broad daylight. During the late afternoon of 14 April radar contact was made with a patrolling Japanese aircraft but, instead of diving, the normal response in such circumstances, Dealey deliberately remained on the surface until the enemy was well within visual range. Then, tolerably sure that the seaplane pilot had seen him, he took the submarine beneath the waves before any retaliatory action could be taken.

The bait worked admirably and, just over an hour later, a destroyer appeared over the horizon to search for the submarine reported by the aircraft. Watching through his periscope, Dealey saw the enemy ship slow down in order to operate her underwater detection gear and, moments later, the unnerving *ping* of the sonar probe bounced off the *Harder*'s hull plating. But the time was not yet ripe. Dealey wanted to make his attack under cover of darkness and, keeping a safe distance from the prowling destroyer, he remained discreetly out of sonar range until dusk.

As the submarine steered towards the target Dealey called the crew to Battle Stations and ordered the torpedoes to be set for shallow running. The slim attack periscope slid upwards and, having centred the enemy in his sights, Dealey relayed details of the enemy's range, speed and course back to Lieutenant Logan, the officer operating the Torpedo Data Computer. The machine clicked as it assimilated the information and the newly calculated deflection angle was passed to the torpedomen in the bow compartment. The range was now down to 1,000 yards and closing.

The first torpedo struck the 2,090-ton *Ikazuchi* amidships below her second funnel. Exactly seven seconds later another Mk 14 smashed into the stern. Two tremendous explosions echoed across the sea and, as a cloud of smoke and steam rose up from the fatally wounded ship, she began to go down by the bows. But the stricken destroyer still had teeth and, with her fantail stacked with depth-charges primed and ready for release, she could still bite. As the *Ikazuchi* sank the hydrostatic valves would trigger the detonators at their pre-set depth and no underwater object in the immediate vicinity would have the remotest chance of survival.

Dealey, however, had no intention of giving the Japanese Captain the satisfaction of a kill in his dying moments. Calling for full right rudder he moved away from his victim at maximum submerged power and, when the depth-charges began to explode four minutes later, *Harder* was safely clear of the danger zone. Instead of destroying the submarine, the depth-charges only succeeded in killing the unfortunate Japanese in the water.

Dealey's log report of the attack was laconic in the extreme: *Range 900 yards. Commenced firing. Expended four torpedoes and one Jap destroyer.*

The sinking of the *Ikazuchi* was not the only moment of excitement during *Harder*'s fourth patrol. In the course of Task Force 58's air operations against Woleai Atoll Dealey's submarine was ordered to act as a rescue boat with instructions to pick up any aviators who crashed into the sea, a mercy mission in which O'Kane's *Tang* and a number of other submarines shared. One aircraft was seen to come down on a small enemy-occupied island and, extending the limitations of his brief, Dealey decided to make a landing in hostile territory. Coming close inshore, he ran *Harder*'s bows aground on a sandy reef and held the submarine in position on her engines while a three-man party, led by Lieutenant Logan, rowed ashore in a rubber boat to search for the downed flier. Fortunately they found him before the Japanese did and, less than thirty minutes after crash-landing on the atoll, the lucky pilot was being helped aboard the submarine.

It was an action typical of Sam Dealey. He had been given a job to do and he intended to do it. Not surprisingly this fourth patrol, of which the air-rescue formed a fitting climax, brought another gold star to his Navy Cross and he was by now officially credited with sinking ten Japanese merchant ships totalling some 100,000 tons, plus the destroyer *Ikazuchi*. But with characteristic modesty Dealey insisted that he owed his success to the two key members of the *Harder*'s team: Lieutenant Frank Lynch, the Executive Officer, whose giant frame earned him the nickname 'Man Mountain', and the Torpedo Officer, Sam Logan. Lynch undoubtedly contributed a leavening of caution when Dealey's enthusiasm got the better of him, while Logan's aptitude for mathematics was invaluable when calculating the vital deflection angles during a torpedo attack, his sharp brain often producing a solution before the mechanical computer.

Harder's fifth war patrol began on 26 May, 1944, when she left Fremantle, her operational base in Western Australia, to patrol the Sibutu Passage, the stretch of water between North Borneo and Tawi Tawi which the Japanese were using as their main fleet anchorage. In fact Dealey had made a special request for assignment to the Tawi Tawi scouting mission because he felt sure it would yield plenty of worthwhile targets. *Harder* was also given the task of lifting off a group of Australian coastwatchers after a hazardous spell of duty in Borneo and, to assist in this latter operation, he was accompanied by an Australian army officer, Major Jinkins, and his NCO, Sergeant Dodds. The submarine was also carrying another important passenger, Captain M. T. Tichenor, the Staff Officer (Operations) of the 7th fleet's Submarine Force. It was perhaps fortunate that Dealey had such a respected senior officer on board as an observer on this trip, for, without Tichenor's confirmation, it is possible that no one would have believed his subsequent claims.

Their first contact with the enemy took place on the evening of 6 June, 1944 – a date already famous in history as the day on which the Allies landed on the Normandy beaches – when *Harder* made radar contact with a heavily escorted convoy of tankers heading for Tarakan. The submarine had been running awash with only her radar aerial protruding above water and Dealey promptly came to the surface so that he could use his speed to reach a good attacking position. The convoy was nine miles away but a full moon afforded excellent visibility and Dealey had to cover his approach by hiding inside a convenient rain squall. At 9.25 pm, however, the submarine emerged into clear weather and she was at once spotted by one of the escorts which immediately steered towards its underwater enemy.

Choosing discretion rather than valour, Dealey turned away and ran for the horizon at 19 knots with the destroyer in hot pursuit. But *Harder*'s skipper still had some shots up his sleeve, and when the Japanese vessel had closed the gap to some 8,500 yards he pushed the submarine below the surface and ordered full left rudder. Confidently expecting to make a kill, the enemy captain hurtled on towards his doom, unaware that *Harder*'s stern tubes were lining up on his beam. Three torpedoes hissed through the water and two struck home. The 1,313-ton *Minatsuki* staggered as the warheads exploded. A searing yellow flame rose amidships, her stern lifted and, with her back broken, she plunged to the bottom. Within four minutes of being hit she had vanished from sight.

Satisfied that the enemy ship had been destroyed, Dealey called for flank speed and chased off into the darkness in search of the convoy. Before many minutes *Harder*'s radar regained contact, revealing a single small vessel heading towards them at high speed. Dealey soon positioned the submarine to meet this new threat. He intended to employ his favourite tactic – a salvo of six torpedoes fired at close range at the enemy's oncoming bows. 'Down the throat' was the description he used in his combat reports.

On this occasion, however, the enemy Captain proved a redoubtable opponent and his instant response to the ambush saved his ship. All six torpedoes missed their intended target and it was suddenly *Harder*'s turn to face death and disaster; but, despite this surprise reversal of fortunes, Dealey still found time grudgingly to acknowledge the enemy's skill.

'Good work, you son-of-a-bitch!' he grunted approvingly. Then, without pausing for breath, he continued, 'Take her down to 300 feet. Rig for silent running. Rig for depth-charges!'

In her efforts to escape destruction, *Harder* found herself facing new perils. A new and inexperienced crew-member working the after hydroplane controls, unaware that the emergency routine would black-out his instruments, and disorientated by the thundering concussion of the exploding depth-charges, set the planes to *Dive* instead of *Rise* during the final moments of the levelling-off routine and the submarine continued her downward plunge until she had exceeded her safe diving limit and was in imminent danger of being crushed by the pressure of the sea.

Realizing the cause of the emergency, the Diving Officer corrected the planesman's error and, adopting similar measures to those used by Lonsdale in the *Seal*, Dealey sent *Harder*'s crew running aft in the hope that the additional weight in the stern would assist the 15° up-angle on the 'planes. But the trim of a submarine is a delicate matter of carefully calculated balance and, virtually out of control, *Harder* shot up 250 feet and almost broke surface under the guns of the enemy before Dealey finally restored trim and brought her back under control.

By exploiting the temperature variations in the sea the submarine's skipper skilfully avoided the enemy's sonar probes and, by midnight, *Harder* was back on the surface and heading for the Sibutu Passage none the worse for her experiences. During the following morning radar contact was again made with another enemy destroyer and, unabashed by the previous evening's failure, Dealey swung head-on to meet her. Visual contact was made at 4,000 yards and *Harder*'s crew was called to Battle Stations. With the range down to 3,000 yards, it was apparent that the destroyer had spotted the periscope, but Dealey made no attempt to dive as the enemy rushed towards him. Only 650 yards separated the two vessels when the first torpedo of a three-shot salvo streaked from the submarine's bows. Fifteen seconds later it struck the 2,077-ton *Hayanami* – one of Japan's most modern destroyers with six 5-inch guns and eight 24-inch torpedo-tubes – followed within moments by another. The third missed but the failure was of little consequence. The destroyer was already doomed. Smoke and steam rose skywards, a vivid white flame cut through the murk, and there was a thunderous explosion as the magazine ignited. But Dealey felt slightly disappointed. The *Hayanami* had taken longer to sink that his previous victim

Minatsuki – all of nine minutes from the first visual contact!

The arrival of a second destroyer allowed no time for reflection and *Harder* headed for the depths as the first depth-charges exploded. The Japanese were playing for real this time and the attack lasted a full four hours before Dealey finally managed to extricate his boat from the trap. An hour later, while cruising at periscope depth, he sighted a flotilla of six destroyers strung out in line of bearing in search of the submarine that had been causing so much mayhem in the Straits.

Dealey, his fighting instincts thoroughly aroused, was in favour of launching an immediate attack, but his Executive Officer, Frank Lynch, urged caution. In any event *Harder*'s crew were still recovering from the previous depth-charge attack and the batteries were low. Sam accepted the wisdom of Lynch's advice and withdrew without further argument. But the presence of so many enemy ships thirsting for his blood indicated the success of the patrol. As he noted in his official report: 'Such popularity must be deserved'.

The time had now arrived for *Harder*'s rendezvous with the Australian coastwatchers and at 2 pm on 8 June the submarine was lying at periscope depth off the pick-up point. Few captains enjoyed these cloak-and-dagger missions and Dealey was fully conscious of the hazards involved. The inshore waters of these lonely islands were poorly charted and, even a mile from the shore, there was insufficient water in which to submerge. The mangrove forests that led down to the beaches were known to be occupied by Japanese troops and naval patrols skirted the islands at frequent intervals. Pin-point accuracy was vital for success, yet no lights could be permitted for fear of alerting the enemy and it was 7.45 that evening before Dealey dared to surface and move closer.

Two small canvas boats were launched and communications were maintained with the aid of short-range walkie-talkie handsets. The boats were guided ashore with the help of *Harder*'s radar and the necessary steering instructions were passed to the Australians by radio. At any moment a burst of gunfire from the beach could herald the disastrous end to the mission and nerves were tense on *Harder*'s conning-tower as the minutes ticked by. Suddenly the walkie-talkie crackled to life and Major Jinkins reported contact. But even at this stage the utmost caution was necessary for it could easily be a Japanese trap. Luckily all was well. Jinkin's coded signal *Eureka and MacArthur* told Dealey that the men had been located and were on their way back. An hour later the two small boats loomed out of the darkness and nosed gently against *Harder*'s ballast tanks. One by one the exhausted

Australian soldiers were hauled on board and hurried below where hot baths, clean clothes, and a good meal awaited them.

Having safely recovered the coastwatchers, Dealey eased the submarine back into deep water and headed south. His next task was to reconnoitre the Japanese fleet base at Tawi Tawi and, having altered course south-eastwards, *Harder* throbbed through the soft tropical night at a steady 15 knots towards the Sibutu Passage. Within minutes of sunrise, however, the submarine was forced to make an emergency dive when a Japanese float-plane which had somehow not been detected by the boat's radar suddenly appeared a mile or so ahead of the port bow.

Harder was only down to 75 feet when the depth-charge exploded and the underwater blast threw many of the sleeping off-duty crewmen out of their bunks onto the deck – an experience shared by Captain Tichenor, the Staff Officer Observer. Any chance of approaching Tawi Tawi by surprise was now out of the question and, to make matters more difficult, the weather conditions were also against the submarine. The sea was so smooth that the whisper of spray from the periscope would be spotted at a range of five miles, while the shadowy bulk of the submarine would be visible to aircraft even at a depth of 100 feet. Dealey went deeper in search of a layer of cold water which would act as a thermal barrier to deflect the enemy's sound-ranging probes and finally found one at 250 feet. Sheltering beneath it he reversed course to the north-east to await developments.

Two destroyers put in an appearance at noon, but, despite searching for several hours, they failed to locate the submerged submarine and, after they had departed, Dealey brought *Harder* cautiously to periscope depth. Taking advantage of an unexpected deterioration in the weather, he headed again for the Sibutu Passage and, as the dusk deepened, he returned to the surface to recharge the batteries, a penance common to all submarines before the advent of nuclear power.

Harder entered the Sibutu Passage at 9 am precisely and, exactly one minute later, she sighted a Japanese destroyer criss-crossing the narrowest stretch of the strait. At 9.02 a second destroyer hove into view steering a parallel course to its companion.

'Radar depth! Battle Stations Submerged!'

With the radar scanner just peeping above the surface Dealey raised the periscope, crouching on his haunches to prevent the column rising too high out of the water. He estimated the range of the destroyers as six miles and decided that they were ripe for plucking. Dusk deepened into night as *Harder* slid down to periscope depth and carefully closed her victims. The scenario was

223

almost too good to be true. The destroyers, both following a carefully pre-arranged zig-zag pattern, were steaming towards each other and Dealey ran the periscope up and down as he judged the range, course and speed of the enemy ships – information vital for the officer operating the Torpedo Data Computer if the machine was to give an accurate deflection setting. The monotonous catechism continued without pause as *Harder* closed the range to 4,000 yards and then to 2,500 yards.

'Up periscope. Speed 15 knots. Bearing – *mark*!'

Lynch read the figure off the periscope's azimuth scale and passed it back to Logan at the TDC. The machine whirred and clicked.

'Solution, captain!'

'Set! Down periscope.'

At 2,000 yards the destroyers turned 30° degrees to port simultaneously, presenting Dealey with an almost perfect target. This time the slim attack periscope remained raised.

'Left rudder . . . Give me the firing course.'

'One-four-five, sir.'

'Bring her to one-four-five. Bow torpedoes stand by.' The green lights on the firing panel in the control room glowed to show the tubes flooded and ready. 'Bearing – *mark*'

'Three-five-zero.'

'Set! Fire One! Fire Two! Fire Three! Fire Four!'

Dealey swung *Harder* to starboard ready to bring the stern tubes to bear as he waited for the torpedoes to complete their 1,000-yard journey. The first missed the bows of the nearest destroyer by inches but the second hit home with an encouraging explosion and, moments later, the third struck amidships. Flames spread rapidly and it was obvious that the *Tanikaze* could not survive for more than a few minutes.

Harder's fourth torpedo ran astern of the sinking destroyer and fortuitously struck the second ship as it emerged from behind the burning wreck of the *Tanikaze*. As with the submarine's third victim, *Hayanami*, the exploding warhead detonated the magazine and a spectacular pyrotechnical display lit the night sky, the blast slamming *Harder* sideways like the lash of an alligator's tail. By the time Dealey handed the periscope over to Lynch the second destroyer had already vanished and all that remained of the other was its stern sticking vertically out of the water. Although the sinking of the *Tanikaze* was subsequently confirmed from Japan's naval records after the war, the identity of the second destroyer has never been clearly established. Some early references show the *Urakaze* as being sunk by *Harder* that day but later sources credit the destruction of the *Urakaze* to the submarine *Sealion*, showing her as being sunk off Taiwan on 21 November, 1944. It is therefore possible that the unidentified second destroyer was the *Urakaze* and that she was only damaged by *Harder* during the attack.

Nevertheless Sam Dealey had succeeded beyond his wildest dreams. His onslaught on the destroyer patrols covering the vital Sibutu Passage convinced Vice Admiral Takeo Ozawa that his main fleet base at Tawi Tawi was encircled by a large force of American submarines. Fearful of what might happen if he waited, he decided to seek the relative safety of the open sea. Although his ultimate departure was prompted by the 5th Fleet's assault on Guam and Saipan there is little doubt that the activities of the American submarines in the Sibutu Passage, especially those of the *Harder*, had a profound influence on Ozawa's movements. It would be true to say that Dealey's successes were an important contributory factor in the events that finally led to Japan's disastrous defeat at the Battle of the Philippine Sea on 19 and 20 June, 1944.

On the afternoon of the next day, 10 June, Dealey arrived off Tawi Tawi just in time to see the Japanese Combined Fleet leaving its anchorage. Peering through his periscope, he could hardly believe his eyes as he saw the masts and funnels of numerous cruisers and destroyers appear over the horizon, followed by the vast pagoda-like bridges of the battleships. Although he had little hope of catching Ozawa's imposing force, Dealey set off in pursuit. But the skies were alive with aircraft and within minutes the spray of *Harder*'s periscope was spotted. While the close escort laid a smokescreen to hide the main fleet units from the submarine, a number of destroyers swung out of line and rushed in for the kill. Dealey turned towards his attackers like a lone cowboy facing an Indian war party. One destroyer in particular seemed more menacing than the others and Sam selected this vessel for one of his famous 'down the throat' shots. With the range down to 1,500 yards he fired three torpedoes from the bow tubes but was then forced to dive deep as the other destroyers closed from starboard. Two of the torpedoes exploded on hitting the target and the effects of the resulting detonation were later described by Dealey as being 'far worse than depth-charging'.

The counter-attack that followed was one of the most severe *Harder* had ever endured. The submarine shuddered and bucked with each blast and the entire surface of the ocean heaved convulsively with an unending barrage of underwater explosions. Loose equipment rattled inside the submarine, cork insulation scattered down from the deckhead seams, lights went out, glass shattered, and the men had to cling to staunchions and other supports to keep their footing. In the midst of the commotion one of the Australian coastwatchers sauntered into the control room to see what was happening. He gave Dealey a cheerful nod.

'If it's all the same to you, sport,' he grinned, 'do you think you could take me back to Borneo? We had a bit of peace and quiet there.'

The attack lasted a full three hours, but somehow *Harder* survived everything the enemy dropped on her. Suddenly the explosions stopped and the listening crew heard the propeller noises of the destroyers gradually fade into the distance. After a long interval the submarine rose quietly to the surface and paused at radar depth for a cautionary scan. The plot showed a clear screen and Dealey ordered the periscope to be raised. He swung the top lens through a full 360°. The sea was empty in all directions. Against all the odds *Harder* had survived. She had set an amazing and never-to-be-broken record – five destroyers sunk in the course of a single patrol!

Dealey returned to Fremantle to a hero's welcome. At a special parade he was given a second Gold Star to his Navy Cross and, on direct instructions from General MacArthur, the Admiral also decorated him with the Army's Distinguished Service Cross – a singular honour for a submarine captain. But Dealey was more concerned with the welfare of his men than the baubles of bravery. After five patrols he was entitled to stand down for a rest and hand the *Harder* over to Frank Lynch. But, while Dealey had no qualms concerning his Executive Officer's ability, he was mindful of the traumas of the last patrol and he considered that Lynch should be allowed a period of leave and recuperation before assuming the awesome responsibilities that went with command of a combat submarine. Sam pulled strings in all directions and even appealed to the Admiral. Finally he was granted permission to remain as captain of *Harder* for her sixth war patrol while Lynch went on leave, the transfer of command to take place on the submarine's return.

Acting as Senior Officer of a six-strong wolf-pack, Dealey left Fremantle accompanied by the rest of his flock on 5 August, 1944, and the little force steered northwards along the Australian coast before cutting west of the Timor Sea through the islands of the Dutch East Indies and into the Makassar Strait. There was virtually no enemy activity in this area by now and the submarines were able to maintain normal routine until they struck out across the Celebes Sea for the waters south and west of the Philippines. *Haddo* drew first blood on 22 August when she sent the frigate

226

Sado to the bottom. But Dealey had no intention of being left out of the action and later the same day he torpedoed and sank the 870-ton escort *Matsuwa* and the 940-ton *Hiburi*, the latter vessel being only seven weeks old when Dealey turned her into scrap metal.

Haddo picked up another scalp the following day when she sank the escort *Asakaze*. Dealey was no doubt well pleased with the achievements of his underwater strike force. Joining up with the *Hake*, he moved down to Dasol, south of the Lingayen Gulf, and at dawn the next day, 24 August, they sighted two Japanese warships on anti-submarine patrol – an obsolete destroyer captured from the Siamese Navy and a minesweeper. Compared with *Harder*'s previous victims they were small fry and the submarines anticipated no problems as they moved in to attack. The destroyer quickly left the scene but the minesweeper stood its ground.

The pulses of sound from the enemy's sonar gear were clearly audible inside the *Hake* and it was obvious that the Japanese vessel had pin-pointed their position. *Hake*'s Captain, however, did not consider the minesweeper to be a suitable or large enough target for a torpedo and he broke off the attack and turned away. As he did so he sighted *Harder*'s periscope cutting through the water some 600 yards ahead. Sam, it seemed, intended to fire a salvo down the enemy's throat in his time-honoured custom.

Eighteen minutes later the men in *Hake* heard the rumbling crack of fifteen depth-charges being dropped in quick succession. Nothing more was ever heard from Sam Dealey or the *Harder*. One of America's greatest submarine commanders had paid the ultimate price.

* * *

Dealey's exploits during *Harder*'s fifth patrol led to the award of the Congressional Medal of Honor to her Captain and a Presidential Unit Citation for the submarine and her crew. Sadly Sam did not survive to receive his medal and it was the lonely figure of his widow, Edwina, watched by their two young daughters, who accepted the decoration from President Franklin D. Roosevelt some months later, the Unit Citation being accepted by a representative of the United States Submarine Force on behalf of the lost *Harder*.

Like any good American Sam Dealey would have been proud of the honours. But the award that meant most to him was a wooden plaque presented to him by his fellow submarine commanders on his return from that momentous fifth patrol. The inscription was brief but apt:

> *To Commander Sam Dealey . . . Destroyer Killer*

—SEVENTEEN—

Chu-Sa* Mochitsura Hashimoto

'Hiriho Kenten – God's Will'

Much was expected from the Japanese Navy's submarines in the weeks and months that followed Pearl Harbor. But, as the statistics show, Japan's underwater offensive was a disastrous failure. Misused tactically and squandered on the altar of military necessity, ultimate success soon became an impossible dream despite the fanatical bravery of the submarine crews. Burdened by poor designs and obsolete equipment, denied such products of modern technology as radar and efficient sonar, and forced to carry out wasteful supply missions to beleaguered island garrisons or equally futile operations with *kaiten* suicide craft, the men of Japan's submarine service were doomed to defeat and destruction from the moment that Rear-Admiral Chuichi Nagumo's dive-bombers hurtled out of the sky on to the unsuspecting American Pacific Fleet lying at anchor in Pearl Harbor's 'Battleship Row' at 7.55 am on 7 December, 1941.

Of the 2,828 merchant ships sunk by submarines of the Axis Powers in World War Two only 175 were destroyed by Japanese vessels – just 907,351 tons from an overall global tally of 14,687,231 tons. Yet Allied submarines operating in the Pacific and Indian Oceans sent 1,153 Japanese merchantmen to the bottom, a bag of 4,889,000 valuable tons of shipping which the Emperor's war lords and admirals could ill afford to lose.

* *Chu-Sa* = Commander

Although the Imperial Navy entered the war with sixty sub-marines in commission and added a further 114 boats to its underwater fleet before the end, it lost no fewer than 130 of them and, by August, 1945, was left with just four large operational submarines, the remainder of its depleted force consisting of unarmed transports, *kaiten* carriers and obsolete craft relegated to training duties. It was, indeed, a sorry tale of high-level in-competence and human waste.

Japan produced no submarine 'aces', despite the undoubted fighting ability of her commanders, and the restrictions which the High Command imposed on its captains were sufficient to ensure that they could never emulate the successes of their American, British and German counterparts. Very few were still alive when the war ended. And of those who survived only a handful had experienced the sharp end of war for more than a few months. But there were exceptions. Commander Hashimoto's career, for example, spanned the entire period of the Pacific War from the midget submarine attack on Pearl Harbor in December, 1941, to the sinking of the *USS Indianapolis* on 30 July, 1945. His first combat cruise began on 18 November, 1941, nearly three weeks before the attack on the US Pacific Fleet, and his final patrol ended on 17 August, 1945, three days after the Emperor's Government had accepted the Allies' surrender terms. Virtually no other Japanese submarine commander could match his experience and expertise.

* * *

Mochitsura Hashimoto, the eighth child of a senior Shinto priest, was born in the ancient Japanese capital of Kyoto in 1909 and, after passing the fiercely competitive public entrance examination, joined the Naval Academy in 1927. The College, built from English-made bricks, was founded in 1873. Situated on the island of Eta Jima close to Hiroshima and overlooking the great naval dockyard of Kure, it had a notorious reputation for harsh discipline. In their smart white uniforms with the distinctive seven brass buttons and ornamental daggers, the young cadets were subjected to a terrifying regime of brutal bullying and officially-condoned physical violence, a system of repression totally alien to Western concepts of education. Punishment for even the most minor offences consisted of heavy blows to the face with a clenched fist while the victim stood to attention before his superior. One leading Japanese destroyer captain, Tameichi Hara, suffered from chronic ear trouble throughout his sea-going career as a direct result of punishment inflicted on him at Eta Jima.

The cadets studied history, engineering, battle tactics and seamanship. And the academic routine was as punishing as the discipline. The working day began at 5.30 am and ended at 9 pm and work continued without respite for seven days a week. There were no periods of stand-easy or relaxation and classroom lectures were interspersed with parade-ground drills and gymnastics, the latter including judo, a martial art at which the young Hashimoto excelled.

During the summer months the cadets were required to swim for three hours every day and the annual camp on Miyajima Island concluded with a mass swim back to the College – a marathon course that covered ten miles and took more than thirteen hours to complete. Not surprisingly about 10% of the cadets had to be invalided from the Academy after this yearly water torture.

But Hashimoto survived and, after the first six months, life became a little easier. Leave was granted and regular beatings ceased. One writer claimed that punishments did not exist at Eta Jima because there was no disobedience. The simple truth was that the cadets were too cowed by the end of their first term to offer any resistance to the regime – a submissiveness to authority that was to continue into service life and which, in part, explains many of the Japanese Navy's failures of World War Two when officers meekly followed orders from their superiors even though obedience meant certain death.

Hashimoto had his first contact with submarines in 1934, but, as a young *Tai-i*, or Lieutenant, he was required to gain experience in surface ships and he soon found himself serving on destroyers and gunboats in China, gaining his baptism of fire on the Yangtse during the mid-Thirties. In 1937 he married the daughter of a wealthy Osaka merchant and spent the next two years ashore studying at the Torpedo and Submarine Schools from which he graduated with high marks and excellent reports. By 1940 he was a junior officer aboard a minelaying submarine and in 1941 he was appointed Executive Officer of *I-24*, a new vessel of the *Type C-1* in which the seaplane hangar and catapult of the previous *Type B-1* boats were removed and replaced by a system of chocks abaft the conning-tower designed to carry and launch midget submarines.

Experiments with two-man submersibles had begun in the early 'Thirties and the first production models, *Ha-1* and *Ha-2*, were launched in 1936 under conditions of extreme secrecy. Unlike the subsequent suicide weapons *kaiten* and *kairyu*, the original *Type-A* boats were truly miniature submarines complete with conning-tower, periscope and two 18-inch torpedo tubes in the bows. Powered by a 600 hp electric motor and measuring 78½ feet in length, they displaced 46 tons in submerged trim and had a range of 80 miles at 6 knots, although their maximum speed was a respectable 23 knots.

In order to protect the secrecy of the two-man submarines security was taken to farcical extremes and, even though the *Type C-1* vessels were specifically designed to act as mother-ships for the midgets, Hashimoto's crew in *I-24* were given no preliminary training in servicing or launching a *Type-A* submersible. When, on 17 November, 1941, the officers of the 1st Submarine Squadron were called to a planning conference and told that they were to leave the next day for an attack on the American Fleet at Pearl Harbor not one of them had even seen the top-secret weapons which they were to take with them. Hashimoto wrote later: 'I saw the craft for the first time at Kure (on 17 November, 1941) and had no chance of learning anything about its construction'.

I-24, with *I-16, I-18, I-20* and *I-22*, left Kure on the night of 18 November and set course for the Bungo Channel and the Pacific. On 2 December Lt-Cdr Hiroshi Hanabusa, *I-24*'s captain, was informed by radio that hostilities would begin on 7 December and Hashimoto was given orders to put the boat into a state of combat readiness – a task that nearly ended in disaster when a blowing valve jammed and the submarine began to sink by the bows. Hashimoto's prompt reaction saved the boat. Running into the forward torpedo compartment he located the jammed valve and hammered at it with a spanner until it came free. Compressed air hissed into the for'ard trimming tank and at 300 feet, the *Type-C-1*'s safe diving limit, the submarine levelled out and began rising again. Hashimoto's calm response to the emergency impressed everyone concerned and Hanabusa was well satisfied with his Executive Officer.

The submarine arrived off Oahu Island during the late evening of 6 December, 1941, in a position some eight miles from Pearl Harbor in exact accordance with the operational plan. With the lights and neon signs of Waikiki Beach clearly visible from their vantage point on the deck, and listening to dance music from Station KGMB in Honolulu, Ensign Sakamaki and his crewman Inagaki busied themselves with the final adjustments to the midget submarine, while *I-24* cruised quietly on the surface parallel to the coast. A gyro failure was discovered shortly before the scheduled launch deadline and, despite Sakamaki's efforts, it proved impossible to rectify the fault. Finally, at 5.30 am local time, it was decided to launch the midget – relying on visual pilotage by Sakamaki to get the tiny two-man submersible to the target. *I-24* dived, the quadruple clamps that held the midget to the upper deck

231

were released, and within seconds the *Type-A* was heading towards the entrance to the main anchorage.

Although no one, least of all the crews, expected the midget submarines to survive, Admiral Yamamoto stubbornly insisted that the parent boats must remain off Hawaii for forty-eight hours in order to recover the submersibles when they came back from their mission. But, as the realists had anticipated, none were to return. *I-24*'s own boat ran onto a reef south of Oahu Island and her commander, Kazuo Sakamaki, was taken prisoner – the first Japanese of the war to fall into American hands. His crewmate, Petty Officer Inagaki, drowned in the surf while trying to reach the shore. The other eight men of the Special Attack Force all perished in the course of this unnecessary and, in many respects, madcap operation.

Having waited for the prescribed period *I-24* and the remainder of the 1st Submarine Squadron withdrew from the recovery zone south of the islands and set course for home, reaching their new base at Kwajalein in the Marshall Islands towards the end of the month. It had been a disappointing start for Japan's submarines, the more so when compared with the outstanding successes of Nagumo's Carrier Task Force during the attack on Pearl Harbor and the destruction of the *Prince of Wales* and *Repulse* by torpedo and dive bombers of the Navy's 22nd Air Flotilla.

I-24 left for her second war patrol on 3 January, 1942, and steered, once again, for her now familiar hunting grounds around Hawaii. While en route, however, Hanabusa picked up a signal from another submarine reporting contact with the *USS Saratoga* and, linking up with units of the 2nd Submarine Squadron, *I-24* joined in a high-speed dash to intercept the carrier. But the blowing valves again gave trouble and Hanabusa was forced to drop out of the chase while temporary repairs were effected. Meanwhile, on 11 January *I-6* had succeeded in torpedoing the carrier and, although the giant flat-top failed to sink, she was so severely damaged that she had to return to America for a lengthy period of dockyard repairs.

I-24 remained on patrol to the north-east of Hawaii but no targets appeared and Hashimoto had no opportunity to use his torpedoes. There was one nasty moment when an enemy aircraft surprised the submarine on the surface but Hanabusa's prompt reaction saved the day. *I-24* crash-dived in record time and was safely down to a depth of 90 feet before the pilot released his bombs.

During the return run to Japan they joined up with *I-18* to carry out a pre-arranged bombardment of shore installations on Midway

Island – a somewhat dubious role for submarines at this stage of the war when their prime targets should have been America's few surviving aircraft carriers. Both boats arrived off the island on the evening of 22 January and, during the night, were forced to dive by an inquisitive patrol vessel. As soon as the immediate danger was past *I-24* rose to the surface to fix her position and identify the target, submerging again at sunrise. There was some excitement during the morning when the Watch Officer sighted a merchant ship through the periscope but closer examination showed that she was inside the lagoon and safely screened from attack by the coral reef. The bombardment – if such a puny effort qualifies for such a grandiose description – proved a dismal failure. Only five shots were fired before the shore guns forced *I-24* to dive. *I-18*'s performance was even worse. Faced by a determined enemy, her captain hastily submerged without firing a single shot!

It had certainly been a disappointing start to the war for Hashimoto. The midget submarine attack, unnecessary and ill-prepared, had resulted in disaster. The so-called bombardment of Midway had yielded equally little success. And no enemy ships had been encountered at sea, a fact that suggested Japanese Intelligence was far from efficient as traffic between the West Coast and Hawaii was increasing daily.

Even if targets had been plentiful it is doubtful whether sinkings would have followed. For the High Command, with typical rigidity, had issued precise instructions setting out the number of torpedoes that could be fired at any particular type of target. Thus attacks on merchant ships and destroyers were limited to one torpedo while cruisers merited three. Only battleships and aircraft carriers qualified for a full salvo of six. Torpedoes are notoriously temperamental weapons and by restricting their captains to a single shot against destroyers and merchantmen the Tokyo Admirals were, in many instances, playing into their enemy's hands. For if a torpedo missed a freighter, or only damaged a destroyer, the submarine commander was forbidden to launch a second, and probably decisive, attack. Most Western officers would have disobeyed such a short-sighted order, or, at least, paid only lip service to it. But, trained at Eta Jima, Japan's submarine commanders submissively obeyed their instructions with the result that many Allied ships were to escape what would have normally been certain destruction.

On *I-24*'s return from the Midway operation, and on Hanabusa's recommendation, Hashimoto was sent to join the Advance Course at the Submarine School – Japan's equivalent of the Royal Navy's 'perisher' course for prospective captains. He graduated with flying colours in July, 1942, and was immediately given command of *RO-31*, an old submarine built in 1923 which had been disarmed and relegated to training duties at Yokosuka. Like Max Morton's *A.1*, Hashimoto's *R0-31* had suffered a disastrous accident earlier in her career when she sank in Kobe harbour while undergoing her acceptance trials, a tragedy that had cost eighty-eight lives.

An obsolete training vessel was not exactly what Hashimoto had had in mind when he graduated but things became more interesting when he was ordered to take part in a series of bizarre experiments in underwater logistics.

As the bloody campaign on Guadalcanal swung against Japan it became necessary to run supplies, equipment and reinforcements to the island under cover of darkness in destroyers – the famous 'Tokyo Express' – and submarines. Severe losses soon forced the destroyers to withdraw while growing American strength, especially in the air, quickly made it unwise for submarines to surface in order to unload. It was Hashimoto's task to test various methods of getting supplies to the surface from a submerged submarine via the torpedo tubes. The results were a total fiasco. They first tried biscuit boxes but these broke up during firing and the rice inside – already scarce in wartime Japan – was scattered all over Tokyo Bay. Hashimoto next tried packing the rice into rubber containers which could be carried on deck and released from inside the boat, but this did not work either and, as a last resort, plywood torpedoes were constructed into which were packed bags of rice. Not surprisingly these also broke up on launching and all that finally reached the surface were pieces of wood and empty paper bags.

Hashimoto himself was not involved in running supplies to Guadalcanal at this stage of his career, which is possibly why he managed to survive the war in one piece. For the campaign to supply the beleaguered garrison heralded the doom of Japan's once-proud submarine fleet. Boats were recalled from operational patrols and, with their armament reduced to a single deck gun and two torpedo tubes, were thrown into the Solomons cauldron as underwater supply ships. At one point, in January, 1943, as many as twenty submarines were engaged in the task of ferrying food and ammunition to the soldiers ashore. Few were to survive the holocaust.

After a long spell of training duties in *RO-31* Hashimoto was given command of *I-158* in February, 1943. But he was again denied combat duties and spent the next six months testing Japan's early and very primitive surface radar apparatus. The trials proved to be very disappointing although Hashimoto was quick to recognize the potential value of this new technology and he soon became a vociferous supporter of submarine radar despite opposition from senior officers and the High Command. Later that Summer he was transferred to the new *RO-44*, a medium-sized submarine of the *Kaichu*-type, displacing 1,447 tons submerged and equipped with a single 3-inch high-angle gun and four torpedo tubes. It was not a lucky class and of the eighteen boats completed only one survived the war – an indictment of the High Command's misuse of their submarines and of Japan's failure to provide her underwater fleet with adequate and efficient surface and sky-search radar.

Having supervised the fitting-out of his new boat, Hashimoto began her trials in September, 1943, and was almost immediately involved in a fierce battle with bureaucratic red-tape in his efforts to acquire radar equipment. Backed by an understanding flotilla captain he succeeded in borrowing a set from the Kure Naval Air Station but it proved somewhat temperamental and, even on a good day, its maximum range was only a miserable 14,000 yards! It was, however, better than nothing especially in conditions of bad visibility. But when Hashimoto tried to obtain similar sets for other RO-class submarines he was reprimanded for carrying out trials without permission and his illicitly acquired apparatus was removed and returned to its rightful owners. By way of compensation, and to show that his senior officers understood the problem, he was allowed to draw one extra pair of binoculars from the stores!

Towards the end of December, 1943, *RO-44* was ordered south. Reaching Truk ten days later the crew basked in the tropical heat of the anchorage, a welcome contrast to the blizzards they had left behind at Maizuru, while their captain reported to the C-in-C 6th Fleet aboard the mighty 18-inch gunned battle wagon *Yamato*, the world's most powerful warship. Hashimoto once more had the temerity to raise the vexed question of radar equipment but, although the Admiral listened to his plea with understanding sympathy, red-tape and inter-departmental rivalry again ensured that no sets were made available for the use of submarines.

RO-44 was sent to patrol off the eastern Solomons but no targets were sighted and on his return Hashimoto found Truk under heavy attack by ships and aircraft of the American 5th Fleet. It was totally impossible to enter the anchorage in such circumstances and, discretion being the better part of valour, he sensibly withdrew to sea and kept out of the way until he received a signal to come in. The harbour entrance and the anchorage itself were strewn with wrecks. 'The sight of capsized and sunken ships, their masts sticking forlornly out of the water, was most desolate,' he recorded later. But worse was to follow. The flotilla's depot ship *Heian Maru* had been sunk at her moorings and her specialist equipment and supplies were now under water. It had been a devastating and totally unexpected assault which had cost the Japanese two cruisers, four destroyers, twenty-six transports and 270 aircraft. Within weeks the Solomon Islands had been abandoned and the Emperor's chastened forces were pulled back to a new defensive line drawn from the Philippines to Okinawa. But until the withdrawal was completed the surviving submarines, including *RO-44*, were ordered to run supplies to the beleaguered troops on Mille Island.

The first mission ended in disaster when the supplies, carried on deck, were swept away by the sea. But fresh containers were embarked and the submarines returned to succour their Army comrades. Desperate weeks full of drama and danger followed but the exhausted submariners were allowed no respite from their increasingly hazardous missions. Amazingly, every boat engaged on these supply runs survived.

On one occasion Hashimoto encountered an American Task Group which included two carriers and a battleship. The big ships altered course at the last minute and ran out of range but the escorting destroyers, steaming in line abreast, were a sitting target. Hashimoto's orders, however, were quite explicit. The supply mission must take priority over attacks on shipping, the only permitted exceptions being battleships and carriers. Despite an understandable and natural instinct to fire his torpedoes Hashimoto's Eta Jima training quickly overcame his personal ambitions. The destroyers were a forbidden target. Reluctantly he ordered his men to stand down from Battle Stations. Taking *RO-44* deeper he waited for the enemy ships to move away.

Although the submarines returned to Truk to refuel and load fresh military supplies they enjoyed little rest for American carrier aircraft continued to pound the base incessantly and *RO-44*, like the other submarines, had to spend the daylight hours lying on the bottom of the harbour in 75 feet of water to escape enemy bombs – a discomfort they shared with the British submarine flotilla based in Malta. But submerging did not always bring protection. On 4 April, 1944, *I-169* had a compartment flooded while she was cowering on the seabed and all attempts to raise her to the surface failed, the task of salvage being made no easier by continual cannon and machine-gun attacks from marauding American aircraft. Hashimoto's boat barely escaped a similar fate when a stick of bombs fell directly over the spot where she was lying submerged. Fortunately the hull was undamaged and there was no flooding, but on returning to the surface it was found that the periscopes had been distorted by the exploding bombs and, unable to effect repairs at Truk, Hashimoto was ordered to take *RO-44* back to Japan.

It was a nightmare voyage. The damaged periscopes made submerged observation difficult and large numbers of American submarines were known to be patrolling the main sea-lanes out of Truk. In addition, without radar or efficient sonar equipment, Hashimoto and his men could only rely on their own eyes and ears when danger threatened. On one occasion an aircraft sighted by a lookout was reported as 'friendly', but when it became apparent that it was decidedly *un*friendly Hashimoto gave the order to dive. It says much for his coolness and presence of mind that he rescinded the order within seconds when he realized that it was preferable to be bombed on the surface than just beneath it with all hatches secured. Fortunately the bombs fell short and Hashimoto was able to take the submarine down into the safety of the depths before the aircraft returned for a second run. Nevertheless *RO-44* was sprayed with machine-gun fire as she dived and a number of bullet holes were discovered in the outer casing when she resurfaced later that day.

The submarine arrived at Kure on 29 April and Hashimoto handed the boat over to her new captain on 15 May when repairs had been completed. Just four weeks later *RO-44* was sunk with all hands by the destroyer *Burden R. Hastings* off Eniwetok.

Hashimoto's next appointment was to the brand-new *Type B-3* submarine *I-58* which was being fitted out in the Yokosura dockyard. With a submerged displacement of 3,688 tons and measuring 356 feet from stem to stern she was a big submarine by the standards of World War Two. Her operational range was an impressive 21,000 miles at 16 knots and she had a maximum diving depth of 325 feet. Her original design included a seaplane hangar and catapult plus a 5.5-inch deck gun. But these were removed and she was fitted to carry four *kaiten* suicide submarines, her capacity being increased to six in March 1945. Much to Hashimoto's satisfaction, she was also equipped with a Type-22 surface radar set to which was added, at a later date, a Type-13 air-warning scanner and receiver.

Having completed fitting-out *I-58* left Yokosuka for diving trials. Apart from finding a bad leak, the first time the vessel exceeded a depth of 200 feet the tests were satisfactory and the submarine was sent to join the Operational Training Squadron in the Inland Sea for her final working-up. It is interesting to note that

Hashimoto shared opinions similar to those of many officers in Western navies: 'In all I saw three submarines built . . . and I was struck by the greater efficiency of the private yards as compared with the Navy dockyards which didn't seem to care how much time and money they wasted.'

I-58 was officially commissioned into the Imperial Japanese Navy on 13 September, 1944, a date that would have certainly dismayed Baron von Spiegel. On completion of her final period of crew training the submarine moved from Sasebo to Kure and then on to Hirao where she picked up her complement of *kaitens*. These one-man suicide torpedoes – the underwater equivalent of the *kamikaze* aircraft – were originally conceived in the spring of 1944 when the admirals realized that conventional submarines could not be built in sufficient numbers, or quickly enough, to match America's fast-growing sea power. Designed around the famous Type-93 *Long Lance* torpedo with its revolutionary enriched-oxygen engine these vessels packed a large warhead of TNT into their bows and were manually steered towards their targets by their one-man crews. The first models had a small hatch through which the pilot could escape at the last moment – but the fanatical young men who manned these vehicles of self-destruction preferred to die with their weapons like the ancient *samurai* warriors of history.

That Japan's submarine fleet should be reduced to such devices is a measure of the slaughter it had suffered at the hands of the Americans. And the loss of trained and experienced personnel was even more serious. Hashimoto noted that of the fifteen officers who had graduated with him from the Submarine School in 1942 only five, including himself, were still alive by December, 1944.

I-58's departure on her first combat mission was an emotional affair with the pilots of the *kaitens* sitting astride their weapons brandishing *samurai* swords and wearing traditional white *hachimaki* scarves tied around their heads. *I-58*'s identification number had been erased from the conning-tower and in its place had been painted the emblem of the Kongo Unit to which the *kaiten* crews belonged – the battle flag of the medieval Japanese warrior-hero Masahige Kusunoki. A brightly coloured banner with the words *Hiriho Kenten** streamed from the periscope standards while hundreds of Navy personnel chanted the names of the men who were about to sacrifice their lives for the Emperor.

Unfortunately the drama and patriotic fervour of *I-58*'s send-off failed to bring success. Hashimoto's high expectations from the

* 'God's Will.'

boat's new air warning radar proved to be somewhat misplaced when the watchful eyes of a lookout spotted an enemy aircraft many seconds before it was picked up on the radar plot. Most of the voyage to Guam had to be carried out submerged – firstly while running the gauntlet of American submarine patrols in the Bungo Channel, and then to avoid being attacked by enemy aircraft. Guam was Admiral Nimitz's advance headquarters for operations against Iwo Jima and Okinawa but despite the increased surface traffic which this generated Hashimoto was under strict orders *not* to make torpedo attacks until the *kaitens* had been launched, the secrecy of the latter operation being of paramount consideration.

With hindsight it is difficult to justify Japan's faith in the *kaiten*. In general terms the suicide torpedoes gained very few successes. In theory, of course, a piloted torpedo should have been far more accurate than a pre-aimed conventional weapon. But it just so happened that the theory did not hold up in practice. Certainly Hashimoto's four *kaitens* achieved little when they attacked Guam in the early hours of 12 January, 1945. No explosions were heard and periscope observation at dawn revealed only some smoke hanging over the anchorage. In the circumstances Hashimoto did not feel there was enough evidence to claim a confirmed victory, although post-war US records suggest that one of *I-58*'s *kaitens* struck and sank an American tanker with heavy loss of life.

I-58 returned to Kure after the attack on Guam and remained at the base until March when, with another *kaiten* group embarked and accompanied by *I-36*, she sailed for Iwo Jima. A radio signal from Combined Headquarters cancelled the operation at the last minute and, having jettisoned the *kaitens*, Hashimoto plodded wearily back to Kure again. It had been a hectic trip with enemy aircraft appearing every time the submarine surfaced, but, thanks to advanced warning by the Type-13 sky-search radar, there was always adequate time to submerge. In fact Hashimoto attributed *I-58*'s survival entirely to the submarine's radar equipment.

Air attacks on the Japanese mainland had now reached a frightening intensity with 334 Superfortresses dropping 2,000 tons of incendiary bombs on Tokyo on the night of 9/10 March causing the greatest man-made fire in history and killing 83,000 civilians – more, in fact, than the Hiroshima atomic bomb! Nagoya, Osaka and Kobe all suffered a similar fate and it was clear that the end could not be long delayed. In addition American aircraft had blocked the Shimonoseki and Bungo Straits with mines. Leaving Kure on 2 April with orders to attack enemy warships off Okinawa, Hashimoto nevertheless succeeded in finding a mine-free exit from the Inland Sea and was soon steering south-westwards. The Okinawa battle-zone proved to be a death trap for Japanese surface warships and submarines alike. After Okinawa even the remnants of Japan's once great fleet ceased to exist. *I-58* was attacked by aircraft *fifty* times in the space of seven days and the longest continuous period she was able to remain on the surface undisturbed was no more than four hours! After a month at sea without maintenance the *kaitens* were little better than scrap metal and the only target, sighted at 3 am on 25 April, proved to be a hospital ship which Hashimoto, with due deference to International Law, allowed to pass unscathed. He finally reached Kure on the 29th, empty-handed as usual, but perhaps not quite so unsuccessful as he at first thought. For *I-58* proved to be the *only* Japanese submarine to return from the holocaust of Okinawa and her sheer survival was testimony to her captain's skill.

American air raids and mine-laying operations intensified still further as the United States' war machine rolled steadily closer to the Japanese mainland. Whole cities had been destroyed by the *B-29* bomber force and virtually every port was sealed by mines. To make matters worse American submarines had now penetrated into the Inland Sea and on 10 June the *USS Skate* torpedoed and sank *I-122* in Toyama Bay. Training exercises, although curtailed, continued despite the risks of enemy attack but *I-58* remained trapped in Kure throughout May and June until minesweepers could clear a channel out of the Inland Sea. But time was not wasted and during this enforced hiatus the submarine was rigged to carry six instead of the original four *kaitens*.

Hashimoto finally left Kure on 18 July and, on emerging from the enemy minefields that were now strangling Japan's inshore waters, he negotiated the cordon of American submarine patrols and headed south to 'harass the enemy's communications'. No shipping was encountered on the normally busy Mariana-Okinawa route, however, and Hashimoto continued to run southwards in search of targets. The weather was hot and sticky and the sky overcast. Exhausted by the debilitating humidity inside the submarine, many of the crew slept naked on sacks of rice as *I-58* rumbled quietly towards the equator.

The Guam-Leyte shipping lane proved equally empty but on Saturday, 28 July, *I-58* finally made an interception, a tanker escorted by a destroyer. Although a conventional torpedo attack was more likely to yield success Hashimoto decided to use two of the *kaitens* because the submarine's hydrophones were malfunctioning and he could not afford to take chances with a destroyer in the vicinity. The *kaiten* pilots wriggled into the domed cockpits of their torpedoes and at 2.31 pm the chocks were released as the first of the suicide craft reported itself ready for launch. The other *kaiten* followed a short while later but no results were observed from the attack, although two explosions were heard some time later. A rain squall made it impossible to see exactly what had happened and Hashimoto made a laconic entry in the log: *Enemy tanker assumed sunk*. It was his way of honouring the dead *kaiten* pilots for, in his heart of hearts, he did not really believe the validity of the claim.

The next day, Sunday 29 July, was overcast with intermittent squalls which, on occasions, reduced visibility to zero. Exhausted by almost continuous watch-keeping, Hashimoto retired to his bunk leaving orders that he was to be roused at 10.30 pm, shortly after moonrise. A Petty Officer woke him as instructed and, having put on his uniform, he offered up a brief prayer in the submarine's Shinto shrine before making his way to the control room. With the crew at Night Battle Stations he brought the boat to 60 feet and cautiously raised the periscope. Nothing was visible but, taking no chances, Hashimoto swept the horizon three times before giving the order to blow main ballast.

I-58 had scarcely emerged from the depths when the navigating officer, the first man to climb through the hatchway and out onto the bridge, reported a ship in sight. Hashimoto raised his powerful night glasses. His eyes confirmed the shouted warning – the dark shape of a ship was just visible against the luminous backdrop of the moon some five miles to port.

'Dive!'

I-58's bows tilted sharply as the four men on the bridge scrambled down the ladder and closed the upper hatch. The whine of the electric motors replaced the rumble of the diesel engines and a cauldron of white bubbles erupted from the sides of the submarine as the sea, flooding through the vents into the ballast tanks, expelled the air.

'Stand-by all tubes . . . *kaitens* to the ready!'

The target was much closer now and Hashimoto tentatively identified it as an *Idaho*-class battleship or a large cruiser. The torpedo-room reported the tubes flooded and ready and the hydrophone operator passed his estimate of the target's speed back to the captain. But Hashimoto's periscope observations suggested that the estimate was excessive and, with supreme self-confidence, he instructed his Executive Officer to re-set the Target Attack Director to 20 knots. The *kaiten* pilots clamoured to be launched but, again, Hashimoto's confidence in his own ability decided him against using the suicide weapons. They had proved too unreliable in the past and, in addition, both the target's speed and the weather conditions were unsuitable for a *kaiten* attack. For once in his career he was free to fight like a true submarine captain. This would be a contest between his own skill and the enemy's alertness. And no one else would be allowed to interfere. The range had now fallen to 1,500 yards and, unbelievably, the enemy was still maintaining a straight course. Hashimoto re-set the Attack Director to Green 60° – range 1500. This was the moment for which he had been waiting through three and a half years of war. It was just two minutes after midnight on Monday 30, July, 1945 when he gave the order.

'Full salvo – at two second intervals . . . *Fire!*'

Six torpedoes shot from the tubes and spread out towards the target as *I-58* swung onto a parallel course to await results. Minutes later three torpedoes slammed home against the enemy ship and Hashimoto saw flames erupt as the warheads detonated. More explosions followed, but the crippled warship seemed reluctant to sink and, while Hashimoto pondered whether to reload and fire another salvo, his hydrophone operator reported that the enemy vessel was using sonar equipment.* Not wishing to be detected, Hashimoto took *I-58* to 100 feet and used the opportunity to reload the empty tubes. By the time he returned to periscope depth to renew the attack, however, the ship had vanished.

Unaware of the true identity of his victim Hashomito moved quietly away from the scene and set off in search of fresh prey. At 3 am on Monday 30 July he sent a brief radio signal to Tokyo reporting that he had 'released six torpedoes and scored three hits on a battleship of the *Idaho* class . . . definitely sank it'. Then he continued his run to the north-east.

On Wednesday he caught a glimpse of a merchant ship, but its high speed prevented a torpedo attack and it vanished over the horizon unaware of its lucky escape. The ensuing week was one of boredom and routine. No targets were sighted and *I-58*'s watch-keepers spent many weary hours staring at an empty sea. Tuesday 7 August brought the first news reports of the atomic bomb attack on Hiroshima. Hashimoto was horrified. He had always found news broadcasts, whether Japanese or American, unsettling. 'My nerves,' he admitted, 'were not capable of taking the strain.' He refused to listen to any more radio news bulletins, deputing the task to Sub-Lieutenant Nishimura.

Three days later morale was boosted when the submarine ran across a small convoy. This time Hashimoto acceded to the pleas of

*The report was a mistake. *Indianapolis* was not, in fact, fitted with underwater sound-ranging gear.

the *kaiten* pilots and agreed to launch the human torpedoes. But two of the craft suffered mechanical problems and only two actually got off – Numbers 4 and 5. Explosions were heard after they had penetrated the convoy and Hashimoto was satisfied that one of the destroyers had now disappeared. Based on this somewhat flimsy evidence he claimed a victory.

Yet another convoy was located by *I-58*'s Type-22 surface radar on 12 August and the last pair of *kaitens* were launched. A merchantman was claimed as sunk but its fate was by no means certain and the loss is not supported by the US Navy's records. But the crew's elation was quickly dampened when, three days later, the submarine's radio picked up a communiqué announcing the end of hostilities. Hashimoto at first discounted the report, thinking it to be another American trick, but further signals were received in the radio room during the day and, despite his orders that all wireless traffic was to be kept confidential, news soon leaked to the crew and rumours spread like wildfire.

I-58 reached Hiraro, the *kaiten* base, on 17 August and was met by stern-faced senior officers carrying the Imperial Rescript – the Emperor's order to his fighting services to lay down their arms and surrender. Hashimoto cleared the lower deck and, calling the men aft, read them the message with tears in his eyes. The war was over. Japan had been defeated. As *I-58*'s war-weary captain readily admitted: 'Most of us were past argument'.

* * *

The sinking of the *USS Indianapolis* was the greatest sea disaster ever suffered by the US Navy, and the tragedy was heightened by the fact that, in addition to the 400 men who died as a direct result of Hashimoto's attack, a further 480 had died by drowning and exhaustion because of an inexplicable delay in confirming that the cruiser was missing. Public opinion, inflamed by press stories of survivors being eaten by sharks or going mad and killing each other, demanded that heads must roll. The Commanding Officer of the *Indianapolis*, Captain Charles B. McVay III, was accused of failing to steer a zig-zag course while steaming through waters known to be patrolled by hostile submarines.

The proceedings of the Court of Inquiry and the subsequent Court Martial fall outside the scope of this brief account but there was an outcry in the newspapers when it was decided to call Hashimoto as a Prosecution witness. The politicians, however, made more of Hashimoto's appearance in the witness box than the facts merited, for he was, in truth, only called to confirm that the cruiser was *not* zig-zagging when he made his attack.

Wearing dark nondescript civilian clothes and speaking in Japanese he answered questions through a US Navy interpreter and his final statement did much to take the sting out of the Prosecution's attack on the unfortunate McVay. When asked: 'Would it have made any difference to you if the target had been zig-zagging in this attack?' Hashimoto answered the question in a soft but firm voice. There was a brief pause and then the interpreter translated his reply to the Court:

'It would have involved no change in the method of firing the torpedoes but some changes in manoeuvring.'

In other words, as he had already told the Court of Inquiry, Hashimoto was quite confident that even if McVay *had* been zig-zagging *I-58* would have still sent the *Indianapolis* to the bottom. But despite this unequivocal statement Hashimoto's evidence was insufficient to acquit Captain McVay of 'through negligence suffering a vessel of the Navy to be hazarded' – the negligence in this context being his failure to steer a zig-zag course. But the Captain won a 'not guilty' verdict on the more serious second charge of 'Culpable inefficiency in the performance of duty'.

And so, in the calm quiet of a courtroom in the Washington Navy Yard, two honourable men who had met so fleetingly and tragically two minutes after midnight on 30 July 1945* some 110 miles north-east of Leyte came face to face once again. It was for Commander Mochitsura Hasimoto and Captain Charles B. McVay the final battle of the Pacific War.

---

* Many reference books show *Indianapolis* as being sunk on 29 July 1945. She was, in fact, sighted by *I-58* at 23.35 on Sunday 29 July. But the torpedoes were not fired until 00.02 on Monday 30 July and this is the correct date of her loss.

—*EIGHTEEN*—

Commander Richard Hetherington O'Kane USN

'The bravest man I know.'

Even before he graduated with the Class of '34 from the Annapolis Naval Academy, the cradle of American admirals since its founding in 1845, Dick O'Kane's sole ambition in life was to command his own submarine. He had a long road to travel before he achieved his ambition but he was fortunate to serve under some excellent masters and he proved an apt and willing pupil. After gaining experience in various training submarines, followed by a spell of compulsory duty with the surface fleet, the outbreak of war found O'Kane as Fourth Officer of *Argonaut*, at that time the Navy's largest submarine with a submerged displacement of 4,164 tons. He did not remain with the giant mine-layer for long, however, and in March, 1942, he was transferred to the *Wahoo* as her Executive Officer.

It was a rapid and well merited jump up the ladder but, despite his obvious satisfaction with the appointment, Dick did not seem over-happy with his lot. *Wahoo* was still on the building slip when he joined her and, like Sam Dealey, he was impatient for combat service, his pent-up frustration increasing when his old boat, *Argonaut*, together with the Marine 2nd Raider Battalion, carried out a highly successful strike against Makin Atoll on 16 August, 1942, shortly before *Wahoo* left Pearl for her first patrol.* To

---

* *Argonaut* was sunk by Japanese depth-charges off New Britain on 10 January, 1943.

aggravate the situation he did not seem to hit it off with his skipper, Lt-Cdr Marvin Kennedy.

Wahoo's Third Officer, George Grider, certainly had reservations about the new Executive Officer. 'A young man who struck me as rather garrulous and potentially unstable,' he wrote after the war. Neither he nor his fellow officers ever dreamt that O'Kane would become one of the US Navy's greatest submarine commanders. Nevertheless Grider found him to be: 'Likeable, obviously a hard worker, and careful about details. But there was something about him that made us feel he was a little out of touch with reality' – a sentiment shared by *Argonaut*'s skipper some months earlier when Dick had suggested laying a minefield in the Sea of Japan. That 'something' later emerged as O'Kane's overriding determination to sink and destroy as many enemy ships as possible. It was a characteristic he shared with many other great underwater fighters like Horton, Weddigen, Kretschmer, Dealey and Wanklyn. The killer instinct!

Things showed little sign of improving even after *Wahoo* arrived at Pearl for combat duties and, during the submarine's second patrol, Grider records that O'Kane 'had grown harder to live with – friendly one minute and pulling rank on his junior officers next. One day he would be a martinet and the next he would display an over-lenient attitude that was far from reassuring.' It was on this second patrol that Mush Morton joined the *Wahoo* as a passenger and it was soon apparent that the two men had much in common. Both shared a passion for apparently hare-brained schemes to attack the enemy and both showed a relish for hitting the Japanese whenever and wherever they could. They shared the same dreams and spoke the same language. In addition the older man seemed to have a steadying influence on the young Lieutenant and by the time *Wahoo* returned to Pearl there had been a noticeable change in O'Kane's attitude.

As soon as Morton assumed command of the submarine he wasted no time in thrusting responsibility onto the shoulders of his Executive Officer. Although Mush always masterminded the details of the actual attack it was O'Kane who remained at the periscope. It was clear that each man trusted the other's judgement implicitly. It proved to be a winning combination and, as related in an earlier chapter, Morton and *Wahoo* soon gained an enviable reputation in the Pacific.

Mush, however, always gave O'Kane and his other officers equal credit for the submarine's successes. They were, as he repeatedly pointed out, a team. He was only the captain of that team.

But all good things must come to an end and on *Wahoo*'s return to Mare Island for overhaul in June, 1943, O'Kane was taken out of the boat and given command of the *Tang*, a submarine of the *Balao*-class of similar dimensions and lay-out to the *Wahoo* but capable of diving to a greater depth, a useful attribute with the underwater war increasing in ferocity every day. When she was completed O'Kane took his new boat out of the Mare Island Navy Yard for her first taste of salt water and spent the next few weeks on diving trials and other routine exercises. Then, moving to San Diego, he began training the crew in combat tactics and attack techniques.

Tang arrived at Pearl in early January, 1944, and left for her first war patrol on the 22nd. Three weeks later the submarine was off Palau and during the small hours of 17 February the radar operator, George Hallahan, reported a contact. A buzz of excitement rippled through the boat and, with O'Kane breathing impatiently down their necks, the radar team quickly prepared a summary of the plot: Target steering 100°; speed 8 knots, zig-zag pattern 40°every ten minutes. It looked to be a promising scenario.

Tang's radar operators were kept busy as the submarine moved ahead and by 2 am O'Kane possessed a comprehensive picture of the enemy – two large ships; one of medium size, possibly a destroyer; five small vessels thought to be anti-submarine units. But the routine was suddenly broken when one of the wing escorts swung out of line and headed towards the surfaced submarine.

The diving klaxon brought the lookouts tumbling down the steel ladder into the conning-tower in double quick time and, as the upper hatch was pulled tight shut, the diesel engines cut out – their throaty roar replaced by the whining hum of the electric motors. *Tang* angled down on her 'planes as the vents opened to flood the ballast tanks and within one minute she was safely beneath the water although O'Kane continued the dive in anticipation of a depth-charge attack. But the reality proved to be something of an anti-climax – just five charges dropped at random. Apparently satisfied that she had done her duty the escort turned smartly away and hurried back to regain station with the convoy. O'Kane waited for sonar clearance and then brought *Tang* cautiously to periscope depth to survey the situation.

The solitary destroyer moved rapidly across his sights seemingly unaware of the danger lurking in the depths but Dick allowed the warship to pass undisturbed. He could see a medium-sized and well-laden cargo vessel approaching and decided that she would be a more rewarding target. He watched the 7,000-ton *Gyotin Maru* carefully as he passed details of her course, speed and range to the officer working the TDC. The periscope ran up for the last time.

'Range 1500.'
'1500 – set.'
'Bearing – mark!'
'Zero-One-Three, Captain.'
'Zero-One-Three – set. Solution!'
'Fire!'

Four torpedoes, spaced at ten second intervals, streaked from the stern tubes and O'Kane's knuckles whitened with tension as he waited. Thirty seconds . . . forty-five seconds . . . sixty seconds.

The first weapon sent up a geyser of dirty water as it exploded in the vicinity of the freighter's propellers. Moments later the second torpedo struck the hull just abaft of amidships. Smoke and flame erupted from the engine-room and the *Gyotin Maru* slowed down. When the third torpedo slammed into the vessel's bows her doom was sealed and a glow of excitement tingled through O'Kane's body as he watched his first victim settle slowly in the water and disappear from view. It was a sight that he never forgot.

Not surprisingly *Tang*'s assault on the *Gyotin Maru* had not gone unnoticed by the convoy commander and one of the escorts was detached to investigate. But again the depth-charge attack was half-hearted and indecisive and the warship quickly scurried off into the darkness to rejoin its companions. Such faint-hearted tactics were unusual – the Japanese were normally tenacious in defence and ferocious in attack. But O'Kane did not stop to reason why. Gift horses should not be examined too closely.

Thirty-three days later *Tang* returned to Pearl Harbor. She had exhausted her entire outfit of twenty-four torpedoes and had scored a commendable sixteen hits. Her final tally of five ships included a fully-laden 21,000-ton naval tanker. It was a more than satisfactory result for O'Kane's first war patrol and it was an encouraging omen for the future. Watching from his underwater Valhalla, 'Mush' Morton must have felt proud of his young protegée.

Tang's second patrol proved to be something of an anti-climax with no ships sighted and no attacks made, but it was not without excitement, for on 29 April O'Kane received radio orders to carry out lifeguard duties during Task Force 58's air strike against Truk and neighbouring islands, a mission he was to share with Dealey's *Harder* and other boats of the Pacific Fleet's submarine force. But, not content to be a passive bystander, O'Kane joined in the fireworks by coming to the surface and using his deck guns on Japanese shore installations while the air-raids were in progress, a tactic that confused and alarmed the enemy but which brought him considerable satisfaction.

The actual rescue operation turned out to be rather more hazardous than expected. Each time *Tang* rose to the surface to scoop a splashed pilot to safety Japanese shore guns opened fire and forced the submarine to dive again. Running submerged was no picnic either, for most of the inflatable rubber rafts had drifted inshore where the water was shallow and whenever O'Kane ventured too close to land razor-sharp coral heads threatened to slice open *Tang*'s keel plating. Finally, in desperation, he sent a radio call to the Task Force commander requesting air cover. Thirty minutes later a swarm of Corsairs and Hellcats arrived and circled overhead so that *Tang* could return to the surface and continue her errand of mercy without disturbance from the enemy.

But this was only one of seven separate pick-up operations carried out by the submarine and of the thirty-five fliers downed by the Japanese defences *Tang* herself saved no fewer than twenty-two. Later that day, when the shallow water made it unsafe to move any closer to the shore, O'Kane showed an unexpected gift for improvisation by making use of a crippled Navy float-plane which, although it was too badly damaged to fly, was still capable of taxiing around the lagoon and picking up survivors who were then ferried back to the submarine.

The rescue mission continued until O'Kane was satisfied that every flier had been saved. *Tang* remained in enemy-controlled waters, under constant threat from Japanese shore guns and aircraft, for two whole days until every known survivor had been accounted for. Then, and only then, did he head for deep water and set course for Pearl. His report to Admiral Lockwood referred to *Tang*'s 'overcrowded bunks' and added that the submarine was 'damned low on fuel'. Almost as an afterthought he added, 'Also no ships sunk'. But O'Kane had nothing to fear from returning home with an unmarked score-card. The Navy, especially the Task Force pilots, never forgot *Tang*'s remarkable and dedicated rescue work off Truk and the submarine's photograph had a place of honour on the bulkheads of many a carrier's flight-room, frequently taking precedent over Betty Grable, Dorothy Lamour and Hollywood's other sex symbols.

Dick O'Kane's third patrol was a humdinger that deserved, and received, a special place in American submarine history. *Tang* sailed from Pearl on 8 June and set course for the East China Sea south-west of Kyushu. Soon after her arrival off the Japanese coast radar contact was made with a large convoy comprising six cargo ships and fifteen escorts. There were, in fact, so many echoes on the radar plot that the operators had difficulty in identifying and separating the targets on their screens and O'Kane decided to resolve the confusion by attacking on the surface under cover of darkness. It proved to be a wise decision and it brought a spectacular success. Closing the convoy at nightfall, he fired a salvo from *Tang*'s bow tubes sinking four ships with six torpedoes, a quite incredible piece of marksmanship that has never been equalled under combat conditions.

Moving further west into the Yellow Sea O'Kane sank another five freighters plus a tanker and by the time he returned to Pearl Harbor *Tang* had destroyed ten ships with just fifteen torpedoes. Her total tally of 39,000 tons for a single patrol remained an American submarine record until the end of the war. Not surprisingly O'Kane was awarded a second Navy Cross – he was to win five in all – while *Tang* and her crew received a Presidential Unit Citation.

The submarine's fourth patrol mirrored the problems and disappointments of *Wahoo*'s fifth mission for, like Morton, O'Kane also had to endure the frustrations and dangers of operating in Japanese home waters with a batch of faulty torpedoes. The cruise opened on a bright note, however, and the morning of 11 August found the *Tang* prowling submerged off Miki Saki on the coast of Honshu. An anti-submarine motor launch and a modern gunboat were in sight to starboard but, although their presence cramped his style to a certain extent, O'Kane carefully kept them at a safe distance and they posed no immediate threat. The patrolling launch finally caught a glimpse of *Tang*'s periscope during the afternoon and began to shadow the submarine, although, for some reason, she made no attempt to ask the gunboat for support.

O'Kane could have gone deep and steered out of the area to escape such unwelcome attentions but his instincts told him that all this anti-submarine activity meant that some juicy targets were likely to appear on the scene in the near future. Two hours later, just before 5 pm, he detected a smudge of smoke on the horizon and closer inspection revealed two medium-sized cargo vessels, the *Joshu Go* and the *Oita Maru*, approaching. They were being shepherded by a solitary escort and, having weighed up the general situation, O'Kane decided to attack. The submarine's crew were called to Battle Stations Submerged, the tubes were flooded ready for firing and he began to stalk his distant quarry.

'Fast screws approaching, Captain! Bearing two-one-five!'

Responding to the Sonar Operator's warning O'Kane swung the periscope to port and saw the gunboat charging towards them, presumably in response to a belated signal from the motor launch. Totally unruffled by this unexpected threat, *Tang*'s captain

250

estimated the gunboat's range and did a quick mental calculation. There was just enough time to attack the two merchant ships and to take the submarine to a safe depth before the gunboat could get near enough to ram. If his gamble was to succeed there was not a moment to lose. He passed the range, speed and bearing of the leading freighter to the officer working the Torpedo Data Computer and the machine whirred and clicked.

'Solution!'

'Fire!'

The first three torpedoes leapt from the bow tubes as O'Kane moved the periscope sight to centre on the other merchantman.

'Shift target . . . second ship. Bearing – *mark*!'

'Bearing two-seven-zero.'

'Two-seven-zero . . . set!'

With his forearms slumped over the guide handles of the periscope and his uniform cap pushed back on his head, O'Kane waited impatiently.

'Solution!'

'Fire!'

'All torpedoes running, Captain.'

O'Kane swung the top lens of the periscope to port just in time to see the fast-moving gunboat shave past *Tang*'s stern with only inches to spare. The enemy boat had been travelling faster than he thought and it was equally apparent that the Japanese commander had made a similar mistake about *Tang*'s speed. Just two or three more degrees of helm and the submarine would have now been plunging to the bottom with sea rushing into the pressure hull through the gaping hole punched by the gunboat's bows. O'Kane forced his mind back to reality.

'Rig for depth-charges . . . take her down!'

Tang dug her nose into the sea but, instead of lowering the 'scope, O'Kane kept it pointing at the first of the two freighters. In those final fleeting moments, before the engulfing water rose up and blanked out the upper lens, he saw the first torpedo strike the target. The *Oita Maru* disintegrated in front of his eyes and, as the smoke and steam cleared, he could see that she had broken in two. The next moment the periscope dipped beneath the waves and all contact with the world above the surface was wiped away. More explosions were heard – the intervals between the reverberating thunderclaps confirming further hits – and a member of the control team dutifully entered the relevant times in the rough log for later evaluation. Having savoured their moment of triumph the submarine's crew waited unemotionally for the crash of the first depth-charges. No one had any illusions about the agony that lay

251

ahead. They knew instinctively that it was going to be bad, but there was nothing they or anyone else could do about it.

Tang rolled violently as the first charges exploded. The pounding beat of the propellers overhead warned the crew that another attack was imminent. The submarine shuddered as the next batch of depth-charges detonated. Crouched in the conning-tower, O'Kane used every stratagem he knew to escape from his tormentor and get *Tang* into the safety of deep water.

But the gunboat was like a tenacious bulldog and the barrage continued with relentless intensity. Light bulbs shattered and glass cracked, each explosion seemingly closer than the last. Cork insulation sprinkled down from the deckhead seams and even the paint began to flake from the bulkheads. O'Kane decided on one last desperate gamble.

'Right full rudder! All ahead full!'

The battered *Tang* swung bows-on to the gunboat and, in obedience to O'Kane's orders, steered to pass directly underneath her assailant, but before she could reach the safety of the dead ground beneath the gunboat's keel a further sixteen depth-charges exploded at point-blank range. The entire hull flexed as the concussion of the blast wave hit the boat. The lights went out and men were hurled from their bunks. Others sprawled on the deck. In the motor room, in the dim glow of the emergency lamps, the electrician's mates were holding the switches in position with their bare hands in an effort to prevent the circuits from arcing and shorting. But from his vantage point in the conning-tower O'Kane smiled. The persistent *ping* of the sonar probe had suddenly ceased. His gamble had paid off. The enemy had lost contact. Taking advantage of his luck O'Kane took the *Tang* seawards into deeper water and thirty-eight minutes later, safe from counter-attack, he returned to periscope depth. The gunboat was still quartering the sea in the vicinity of her last contact while an aircraft, which had joined the hunt, circled overhead. Closer inshore the motor launch and the other escort were busy picking up survivors. Both freighters had now completely vanished and there was little doubt as to their fate. O'Kane lowered the periscope and stole quietly away.

The next eleven nights failed to yield a single target and the seas remained empty from dusk to dawn. It occurred to O'Kane that, in view of the heavy losses which the Japanese were suffering as the result of night submarine attacks, they were keeping their ships at anchor through the hours of darkness and only sailing in daylight when the American boats were submerged. To test his theory, O'Kane returned to Miki Saki at dusk on 22 August.

Probing into the near-by bay of Owase Wan he quickly located a target which, on closer inspection, proved to be the self-same gunboat that had nearly sunk them eleven nights previously. As O'Kane brought the submarine to Battle Stations Surface he could not help thinking that revenge was sweet. The enemy was at anchor and, bringing *Tang* to the surface, he took her around the stern of the sleeping warship so that he could attack from her landward side. The after tubes were prepared and, optimistically confident, O'Kane fired a single electric torpedo. But instead of striking the gunboat the weapon misbehaved and, after a run of less than 100 yards, it lost buoyancy and sank to the bottom. A second Mark 18 followed, but this, too, developed depth-keeping problems and passed underneath the target without exploding.

It was difficult to understand how the normally alert Japanese lookouts could have missed seeing the two torpedo tracks but there was absolutely no sign of life on the enemy vessel and, taking advantage of their laxness, O'Kane brought *Tang* around so that her bow tubes were in line with the anchored gunboat. This time he took the precaution of using a conventional model but even this well-tried and obedient weapon unexpectedly developed a mind of its own. A gyro malfunction knocked it off course soon after launching and, swerving to starboard, it passed clear of its target by several hundred feet. It was totally unbelievable. Three shots and three failures. O'Kane was busy composing some suitably acid phrases to throw at the Bureau of Ordnance on his return to Pearl when the second thermal-engined torpedo was fired. As if atoning for the antics of its sister and two half-brothers it ran as straight as an arrow and plunged into the gunboat's belly with a satisfying explosion that lit the night sky. By the time the smoke and steam had dispersed the warship had already gone to the bottom and only small pieces of wreckage and debris remained floating on the surface.

O'Kane started his next patrol on 24 September. With seventeen ships already standing to his credit he had high hopes of further successes as he steamed out of Pearl Harbor and headed west-wards. Anticipating an early naval and military assault on the Philippines, the Japanese were rushing reinforcements to the islands with frantic haste. In an effort to circumvent American submarine attacks the Tokyo High Command routed the bulk of their convoys to the west of Formosa, an area which they considered to be relatively safe from the enemy's underwater predators. The Japanese view was, in fact, shared by the Staff of Admiral Nimitz's Pacific Fleet headquarters for extensive and uncharted minefields made the seas to the west of the island exceedingly dangerous, while saturation air patrols from bases on Formosa and the Chinese mainland threatened to make it a graveyard for any submarine that dared to operate along these vital shipping routes. O'Kane, however, had volunteered to stick his head in the lion's mouth to see if he could extract any titbits. With implicit confidence in his finest Captain, ComSubPac had given his consent.

Tang entered the Straits of Formosa on the night of 10 October and within hours had sunk her first victim, a cargo vessel which she sent to the bottom after hitting her with two torpedoes from a three-shot salvo. Thirsting for more Japanese blood, O'Kane penetrated further into the Straits and, soon after dawn, met up with another freighter. With land in sight to starboard and shallow water under the keel, O'Kane sensibly decided to defer his attack until nightfall and spent the rest of the day carefully shadowing the merchant ship at periscope depth. *Tang* was some 4,000 yards astern of the cargo vessel when she surfaced after dusk but she was considerably faster and, although O'Kane kept the diesels throttled back, he had no difficulty in overhauling his intended prey. Having passed safely ahead he swung the submarine to port and waited. *Tang* was rolling heavily in the onshore swell and spray splattered her bridge each time the waves broke against the conning-tower. Seeking protection from the weather O'Kane crouched behind the bridge screen as the enemy ship came into range. In his anxiety to conserve his stock of torpedoes he had decided to launch only one weapon instead of the usual salvo and, in an uncharacteristic moment of self-doubt, he wondered whether he was being over-confident. The range had narrowed to 500 yards when he gave the order to fire and less than half a minute later he saw the flash of the explosion. Having moved closer to confirm that his victim was sinking he turned seawards and, taking the submarine beneath the surface, he set off in search of more scalps.

O'Kane's next brush with the Japanese came on the morning of 20 October when he sighted a small battle group consisting of a light cruiser and two destroyers. They were steaming south at high speed but their intricate zig-zagging course had the effect of slowing their progress and *Tang* came to the surface to give chase. O'Kane had, in fact, almost caught up with the squadron when the cruiser's searchlights suddenly sprang out of the darkness and settled on the submarine. Within moments the enemy's 6-inch guns had opened fire but *Tang* was already submerging fast and by the time the cruiser found the range the submarine was safely out of reach of its shells.

The next forty-eight hours yielded only empty seas until, just after midnight of the second day, *Tang* made radar contact with an approaching convoy. O'Kane steered towards it on the surface and then paralleled its course while he and his Executive Officer, Frank Springer, examined the huddled mass of ships through their binoculars. The convoy was steaming in an unusual cross-shaped formation – a centre column of three tankers in line-ahead with a cargo vessel or transport on each of the port and starboard wings. It was protected by a group of small anti-submarine escorts.

'Full ahead flank!'

Tang's 5,400 HP diesel engines roared to maximum power as she surged ahead of the convoy and O'Kane kept his fingers crossed that the exhaust noise and bow-wave would not attract the attention of the enemy lookouts. Then, having drawn sufficiently ahead, he brought the submarine onto an attack bearing and, as the convoy appeared out of the night, he hurled *Tang* into its centre at battle speed. Five torpedoes leapt from the bow tubes and sped towards the middle column of tankers before the Japanese had even realized that an enemy submarine was in their midst. The ensuing mayhem exceeded even O'Kane's wildest dreams. Two struck the leading tanker, one exploded against the centre ship, while the final two weapons smashed into the third. All three vessels erupted in flames simultaneously and the individual fires quickly linked together to form a continuous wall of flame as the oil floating on the surface of the sea ignited and added to the conflagration.

O'Kane had intended to use *Tang*'s stern tubes on the nearest of the two wing merchantmen but his plans were thwarted by the spectacular fruits of his own success. The glare of the flaming pyre had transformed the darkness of night into the brilliance of day and the surfaced submarine was starkly revealed to the enemy like an actor standing centre-stage in the spotlights. With the submarine seemingly at its mercy, the nearest freighter altered course and steered to ram the vessel responsible for the horrifying holocaust of death and destruction that had engulfed the convoy. In the distance, lit by the glow of the fires, O'Kane saw the merchant ship on the outer wing port her helm to support her companion.

For once O'Kane's boldness had landed him in deep trouble. There was no time left to fire his torpedoes – and to dive with the enemy at such close range was tantamount to suicide. Calling for flank speed and full right rudder, he tried to run clear of the freighter's menacing bows. But the enemy ship matched the movement and swung even closer. With sweat beading his face O'Kane reversed helm and, with only seconds to spare, *Tang* wriggled free. A burst of machine-gun fire swept the submarine's exposed bridge and, with the same disregard for personal danger demonstrated by Rupert Lonsdale during *Seal*'s final agony, O'Kane ordered everyone below while he remained topsides to face the enemy. His courage brought a well-deserved reward. Both Japanese vessels were now in frighteningly close proximity as the two captains threw caution to the wind in their determination to ram the submarine. Seizing his opportunity, O'Kane loosed a full salvo of four torpedoes from the stern tubes. At this moment the two enemy ships collided heavily and were still locked together when *Tang*'s torpedoes crashed into the wreckage. Satisfied with a good night's work, O'Kane turned the submarine away from the burning and sinking ships and sped northwards. The assault on the convoy which had ended with the destruction of all five vessels had taken exactly ten minutes!

Less than 24 hours later, at 11 pm on the night of 24 October – exactly one month after leaving Pearl Harbor – O'Kane made radar contact with another convoy. The confusion of echoes on the plot indicated an unusually large group of ships and, eager for a repetition of the previous night's spectacular victory, he took the submarine into visual range. Although the convoy was not steering a zig-zag pattern the escorts were nervously alert and every few minutes their guns opened fire on unseen and imaginary targets. O'Kane studied the situation carefully through his glasses. He had eleven torpedoes left and he did not intend to waste a single one of them.

Tang slid inside the convoy with the precision of a surgeon's scalpel entering a patient's body. O'Kane had already selected the first column of ships as his initial target – two transports with conspicuously large deck cargoes and a well-laden tanker – and, turning the submarine towards them, he unleashed a salvo of six torpedoes from the bow tubes. Vivid flashes lit the darkness as the weapons did their deadly work and, with quite astonishing marksmanship, each of the three ships fell victim to two torpedoes apiece. The sudden attack led to utter confusion. Signal lamps flickered urgently, searchlights swept the sea, and every available gun opened fire, their crews, seized by blind panic, shooting indiscriminately in all directions. Reflected against the night sky the ruddy glow of the burning ships formed a dramatic backcloth to the scene of carnage and chaos.

But O'Kane was unmoved by the grand panorama of destruction unfolding in front of his eyes and, even before the first torpedoes had exploded, he had swung *Tang* around and pointed her stern towards two more likely targets – a cargo ship and another tanker. Range, speed and bearings were passed to the TDC operator in the control-room below by the talker manning the battle-phone at the skipper's elbow and O'Kane waited tensely for confirmation of the attack settings.

A vicious salvo of 5-inch shells screamed out of the darkness and exploded all around the surfaced submarine as a previously unnoticed Japanese destroyer loomed out of the night a short distance astern of the tanker. Its guns sparkled again and O'Kane willed himself not to duck for cover as the next salvo of projectiles started their lethal journey.

'From TDC, Captain . . . solution.'

'Fire! All ahead flank!'

The events of the next few minutes almost defy credibility. The first of the three torpedoes exploded against the freighter. Moments later the second weapon detonated magnetically as it passed under the tanker and the vessel, plus its cargo of aviation spirit, erupted in a sheet of dazzling white flame. Simultaneously the destroyer, struck either by the third torpedo or falling victim to an internal magazine explosion triggered by the heat of the blazing tanker, blew up and disintegrated into millions of tiny burning fragments of steel and human flesh.

O'Kane steered *Tang* away from the holocaust and, seeing a hiding-place in the darkness to seaward of the convoy, he gave orders to reload the bow tubes with the submarine's last two torpedoes. Five minutes later he returned to renew the attack. The freighter which had been torpedoed earlier was lying stopped in the water but as she seemed to be in no immediate danger of sinking O'Kane decided to put her down with his two remaining 'fish'. A pair of escorts were circling the crippled vessel and, to avoid detection, he took the submarine around the stern of the merchantman to attack her unguarded side.

The first torpedo struck the target amidships causing her to list sharply and, to ensure that she joined her companions on the bottom with the least possible delay, O'Kane fired his final weapon. But Torpedo No 24 was the joker in the pack. It wandered to port within seconds of launching and O'Kane watched with growing horror as it began to circle with ominous intent.

'All ahead emergency! Right full rudder!'

Suddenly the hunter had become the hunted, the threat coming, not from the enemy, but from one of *Tang*'s own torpedoes! Within half a minute the treacherous weapon had swung through a complete half-circle and was speeding back towards the submarine at 45 knots. O'Kane did everything he could to escape but the torpedo seemed imbued with a life of its own. The distance was narrowing with every passing second and he was powerless to do anything about it.

The torpedo struck *Tang* in her after torpedo-room and the shock of the explosion nearly threw O'Kane to the deck. Clinging to the base of the radar scanner for support he shouted an order to close the upper conning-tower hatch bare seconds before the submarine sank beneath his feet. As *Tang* vanished into the depths he kicked himself to the surface to join the other eight members of the bridge party who were swimming in the water. A few minutes later the shocked and dazed survivors were joined by a ninth man –Lieutenant Savadkin who had been in the conning-tower occurred.

Conditions for the men still trapped inside the boat were desperate. The submarine was lying in 180 feet of water and, with three compartments flooded, there was insufficient buoyancy to get the vessel back to the surface again. There had been a number of casualties and a fire which had started in one of the battery compartments was filling the interior of the boat with fumes and smoke. The damage control party quickly extinguished the flames but the sudden blaze had consumed precious oxygen and the rubber-covered cables were still smouldering. Then, as if they were not suffering enough, the convoy escorts began a fierce depth-charge attack which was to last for four terrifying hours.

When the roar of the underwater explosions finally died away *Tang*'s crew prepared to abandon the crippled submarine. The first four men squeezed into the escape chamber and an inflatable rubber dinghy was passed through the hatch before the watertight door was sealed and the flood valves opened. Thirty-five minutes later the chamber was drained down and the door opened. Three of the men, half-drowned and barely conscious, were still inside. The fourth had escaped, although, unbeknown to the trapped crew members inside the submarine, he did not succeed in reaching the surface.

Five men grouped together to make the next attempt but two failed to get through the escape hatch and they were still inside the chamber when it was opened forty-five minutes later. The submarine's central oxygen supply was now running low and the next four men to escape were unable to top up the reservoirs of their Momsen Lungs* before entering the chamber. But by a miracle all four successfully exited through the hatch.

When Lieutenant Flanagan and a second group of four men climbed into the chamber the fire in the battery room had flared up

*An underwater breathing kit used by the US Navy and similar to the Royal Navy's DSEA equipment.

again and the fierce heat was blistering the paint on the outside face of the bulkhead. In addition the rubber gasket forming the watertight seal of the bulkhead door was beginning to smoulder and it was clear that those left behind in the flooded submarine now had virtually no chance of survival.

Although Flanagan's party all reached the surface safely only five of the thirteen men who successfully escaped from the sunken *Tang* were still alive when they were dragged from the sea by a searching enemy destroyer the following morning.

O'Kane, Lieutenant Savadkin, and the eight survivors from the bridge party who were thrown into the sea when the torpedo exploded spent a considerable time in the oil-polluted water before they were hauled to safety. But their ordeal had only just begun. Their Japanese captors forced the exhausted men to strip and then beat them unmercifully with their clenched fists and bayonet scabbards until they could scarcely stand, but not a single man divulged any information of importance and, after further routine interrogation ashore, O'Kane and his men spent the remainder of the war in various prison camps on the Japanese mainland.

Of the fifteen officers and men who survived the sinking only nine were to return home at the end of hostilities. Japanese prison-camp brutalities and the privations of captivity killed their six shipmates. Happily O'Kane was one of the fortunate nine and in 1946, having recovered his health and resumed his naval career, he was personally decorated with the Congressional Medal of Honor by President Harry S. Truman.

In all, *Tang* sank twenty-four enemy ships – more than any other American submarine with the exception of the *Tautog* which, it should be noted, ran up her record-breaking score under the command of three separate captains. And in terms of merchant tonnage sent to the bottom *Tang*'s final total of 93,824 tons placed her fourth in the underwater stakes. O'Kane had good reason, indeed, to be proud of his submarine and her gallant crew.

The legendary 'Mush' Morton once described his former Executive Officer as 'The bravest man I know'. It was an accolade that Richard Hetherington O'Kane earned many times over.

Quotation Sources

p.(ix)	'We had competent navigators . . .'	*The World Crisis* (Vol I) Winston S. Churchill (Thornton Butterworth 1923)
p. 11	'We played auction . . .'	*The Great War* (Vol I) Ed. H. W. Wilson. (Amalgamated Press. 1914)
p. 12	'I knew nothing . . .'	*Max Horton and the Western Approaches* W. S. Chalmers. (Hodder & Stoughton 1954)
p. 12	'If it ever comes off . . .'	*Max Horton* Ibid.
p. 12	'Submarine very lively . . .'	Quoted in *Max Horton* Ibid.
p. 12	'Trawlers where cruisers . . .'	Quoted in *Max Horton* Ibid.
p. 13	'She went up . . .'	Quoted in *Max Horton* Ibid.
p. 13	'To get one of these . . .'	*Naval Memoirs* (Vol I) Roger Keyes. (Thornton Butterworth 1934)
p. 14	'Good at his boat . . .'	Quoted in *Submarine Boats* Richard Compton Hall (Conway Maritime Press 1983)

p. 14	'His reputation as . . .'	*Max Horton* Ibid
p. 20	'If they are so cold . . .'	*Max Horton* Ibid
p. 22	'We hit her . . .'	Quoted in *Max Horton* Ibid
p. 24	'Due and proper . . .'	quoted in *Baltic Assignment* Michael Wilson. (Leo Cooper 1985)
p. 24	'You are in Swedish . . .'	*Baltic Assignment* Ibid
p. 25	'I understand that . . .'	Quoted in *Max Horton* Ibid
p. 25	'I learn that . . .'	quoted in *Max Horton* Ibid
p. 28	'Spiess, you see how . . .'	*Raiders of the Deep* Lowell Thomas (Doubleday & Co Inc. 1928)
p. 30	'Was the very . . .'	*Raiders of the Deep* Ibid
p. 36	'A fearful picture . . .'	*Raiders of the Deep* Ibid
p. 36	'Her men stayed . . .'	The Great War (Vol 2) Ibid
p. 36	The loss of nearly . . .'	Quoted in *The Times History of the War* (Vol 2) 1915.
p. 37	'We wish no lives . . .'	*The Times History of the War* (Vol 7) 1916
p. 38	'Present his compliments . . .	*The Times History of the War* Ibid
p. 41	'Assume command . . .'	*The World Crisis* Ibid
p. 48	'I put the helm . . .'	Quoted in *Submariners VC* William Jameson (Peter Davies 1962)
p. 49	'If in any action . . .'	Quoted in *The Great War* (Vol 10.1918) Ibid
p. 50	'Please accept . . .'	*Smoke on the Horizon* C. V. Usborne. (Hodder & Stoughton 1933)
p. 50	'Communicate to the . . .'	*Smoke on the Horizon* Ibid
p. 50	'The Turks were so . . .'	*Smoke on the Horizon* Ibid
p. 51	'It was a mighty . . .'	*Smoke on the Horizon* Ibid

p. 53	'I have to report . . .'	*Raiders of the Deep* Ibid
p. 54	'They ate together . . .'	*Raiders of the Deep* Ibid
p. 55	'Nerves are the . . .'	*U-Boat 202* Baron von Spiegel. (Mews Books 1976) Originally published in Germany Ca 1916
p. 55	'I mustered my best . . '	*U-Boat 202* Ibid
p. 56	'It is exactly. . .'	*U-Boat 202* Ibid
p. 60	'Submarine men are . . .'	*Raiders of the Deep* Ibid
p. 60	'The ship with the . . .'	*U-Boat 202* Ibid
p. 62	'German submarine captains . . .'	*The Killing Time* Edwyn Gray. (Seeley Service & Co. 1972)
p. 62	'My men were . . .'	*Raiders of the Deep* Ibid
p. 64	'I couldn't forget . . .'	*Raiders of the Deep* Ibid
p. 65	'I have wanted to . . .'	*Raiders of the Deep* Ibid
p. 66	'You know this book . . .'	*Strange Intelligence* Hector Bywater & H. C. Ferraby (Constable & Co., 1931)
p. 68	'The finest feat . . .'	*The World Crisis* (Vol 4) Ibid
p. 70	'The intended operation . . .'	*Roger Keyes* Cecil Aspinall-Oglander. (The Hogarth Press. 1951)
p. 72	'Stouthearted and enterprising . . .'	Quoted in *Submariners VC* Ibid
p. 76	'It was a silent . . .'	*Daily Mail* 25 April 1918
p. 77	'She was going full-tilt . . .'	*Daily Mail* Ibid
p. 78	'I never saw such . . .'	Quoted in *Zeebrugge and Ostend Despatches and Narratives*. Ed. C. Sanford Terry (Oxford University Press. 1919)
p. 79	'We were lucky . . .'	*Daily Mail* Ibid
p. 79	'The execution of this . . .'	*Blocking of Zeebrugge*. A. F. B. Carpenter. (Herbert Jenkins 1922)
p. 80	'Well done Uncle Baldy . . .'	*Submariners VC* Ibid

p. 85	'The submarine showed her . . .'	*Q-Ships and their story* E. Keble-Chatterton (Sidgwick & Jackson. 1923)
p. 86	'very rarely torpedoed . . .'	*Raiders of the Deep* Ibid
p. 86	'Many officers sank . . .'	*Raiders of the Deep* Ibid
p. 86	'Four torpedoes to sink . . .'	*Raiders of the Deep* Ibid
p. 87	'Yet we encountered . . .'	*Raiders of the Deep* Ibid
p. 88	'The sea became . . .'	*Raiders of the Deep* Ibid
p. 88	'It was like looking . . .'	*The Killing Time* Ibid
p. 89	'After what I had . . .'	*Raiders of the Deep* Ibid
p. 89	'I cannot leave . . .'	Quoted in *Raiders of the Deep* Ibid
p. 93	'To surrender at ports . . .'	Quoted in *The Killing Time* Ibid
p. 95	'To the Hang Lee's. . .'	Quoted in *Armed with Stings* A. Cecil Hampshire. (William Kimber. 1958)
p. 95	'We understand your . . .'	*Armed with Stings* Ibid
p. 98	'Distinctly clever . . .' and other official reports.	By courtesy of the Royal Navy Submarine Museum, *HMS Dolphin*
p. 104	'It was sheer hell . . .'	Unidentified Hong Kong newspaper.
p. 110	'Our Lady of Poland . . .'	*Orzel's Patrol* Eryk Sopocko. (Methuen. 1942)
p. 113	'Good luck . . .'	*Navies in Exile* A. D. Divine. (John Murray 1944)
p. 120	'Stop engines . . .'	*Orzel's Patrol* Ibid
p. 120	'Abandon Ship . . .'	*Orzel's Patrol* Ibid
p. 121	'They keep together . . .'	*Orzel's Patrol* Ibid
p. 126	'A quiet and . . .'	*Will not we fear* C. E. T. Warren and James Benson (Harrap. 1961)
p. 126	'Too much of . . .'	*Will not we fear* Ibid
p. 128	'A ruddy marvel . . .'	*Will not we fear* Ibid

p. 135	'Dear God, we have . . .'	*Will not we fear* Ibid
p. 137	'We'll have to surrender . . .'	*Will not we fear* Ibid
p. 138	'Jump into the water . . .'	*Will not we fear* Ibid
p. 139	'Safety of personnel . . .'	Quoted in *Will not we fear* Ibid
p. 141	'Few U-boat commanders . . .'	*The Second World War* Winston S. Churchill (Cassell. 1948)
p. 143	'I don't think I missed . . .'	Quoted in *Enemy Submarine* Wolfgang Frank. (William Kimber. 1954)
p. 145	'I have no intention . . .'	*The Golden Horseshoe* Terence Robertson. (Evans Bros. 1955)
p. 152	'From captain to captain . . .'	*The Golden Horseshoe* Ibid
p. 153	'I should like to say . . .'	*The Golden Horseshoe* Ibid
p. 153	Details of losses table.	*U-Boats in action* B. Herzog. (Ian Allen/ Podzun Verlag. 1970)
p. 157	'This was a skilful . . .'	Quoted in *War under the waves* Fred Warshofsky. (Pyramid Books. 1962)
p. 177	'Were rather a nuisance. . .'	*Sea Devils* J. Valerio Borghese (Andrew Melrose. 1952)
p. 178	'I at once ordered . . .'	*A Sailor's Odyssey* Viscount Cunningham (Hutchinsons. 1951)
p. 178n	'But no physical . . .'	*Oppenheim's International Law* (7th Edtn. Vol 2) Ed. H. Lauterpacht. (Longmans Green & Co. 1948)
p. 180	'Meanwhile something . . .'	*A Sailor's Odyssey* Ibid
p. 180	'Please report what is . . .'	*The Second World War* Ibid
p. 184	'Built like a bear. . .'	*War Fish* George Grider with Lydel Sims (Cassell. 1958)

p. 185	'A cautious look. . .'	*War Fish* Ibid
p. 185	'Hell, no . . .'	War Fish Ibid
p. 186	'When do I fire . . .'	*War Fish* Ibid
p. 192	'In ten hour running . . .'	Quoted in *War Fish* Ibid
p. 193	'Come on home . . .'	Quoted in *War Fish* Ibid
p. 194	'Another running gun . . .'	Quoted in *War Fish* Ibid
p. 195	'Admiral I want to . . .'	*Submarine* Edward L. Beach. (William Heinemann. 1953)
p. 205	'I think it's time . . .'	*Submariners VC* Ibid
p. 206	'What the hell are . . .'	*Stand by to surface.* Richard Baxter (Cassell & Co. 1944)
p. 208	'While picking up . . .'	*Italian Warships of World War II* Aldo Fraccaroli (Ian Allen. 1968)
p. 209	'Liked to be comfortable. . .'	*Stand by to surface* Ibid
p. 209	'A very severe supply crisis . . .'	*Submariners VC* Ibid
p. 212	'There had been no . . .'	Quoted in *Beneath the Waves* A. S. Evans (William Kimber 1986)
p. 213	'Such was the standard . . .'	Quoted in *Submariners VC* Ibid
p. 216	'The headlights of cars . . '	*The Far and the Deep* Edward P. Stafford (Arthur Barker 1968)
p. 221	'Good work you . . .'	*Submarine* Ibid
p. 222	'Such popularity . . .'	Quoted in *Submarine* Ibid
p. 225	'Far worse than . . .'	Quoted in *War under the waves* Ibid
p. 227	'To Commander Sam Dealey . . .'	*Fighting under the sea* Ibid
p. 231	'I saw the craft . . .'	*Sunk* Mochisura Hashimoto (Cassell 1954)
p. 235	'The sight of capsized . . .'	*Sunk* Ibid
p. 238	'In all I saw three . .'	*Sunk* Ibid

p. 238	*'Hiriho Kenten . . .'*	*Abandon Ship* Richard F. Newcomb (Quality Book Club. 1960)
p. 241	'Enemy tanker assumed . . .'	*Abandon Ship* Ibid
p. 242	'Released six torpedoes . . .'	Quoted in *Sunk* Ibid
p. 242	'My nerves were not . . .'	*Sunk* Ibid
p. 243	'Most of us were past . . .'	*Sunk* Ibid
p. 244	'Would it have made . . .'	*Abandon ship* Ibid
p. 244	'It would have involved . . .'	*Abondon ship* Ibid
p. 246	'A young man who . . .'	*War Fish* Ibid
p. 246	'Likable, obviously a hard . . .'	*War Fish* Ibid
p. 246	'Had grown harder to . . .'	*War Fish* Ibid
p. 249	'Overcrowded bunks . . .'	Quoted in *Pass the ammunition* Stan Smith (Manor Books 1976)
p. 259	'The bravest man . . .'	*Submarine* Ibid

—APPENDIX ONE—

Warships Sunk by Submarines in World War I

| | *Sunk by submarines of:* | | | | | |
	Germany	*Britain*	*Austria*	*Italy*	*France*	*USA*
Battleships	9	2	1	1	–	–
Cruisers	14	4	2	–	–	–
Destroyers	15	5	4	–	–	–
Submarines	7	17	4	3	2	–

—APPENDIX TWO—

Warships Sunk by Submarines in World War II

	Sunk by submarines of:						
	Germany	USA	Japan	Britain	Italy	Holland	USSR
Battleships	2	1	–	–	–	–	–
Carriers	8	8	3	–	–	–	–
Cruisers	7	12	2	6	2	–	–
Destroyers	50	41	8	5	2	1	–
Submarines	5	19	1	35	3	4	3

Index

270

272

273